Arnulfo L. Oliveira Memorial Library

UTB
TSC

In the Shadow of the Polish Eagle

In the Shadow of
the Polish Eagle

The Poles, the Holocaust and Beyond

Leo Cooper
Senior Research Associate
Contemporary Europe Research Centre and
Centre for Russian and Euro-Asian Studies
University of Melbourne
Australia

First published 2000 by
PALGRAVE
Houndmills, Basingstoke, Hampshire RG21 6XS and
175 Fifth Avenue, New York, N. Y. 10010
Companies and representatives throughout the world

PALGRAVE is the new global academic imprint of
St. Martin's Press LLC Scholarly and Reference Division and
Palgrave Publishers Ltd (formerly Macmillan Press Ltd).

ISBN 0–333–75265–1 hardback
ISBN 0–333–96210–9 paperback

This book is printed on paper suitable for recycling and
made from fully managed and sustained forest sources.

A catalogue record for this book is available
from the British Library.

Library of Congress Cataloging-in-Publication Data
Cooper, Leo.
    In the shadow of the Polish eagle : the Poles, the Holocaust, and
    beyond / Leo Cooper.
        p. cm.
    Includes bibliographical references (p.) and index.
    ISBN 0–333–75265–1
    1. Jews—Poland—History—20th century. 2. Holocaust, Jewish
    (1939–1945)—Poland. 3. Antisemitism—Poland. 4. Poland—Ethnic
    relations. 5. Holocaust survivors. I. Title.
    DS135.P6 C655 2000
    943.8'004924—dc21
                                                        00–059125

10   9   8   7   6   5   4   3   2   1
09   08   07   06   05   04   03   02   01   00

Printed and bound in Great Britain by
Antony Rowe Ltd, Chippenham, Wiltshire

To my grandfather,
father,
mother,
sister,
and many relatives and friends,
whose ashes have fertilised the soil of Poland

We, in history the most magnificent heap of bloody manure with which we have fertilised Poland, so that the bread of freedom will taste better to those who will survive us.

'My Żydzi Polscy' ('We, Polish Jews'), Juljan Tuwim, 1942

Contents

Foreword

This book was a long time in the 'making', or rather writing. It is the product of several decades of refreshing my memory, of research and of a great deal of soul searching. Often, I was overcome by doubts whether a work of this nature should see the light of day. Some years ago, I was told by a French publisher that it is inappropriate to extrapolate from personal memories to speak about the relations between Poles and Jews; it should be left to historians. I am not, strictly speaking, an historian, but I maintain that personal testimonies by witnesses to historical events are as relevant as documentary evidence.

With the passing of time, and the emergence of a plethora of books on the Holocaust, I became convinced that it is imperative to probe into the past of the country where I was born and spent the years of my prime youth. It pained me to see that of all the European countries who subjected themselves to historical examination of the Second World War period, Poland was the only exception. For most Poles, Poland is a martyr nation with no 'black pages'. My research proved this to be incorrect.

The question of Polish–Jewish relations and in particular the question of reconciliation have lately become a subject of some, albeit subdued, discussion in Poland. Some years ago, replying to my letter in which I complained about the dearth of writing about anti-Semitism in Poland, the well known Polish journalist Jerzy Turowicz, admitted that 'unfortunately some anti-Semitism still exists in Poland, but it is a marginal phenomenon'. He assured me that dozens of articles on that subject have appeared in the Polish press and referred to the commemoration of the fiftieth anniversary of the Warsaw Ghetto uprising as proof that Poland is not indifferent to the problem of anti-Semitism. I could not find evidence of this; I believe there is a general silence which is the greatest obstacle to reconciliation between Jews and Poles. I hope the present work will make some contribution toward this objective.

If I had to name the people who encouraged me to undertake this difficult task, I would have to place at the top of the list my wife, Fanny, who patiently read every bit of every draft I wrote and offered valuable advice. Encouragement came also from Leslie Holmes of Melbourne University, to whom I showed the outline of this study, and who thought it 'looked terrific'. My good friend Harry Redner of Monash University made a similar assessment.

I received practical assistance from professor Hanoch Gutfreund, former President of the Hebrew University in Jerusalem. Thanks to him I obtained easy access to the vast material in the University Library where Dr Michael Rigler was of great help.

My thanks must also go to Cameron Laux, one of the editors of my book at Macmillan. He warned me that 'a book of my sort, is likely to give rise to heated debate, scholarly or otherwise'. If it does, I have achieved my objective.

Introduction

Despite the time-lapse since those tragic events, the Holocaust continues to be the subject of research, writings and of general public interest. The trial of Papon in France, the Swiss involvement in dealing with Nazi stolen gold, the recent international Holocaust conference in Stockholm, and the probes into the attitude toward the Jews by a number of other countries during the war are but a few indications of that interest.

It is rather surprising that relatively little attention has been devoted to Poland – the country where Nazi extermination plans were most fully executed. Unlike Germany, France and other European countries, whose role during the Holocaust has been investigated, Poland has so far escaped historical scrutiny. This book attempts to fill that gap.

The Jewish population in pre-war Poland numbered about 3.5 million. In 1944 – after Poland's liberation from German occupation – there were only about 80,000 survivors. An estimated 300,000 returned from the Soviet Union, but after the Kielce pogrom in July 1946 a mass exodus of Jews took place, which further reduced the size of the Jewish community. Poland is the only European country in which it can be said that Hitler's Final Solution has been successfully carried out (Poland is *Judenrein*). Furthermore, in contrast to other countries where Jewish life has slowly been rebuilt by the survivors after the war, the Jewish presence in Poland today is only minimal and there is no prospect that it will be revived.

Compared to other countries, Poland is a special case. It was the first victim of Nazi aggression and the Poles are supposed not to have collaborated with the invaders. Poland can also boast of having the largest number of individuals who were awarded by the Israeli government the honourable title of the Righteous among the Nations for saving Jewish lives.

There is, however, another, darker side of the coin – Polish anti-Semitism and its role in the almost total disappearance of the Jews in Poland. This problem begs an answer to one important question: given the large Jewish community in Poland, why was the percentage of survivors in Poland relatively small compared with those in other European countries?

The present work attempts to find an answer to this vital question. It tries to avoid generalisations, for not all Poles can be said to have behaved badly during the war – however, only few behaved in a noble manner by saving Jews. The vast majority could be defined as onlookers, that is, indifferent to the fate of their Jewish countrymen, and a large number may be considered as perpetrators, that is, those who have personally participated in the murder of Jews and others who have contributed to the death of thousands of Jews by denouncing them to the Germans. Among the perpetrators were also members of the Polish underground movement connected to the Polish government-in-exile in London. Poland is the only country where denouncing Jews to the Germans and tracking down those who attempted to hide, were defined in wartime as a profession – the so-called 'szmalcownik'.

It is for this reason that the line between Polish onlookers and perpetrators is very thin indeed. The practice of blackmail and extortion by the 'szmalcowniks' was widespread and was well known to the majority of the Polish population. Yet, there was little attempt to stamp it out, or to discourage those who were involved. Denouncing Jews had the tacit approval of the population at large; the Polish resistance did little to stop it, and the Catholic clergy when it did not openly preach anti-Jewish sentiments, kept an ominous silence about it.

This period in Polish history has been swept under the carpet or simply falsified by Polish historians in Poland and elsewhere. Most Polish intellectuals assert that Polish society in its vast majority felt compassion for Jews and helped them whenever it was possible. They consider the activities of the Polish blackmailers who denounced Jews to the Germans as exceptions.

The testimonies of survivors and recently found documents tell a different story. Poles in general, with a few commendable exceptions, did not show any commiseration and did not render assistance to Jews who attempted to hide. On the contrary, a Jew in hiding lived in constant fear not only of the Germans, but of his Polish neighbour or a passerby who, in contrast to a German, had an acute ability for recognising a Jewish face in the crowd. Had the Poles displayed neutrality – that is, looked the other way – thousands of Jews would have been saved. No act of heroism was required.

Documents uncovered in the German Federal Archives in Koblenz contain correspondence between the Gestapo and the NSZ (National Armed Forces – a Polish underground organisation) clearly indicating close collaboration as far as tracking Jews was concerned. Particularly active in this respect were Polish units of the so-called 'Świętokrzyska Brigade' in the district of Radom, which cooperated with the Germans during the occupation and withdrew from Poland together with the German army in January 1945. It is rather surprising that the NSZ has been awarded the highest honour for resisting the Germans by the former President, Lech Wałęsa.

The controversy has been, and still is, a subject of fierce discussions among historians. The accusations directed against the Polish nation for its behaviour during the Holocaust have, so far, not been convincingly refuted. Polish apologists are constantly devising ways of absolving the Polish nation of any responsibility. They tend to exaggerate the assistance rendered to the Jews by the Poles during the war. It is true that many Poles have indeed saved Jews, but the percentage of those saved by the Poles relative to the entire Jewish population in Poland was very low – the lowest of any European country.

One of the darkest pages in Polish history, however, consists of events which took place long after the chimneys of the Nazi crematoria ceased to smoke. On 4 July 1946, the word spread over the town of Kielce in Poland: the Jews had kidnapped a Polish boy in order to kill him for ritual purposes. Within hours a large crowd gathered in front of a tenement housing about 200 Jews – many survivors of the Nazi extermination camps and some who returned from the Soviet Union. They were all about to leave Poland due to the hostile environment in the country at the time. The mob attacked the house. Jews were thrown out of the windows, trampled underfoot by the bystanders and beaten with metal rods. The participants in the killings were civilians, workers of the neighbouring steel mill, soldiers of the Polish army and militiamen. According to some estimates half of the Kielce population of 50,000 took part in the disorder – it was a public outburst of hatred directed against the Jews and of a sort unseen since the dark ages.

What was significant in all the material published in Poland about this event is the variety of theories on the identity of the instigators. Among the suspects were the Communists, the Zionists and the Jews themselves. So far, not one Polish historian has considered Polish anti-Semitism as a catalyst of a spontaneous eruption of nationalism and religious zeal. To this day any reference to this tragic event is met by hostility from Poles who claim that it denigrates the honour of the Polish nation.

Polish hostility against Jews did not begin and did not end with the Kielce pogrom. Killing of Jews took place in many towns and villages in liberated Poland before the pogrom, and in 1968, after a vigorous anti-Jewish campaign by the Polish government, most Jews left Poland. Only a tiny community, mostly of old Jews, remained.

This book is not only a survey of the Holocaust period in Poland and beyond, but goes one step further – it attempts to uncover the sources and origins of Polish animosity toward the Jews. To understand what happened during the war one must go back to pre-war Poland. Polish anti-Semitism did not begin with the German occupation. It existed in Poland for a long time, but came to the surface when Poland regained her independence in 1918 after 150 years of foreign rule.

It was during the period 1918–39 that Polish anti-Semitism grew in intensity not only among the population at large, but also became official government policy. Restrictive laws were introduced in the early thirties and a *numerus clausus* at Polish universities preceded similar restrictions in Germany by a number of years. Anti-Semitism expressed itself in the persecution of Polish Jews long before Hitler came to power in Germany. Poland was the theatre of numerous pogroms in which Jews were killed or wounded long before the Kristalnacht in Germany. Anti-Semitic propaganda was spread by almost every Polish newspaper and there were calls for the expulsion of the Jews from Poland. This period is well documented and there is no shortage of evidence of a virulent anti-Semitism as a precursor to Polish behaviour during the Holocaust.

In this respect Poland must be singled out for yet another reason. In Germany and France, for example, there has been much soul-searching about this matter over the years. Poland is the only country which refuses to come to terms with its past. There were numerous, albeit feeble, attempts by some more enlightened Poles to probe into the dark pages of Poland's history; but faced with general hostility, these attempts came to nought. Little of that part of the Polish past can be found in Polish literature. In fact, Jewish presence in Poland, which goes back 1,000 years, occupies only a few paragraphs in Polish history text books.

The history of Polish Jewry was, and is still being, written almost exclusively by authors of Jewish descent. It represents a topic important to Jews, above all, and is one that is most familiar to them. It seems that Polish anti-Semites, when writing history, are capable only of producing contemptible misrepresentations. Polish non-Jewish authors who are not anti-Semites prefer to avoid the subject altogether. Generally, Polish authors who maintain the taboo on unpleasant subjects believe that they are acting in the national interest. They want to construct a blameless historical past for their native land, free of any stain (Lewandowski, 1987, p. 69).

It is only in the last few years that some Polish intellectuals have been brave enough to face the past. They are encouraged by the present Polish president Kwaśniewski, who on several occasions has indicated a genuine desire for Jewish–Polish reconciliation.

Is Polish–Jewish reconciliation possible? That this question should be under discussion is a clear indication that there are problems affecting Jewish–Polish relations. It was debated in May 1987 during the Fifth World Congress of Polish Jews in Israel. Hundreds of representatives from 15 countries, including a six-man delegation headed by a member of the Polish parliament, participated in the Congress, whose theme was '1000 Years of Polish Jewry'. Most delegates were in favour of reconciliation between the two nations, while others argued that Polish behaviour during the Holocaust and lack of repentance afterwards makes an improvement in Polish–Jewish relations unlikely. Jewish and some Polish commentators saw the root of the problem in the unwillingness of Polish society to look closely into its past, especially at the behaviour of many Poles prior to, during and after the German occupation of Poland (*Jerusalem Post*, 13 April 1987).

This book is an attempt to convey the latter message to Poles who lived through and know what took place in Poland during the period in question, as well as to the younger generation, so that they may reflect upon the dark moments of Polish history. Perhaps, given enough time, such reflections may lead to a genuine reconciliation.

Prologue: Poland Welcomes Back Survivors – May 1946

> We, Polish Jews ... We eternally alive – that is, those who
> perished in the ghettos and camps, and we, the ghosts – that
> is those who will return to the country from over the seas,
> and will haunt among the ruins with our wholly preserved
> bodies and our obstinately kind-of preserved souls.
>
> ('My Żydzi Polscy' ('We Polish Jews'), *Juljan Tuwim, 1942*)

It was late spring of 1946. The war had ended twelve months before,
but the memories of those terrible years still lingered in my mind. I
should have been full of joy as the moment I had been waiting for
over the past seven years had finally arrived. Soon I would be crossing
the border separating the Soviet Union from Poland and I would be
back in the country where I was born and where I had spent the prime
years of my youth. I was in a state of excitement at the thought of
returning home. All that separated me from my native country was
the river on the shores of which I was standing. It was the same river
I had crossed in 1939 while escaping the Nazis. That crossing point
was further to the north about 60 kilometres from where I was now.
At that time, when I made the crossing in a dinghy under the protection of night, I had not realised that ahead of me were seven long
years of exile.

My return journey began in the small town of Komarovo located
half way between Moscow and Leningrad. I had spent the past two
years in that town and when, after the end of the war, the order came
for all former Polish citizens to be repatriated, the local Soviet authorities organised a goods-train that would take us back to Poland. All
along the journey we were singing Polish, Russian and Yiddish songs
accompanied by the sounds of a guitar, which one of the repatriates

took back with him, and a mandolin, which I played. I bought the mandolin for a few roubles at the Komarovo market. It wasn't really a bargain, for it had quite a large hole in its bottom part, but this didn't worry me. I, and everyone else, thought the sound was quite good and the tunes I had been playing were recognisable.

Before leaving Komarovo my friends and I made sure to be seated together in the same carriage. Amongst them was my good friend David, who could boast close knowledge of the Soviet system. He spent some time in a Soviet labour camp and was set free in 1941 after the Nazis invaded the Soviet Union. Just prior to our departure, he was again arrested by the secret police but released after a few days of interrogation. A pre-war staunch communist, he had become a sworn enemy of the regime. 'They [the communists] should burn in hell', he would say in front of people. I used to warn him of the danger he was facing from the Soviet police, but he would not listen. Now, however, as we were about to leave the workers' paradise, he suddenly started to preach his old ideas and voice his intention to help build a democratic Poland.

Kuzka, the sheet-metal worker, a former member of the social democratic party Bund, had never been a friend of the Bolsheviks and was eagerly awaiting the moment of liberation from Soviet rule. Marek was a Zionist and retained his dream of going to Palestine. As for Yosif, Nute, Ivan Ivanovich and others, they had never disclosed their political views for fear of the Soviet secret police. Now, all our fears had gone and everyone felt free to express his opinion. We all agreed that there was no future for us in the Soviet Union.

As for myself, I was torn between hope and despair. I simply could not grasp the extent of the terrible catastrophe, and the enormity of the calamity did not sink into my consciousness. I could not believe that a Jewish community of three and a half million could have been wiped off the face of the earth. Yet, the confirmation of the great tragedy had come to me a year before.

At the end of 1944, or perhaps at the beginning of 1945, I was constantly glued to the loudspeaker in my room. After the offensive that began in August 1944, when the Red Army entered into the territory of former Poland, the Russian radio kept repeating messages calling to listen to an important announcement. This was usually a news item announcing the liberation of a Polish town – an announcement preceded by the sound of Polish music. Tears came to my eyes when I heard a familiar tune of a song I used to sing while at school in Warsaw. Names such as Lublin, Białystok and Brest Litovsk were a clear indication that the turn of my native town was not far away. The much awaited day arrived when in January 1945 the radio announced the fall of Warsaw to the Red Army. I was overjoyed and so were all my Jewish friends.

The first thing I did was to write home. I must have written at least twenty postcards to my parents, all my uncles, cousins and other relatives whose addresses I still remembered. 'My dear parents', I wrote, 'the war is now over and I hope that this card will find you all in good health. I am well and I am looking forward to some good news from you. Your loving son.'

Everyone I knew was busy writing similar letters. There was an air of excitement and happy expectation in anticipation of receiving some replies. About six months later one of the postcards that I had sent to Warsaw came back. It bore a large stamp in the Polish language: 'dom spalony' – this house is burnt out. More cards bearing the same imprint kept arriving until I received every card I had written. With them came the terrible realisation that not one of my family was alive. Yet, the confirmation of my worst fears still did not sink into my consciousness and the hope that perhaps I would find some survivors made me eager to leave Russia as soon as possible.

While the train was moving westward towards the Polish border, the door of the carriage was wide open, and looking out I could observe the passing scenery – the typical Russian birch-tree forests and green meadows. As on my previous journeys through the Soviet Union the train was making very slow progress. It had to give way to all civilian traffic that was getting back to normal after the war. Like in a motion picture running backwards, names of towns which I had seen seven years earlier began to appear but in reverse order. We reached the Soviet–Polish border at the town of Brest Litovsk.

It was here that train-loads of former Polish citizens, who escaped to the Soviet Union from Nazi occupied Poland in 1939–40, had been arriving almost daily to be repatriated. Clearly there was little coordination between Soviet authorities in charge of repatriation and those responsible for the railway transport. Trains continued to arrive with only a few crossing the bridge towards the Polish side. It took sometimes up to two weeks for a single train to cross the bridge. This created a huge bottle-neck – and a long wait. The train which was to take me back to Poland had been standing for some days at a siding near the Brest Litovsk railway station waiting for the order to cross into Poland when a goods-train arrived from the Polish side. The locomotive stopped on the track almost opposite our carriage. The train-driver, a Russian man dressed in greasy overalls, stepped down from the locomotive and started to talk to Kuzka who happened to be standing nearby. They were soon surrounded by a few more people. When the Russian found out that we were Jews going back to Poland he could not hide his surprise:

'Fools, where are you going? If you Jews are going back to Poland, I don't envy you', he said.

Before we had time to ask him further questions, he began to describe the situation in the country to which we were returning after seven years of exile.

'If I were you,' he continued, 'I would not return to Poland. The Poles are killing Jews anywhere they can find them. They are stopping trains with repatriates and shooting them. The Polish army and the police are helpless so don't count on any protection. Believe me, if you go back, you stand a good chance of being killed. You would be much wiser if you stayed here.'

We just stood and listened in silence. Then a discussion about what we just heard began. Some objected and tried to prove that what the Russian just told us could not be true. I myself wished it weren't true.

I went for a walk to digest the latest news. I reached the shores of the river separating me from Poland. Everything around me was so peaceful. The air was calm with no breeze. High above was a blue sky and below was the river that seemed like a lake whose surface was only slightly disturbed by the current. From where I was standing I could see the Polish side of the river-bank full of tall birch and pine-trees whose shadows were reflected in the mirror-like waters.

As I stood there and looked across to the opposite side I was suddenly overwhelmed by a feeling of anxiety bordering on fear. I was unable to precisely locate the source of my apprehension, but I felt as if something sinister were going to happen to me, as if I were in imminent danger. Was it perhaps the warning conveyed by the driver of the train which had just come from the Polish side? I tried to reason. Surely it cannot be as bad as the man had said. After all, Poland had experienced the Nazi occupation and had shared together with the Jews the horrors of the war. And if it were true that most Jews perished, why would the Poles wish to kill the few that survived? I tried to console myself with the thought that after all my dreams of returning home were about to become a reality. Images of happier times began to emerge in front of my eyes. I saw the streets of my home town, Warsaw, through which I used to walk, and the house in which I used to live.

My thoughts were interrupted by the whistle of the train – a signal of the imminent departure. As soon as I returned to the carriage the train began to move. At first it moved very slowly then it gathered speed before slowing down again as it approached the temporary wooden bridge which replaced the old one destroyed during the war. From where I was standing in the carriage I could see the outlines of the Polish side of the river. My heart was beating to the rhythm of the train.

I stretched my head out of the carriage to see the slowly approaching shores. I saw trees and among them, standing near the edge of the bridge, a group of people. They were gesticulating and appeared to be shouting, but their voices could not be heard because of the rattling of the train, the clatter of the wheels over the track, and the constant whistling of the steam engine. The carriage in which I was travelling was at the far end of the train so it had taken some time before it had reached land. By then I could distinctly see the raised hands of the people and I could also hear their voices:

'Look, they are all Jews! The filthy Jews are coming back!'

The shouting was accompanied by the sound of stones thrown at the train. Some fell inside the carriage. Instinctively I stepped back, and although I wasn't hit I felt as if every stone was aimed at me. For a short moment everyone in the carriage remained motionless.

'Shut the door!', someone screamed.

Pushed by two people the door began to slide, and as dimness enveloped the carriage, I suddenly realised that I had re-entered the shadow of the Polish eagle, the domain of dark hatred, which I had feared so much, but which I had hoped had gone with the end of the war.

Part I
The Polish Exile

1
The Dawn of the Jewish Community in Poland

> Now there arose a new king over Egypt, who did not know Joseph. And he said to his people, 'Behold, the people of Israel are too many and too mighty for us.'
>
> (Exodus 1:8–9)

When a certain Jew by the name of Abraham Prochownik entered the Polish town of Gniezno, he was met by dignitaries who greeted him as the ruler of Poland. The Polish sovereign, Popiel (*circa* the first half of the ninth century), known for his cruelty, had just died and for the last few days dignitaries were busy debating whom to appoint as the prince of what was to become later the Polish kingdom. After lengthy and fruitless discussions it was decided to designate the first man who entered the gates of the town the following morning. It happened to be the Jew, Abraham Prochownik. However, he declined the offer in favour of prince Ziemowit, who established the Piast dynasty of Polish kings (Dubnov, 1951, p. 328).

Another legend, ascribed to the sixteenth-century rabbi Moses Isserles, speaks about Jewish wanderings over Europe in search of safer ground. When the first Jews arrived close to the Polish territory, one of them said 'Po Lin', which in Hebrew means 'here you should rest' – hence the Yiddish and Hebrew name of Polin for Poland.

Thus begins the history of Jewish settlement in Poland; that is, the period of Jewish history before the introduction of Christianity into that country in 966. It is steeped in obscurity and shrouded in some mystic legends. Except for the legend about the first Jew in Poland, which can be placed in the early tenth century, there is practically no evidence of their early presence. There are several theories regarding the beginning of Jewish settlements in Poland. According to one

9

theory, the first Jewish settlers came from the West escaping the Crusades and the subsequent systematic persecution of Jews in western Europe.

Some historians claim that Polish Jews are the descendants of the Khazars. The Khazars were a tribe which settled in the lower Volga region. In about 786–809, their king Bulan and 4,000 of his nobles adopted Judaism as a state religion. They became a powerful state which lasted from the eighth to the tenth centuries, but disintegrated after the conquest by the Russian archduke Yaroslav in 1083. Some of the Khazars are said to have fled the Tartar invasion of 1237 and found shelter in Poland (Roth and Wigoder, 1970, p. 1543).

From its very inception, Poland had to fight the German expansion to the east. The first Polish King, Mieszko I, was forced to adopt Christianity in 966 in order to avoid an armed conflict with the Saxons, who justified their drive towards the east by a missionary objective of converting the pagan Poles. Mieszko I became, therefore, a vassal of the Roman-German emperor Otto I, and the Catholic Church became the religion of the Polish state.

About the middle of the thirteenth century the steppes of Russia were invaded by the Tartars. Much of the population fled westward, including the Jews who lived in the areas of the Tartar invasion. They moved to territories which later became the Polish state. Thus, two migrations, one from the east and the other from the west, led to the foundation of the Jewish community in Poland.

To restore its economy after the Tartar invasion of 1240, the Polish kings encouraged the immigration of German merchants. In their attempt to increase the income from the land they owned, large land-lords fostered an intensive colonisation campaign offering various concessions for the immigrants. Most settlers came from western Europe, mainly Germany (Arnold and Żychowski, 1966, p. 27). It is safe to assume that this policy attracted Jews as well, but Polish history books do not mention the arrival of Jewish immigrants. It would seem as if for Polish historians the arrival of the Germans is more deserving of mention than the arrival of Jews, who contributed to the Polish economy as much as the Germans did, and were much more loyal to the Polish state than were the Germans. Even modern Polish historians ignore the early Jewish presence in Poland. A 1966 history textbook, when speaking of the influence exercised by ethnic minorities in the formation of the Polish state, speaks of German and Celtic nationalities without mentioning Jews at all (ibid., p. 7).

A decree by German princes dated 906 AD, which requested payment on the Bavarian–Bohemian border 'from Jewish and other traders' travelling to the east, is one of the first mentions of a Jewish presence in Poland, but concrete evidence of the existence of Jewish settlements dates from the second half of the twelfth century. Historical records point to the importance of the Jews in the Polish economy of that time, when Polish princes and kings granted to the Jews the minting of Polish coins. Archaeological finds of Polish coins of the twelfth and thirteenth centuries with inscriptions 'Meszko the King of Poland' and 'Bracha Meszko' (in Hebrew), indicate that at the time the Jews in Poland occupied an important position in the Polish economy.

At first the Jews were welcomed and they appear to have lived on good terms with the Christians. The Jews brought with them the experience of western civilisation, thereby contributing to the advance of a primitive economy. Recognising the benefits that the Polish state would derive from the Jews, the Polish king Bolesław the Pious issued in 1264 the so-called Statute of Kalisz – a highly favourable charter of privileges to the Jews already residing in his domain. It granted the Jews freedom of commerce, the right to deal in money, the right to purchase property and autonomy of spiritual and urban jurisdiction (Abramsky et al., 1986, p. 3).

At the time of the arrival of the first Jews, Poland was a relatively primitive society. It was an agricultural country, consisting of large estates which belonged to the nobility, with little commerce. Polish cultural and economic development lagged very much behind that western Europe, where money as a means of exchange was already developed. Poland was economically backward, and the nobles had a traditional aversion to occupations connected with trade. But trade and economic activities in general were needed if the country was to become part of western Europe, which many Poles desired. The people who could contribute in this area were the Jews with their experience and tradition. 'They were the only group in Poland ... to take on the task for which the others were not prepared or for which they had contempt' (Hertz, 1988, p. 69).

In an era of universal illiteracy, the Jews were the only stratum of the Polish population to whom education was of prime importance. Jews who entered Poland during the thirteenth and fourteenth centuries were on a much higher cultural level than the Poles – something no Polish historian would admit. For the Jews, knowledge was not always confined to the study of the Scriptures but also included other areas such as medicine. From the early Middle Ages, Jews studied medicine and sometimes became court physicians in all the lands of the diaspora, including Poland. A Jew, Jakub Izaak, was the Polish king Zygmunt I's court physician, Salomon Aszkenazy was Zygmunt August's, and Jonas Casal and Abraham of Troki treated Jan III. Another Jew, Nisanowicz, was count Radziwill's doctor.

Many of the early Jewish immigrants into Poland who came from the West engaged in finance, at which they had considerable experience. The landed nobility required money to develop agriculture on their large estates, and they obtained their financial resources from Jews. The rise of towns in the thirteenth and fourteenth centuries also stimulated the need for more capital, which could be supplied mainly by Jews.

It was the main reason why Polish rulers granted the Jews many privileges. But a careful reading of these privileges indicates that they were not granted as acts of kindness towards strangers. The Polish state greatly benefited from their presence, and were it not for the strong influence of the Church, the Jews would have obtained equal rights to the indigenous Poles. For a number of years Poland was a destination for Jewish migrants and their situation in that country was relatively secure until the Poles fell under the influence of the teachings of Christianity; that is, until they were taught to nurture special prejudices against the race who committed deicide (Poliakov, 1974, p. 246). An analysis of the special character of Polish anti-Semitism can therefore be related to the influence of the Church.

The history of Polish Jewry followed the pattern that began in biblical times during the reign of the Pharaohs. After having saved Egypt from the great famine, the Jews came under the rule of a king who saw that 'the people of Israel are too many and too mighty for us'. In Poland, that king was the Catholic Church. When the Church had become firmly entrenched in that country, the Jews became the target of persecution. The Jewish presence in Poland had been perceived by the church as a danger, 'lest the Christians become infected with the superstitions and evil practices of the Jews' (Mahler, 1942, p. 112). The Church began a campaign against the privileges granted to the Jews by the 'Kalisz Statute'. A Church council was held in Breslau (a Polish city at that time) in 1267, during which a number of resolutions aimed against the Jews were adopted. The Church attempted to introduce in Poland, whose population was Roman Catholic for only about one century, the same restrictions on Jewish life as developed earlier in western Europe during the previous thousand years (Grayzel, 1968, p. 391). The synod also demanded the strict segregation of Jews from Christians through the creation of separate Jewish sections in the towns. The reasons advanced by the Church were that 'the Polish land is a new part of the Christian organism'; and 'in order that the Christian faith be sooner and more easily inculcated into the hearts of the faithful'.

Anti-Jewish sentiments within Polish society have a long history. They are virtually embedded in the Christian faith. Poland was relatively late in adopting Catholicism as a state religion, but because of efforts on the part of the Catholic Church, the faith was primarily based on the New Testament with its story of the Crucifixion. The Catholic Church, who had already much experience in anti-Jewish activities in Europe, had no difficulties in inculcating the hatred of Jews in the hearts and minds of the Polish population. It had in fact a relatively easy task, because Polish society, which had just abandoned paganism, was still at a primitive stage and prone to religious influences. Furthermore, Christianity being by now a state religion, could widely spread its influence over the masses.

The entire history of Polish Jewry can be viewed as a perpetual process of growing anti-Semitism instigated by the Church. According to the eminent historian Leon Poliakov, 'a bloody tradition was perpetuated, as evidenced by the pogroms of the late nineteenth century, the massacres of 1918–1920, the cooperation given to Nazis a generation later ... [and the pogrom in Kielce in 1946]' (Poliakov, 1974, p. 271).

The first pogroms are recorded in a chronicle of 1349, but without any indication as to the localities in which they took place. Another source indicates a pogrom on Jews in Wroclaw on 28 May 1349, provoked by the accusation that they were spreading the 'black death' epidemic. The entire Jewish quarter was burned down and many Jews were murdered. There were anti-Jewish events in Kalisz, in Cracow, and in 1367 there was a pogrom in the city of Poznan.

One Polish historian emphasises that bloody pogroms of Jews were at that time widespread in Germany and spilled over into Poland, and 'that the responsibility for these shameful events does not lie on the conscience of the Polish state policy, because the Polish king Kazimierz the Great adopted a policy of tolerance, and his policy was not a result of any weakness, but on the contrary, of wise decisions and power' (Jasienica, 1966, p. 346). Indeed, in 1334, the Polish king Kazimierz the Great (1333–70), reaffirmed the charter of Bolesław and even added further regulations to safeguard the Jewish population. In fact, royal protection prevented many attacks against the Jews during the 'black death' epidemic when Jews were accused of poisoning water wells (Grayzel, 1968, p. 390).

Kazimierz Wielki is said to have opened the gates of Poland for the Jewish immigrants from Germany, from where they were being expelled. Like the previous kings, he exploited the Jewish element against the growing German urban colonisation of Poland. He also understood the importance of the Jews for the Polish economy, especially for the transformation of a primitive form of commercial exchange into a money economy, which he thought would raise state revenues and economically consolidate the country. His ambitious plans for changing the economic system required large financial resources. He expected the Jews to supply the needed money and to bring with them their knowledge and financial experience. The state banker on whom the king conferred the task of managing state finances and the minting of money was the Jew Lewko. The Kazimierz period is characterised by rapid economic and cultural advancement of Poland and an increase in general well-being and education.

There is a popular belief among the Poles (and the Jews) that Kazimierz was a protector and benefactor of the Jews because he had a Jewish mistress – Esterka. According to this legend, Esther's origins were in the Cracow ghetto. She bore the king a few children who remained Jewish. Polish historians generally consider this to be a historical myth.

Kazimierz's fair treatment of Jews met with great appreciation by the Jewish community: 'the Kazimierz hospitality we paid back by work. What we managed to save from the burning stakes of the Spanish Inquisition and from the hands of the mad mobs of German crusaders, we brought into this country. It was not only gold and precious stones, but a spirit rich with experiences, new ways of economic development unknown to the inhabitants of this country' (Oberlaender, 1935, pp. 101–2).

Early attempts by the clergy and Christian merchants to restrict the rights of the Jews met with resolute opposition from King Kazimierz, but his successor, Władysław Jagieło (1386–1434), refused to confirm Jewish privileges and persecution began to be applied. In 1399, the archbishop of Posen instituted proceedings against the Jews in that town on the alleged charge of their having desecrated three Hosts from the Dominican church. The rabbi of Posen and thirteen elders of the Jewish community were roasted alive. In 1407, at Easter time, a priest of Cracow spread a rumour that the Jews killed a Christian child. In response, the Jewish quarter was attacked and many Jews were killed. Their property was looted and their children were baptised (Margolis and Marx, 1956, p. 529).

The Church was particularly active in the anti-Semitic movements of the fifteenth century Poland. It initiated a vigorous anti-Jewish campaign by inciting the Polish populace against their Jewish neighbours. An avalanche of accusations was let loose by the clergy. Jews were accused of blaspheming against Christianity, desecrating the Host, and murdering Christian children in order to use their blood for ritual purposes. John Capistrano, who came to Poland in 1454, aroused the population against the Jews and this led to pogroms in several Polish towns. In the same year, yielding to the urging of John Capistrano, King Kazimierz Jagiellonczyk (Kazimierz IV) abrogated some of the Jewish privileges. Thirty years later in 1483 the expulsion of Jews from Warsaw took place, followed by the expulsion from Cracow in 1491.

Conditions improved in the sixteenth century under the liberal Sigismund I (1500–48) and Sigismund II August (1548–72), when once more the Jews were needed for the further economic advancement of Poland. Sigismund August, the last of the Jagiello kings, issued an edict granting the Jews a large measure of autonomy. The edict of 13 August 1551 has been called the 'Magna Carta' of Jewish self-government in Poland (Margolis and Marx, 1956, p. 535). A number of Jews managed to reach key positions in the economic and political life of the country.

Jewish contributions to the economic advancement of Poland between the fourteenth and seventeenth centuries is beyond any doubt, for with the exception of a small middle class, there was no other effective economic force in Poland but the Jew. They were the main intermediaries between the producer and consumer over the vast territory of Poland. The Jew served as a key element in a broad colonisation process, marked by a rapid expansion in agriculture and trade. According to the Polish historian Halecki, 'the king with the help of urbane and even Jewish brains, managed to balance the state treasury' (Oberlaender, 1935, p. 102).

Jews also participated in the expansion of the Polish economy to the Baltics. Being a mostly agrarian country, Poland became the 'granary of Europe'. However, to obtain economic benefits it was necessary to find markets for the grain. It was the Jews with their trading experience who to a large degree contributed to the export trade in agricultural commodities (Hundert, 1986, p. 58). This period of development of foreign trade is a period of economic advancement in Poland. It is also known as a fine period in the history of Polish Jewry. At that time, Poland was the only country in Europe in which Jews were allowed to participate in a wide range of trades, crafts and skills.

The period between the thirteenth and sixteenth centuries was one of formation and adjustment of the communal life of Jews in Poland. By the sixteenth century they constituted a community with its own particular way of life. They formed autonomous communities called the Kahal. The Kahal had its head, the Rosh ha-Kahal, and its trustees, the 'gabbayim'. In 1503, the Polish monarchy appointed Rabbi Jacob Polak 'Rabbi of Poland', and the emergence of a chief rabbinate, backed by the crown, allowed the development of a form of self-government which the Jews had not known since the end of exilarchate (a Jewish institution headed by an exilarch – the head of the Jewish community in Babylonia). From 1551 the chief rabbi was elected by the Jews themselves.

The papal legate, Commendoni, described in about 1565 the status of the Polish Jews in the following terms: 'In these regions masses of Jews are to be found who are not subject to scorn they meet with everywhere. They do not live in abasement and are not reduced to menial trades thereby. They own land, engage in commerce, study medicine and astronomy. They possess great wealth and are not only counted among respectable people but sometimes even dominate them. They wear no distinctive insignia, and are even permitted to bear arms. In short, they have all the rights of citizens' (Poliakov, 1974, p. 249).

From the late sixteenth century, when the number of Jews in Poland began to increase, until the Age of Haskalah (Jewish Enlightenment) in the mid-eighteenth century, Jewish life was concentrated in small villages – in the so-called *shtetl* – around the synagogue, and in the usually adjoining house of learning (Beth Midrash). Depending on its size, the community had various institutions whose tasks ranged through administrative, educational and charitable activities. It usually had a synagogue, ritual bath, and a combined hospital and home for the aged. It invariably had a charitable fund, which supported the poor.

In such a small community the highest authority was the rabbi, usually a man of considerable knowledge of Jewish law, which he would have studied for a number of years. Each Jewish synagogue was independent of any other and, in contrast to the Church, did not have a hierarchal structure – that is, there was no other power above the rabbi except the community itself, by whom he was appointed in his role as a teacher and a judge according to the Jewish law. The Kahal had the power to impose various penalties, including flogging, imprisonment and in extreme cases excommunication. It had no right to impose the death penalty. It should be noted, however, that criminal offences among Jewish communities of that time were extremely rare (Grayzel, 1968, p. 394).

During the reign of the Polish king Stefan Batory (1576–86), who confirmed Jewish privileges and sharply attacked blood libel accusations, Jewish autonomy was extended even further. By the end of the sixteenth century the Jews governed themselves through a sort of parliament, the Council of Four Lands – 'Vaad Arba Aratzot' – the four parts of the Polish-Lithuanian Commonwealth (Great Poland, Little Poland, Lithuania and Ukraine). It lasted from 1580 to 1764. Such an organisation of the Jewish community was favoured by the Polish authorities because they found it more convenient to collect taxes from one source rather than from many individuals. Polish authorities realised that it was more convenient to impose a single annual tax on the entire Jewish community and leave the allocation and collection to the Jews themselves (Poliakov, 1974, p. 252).

The royal purpose in devolving power to the Jews was clearly self-interest. The kings could make more money by allowing the Jewish communities to develop, and taxing them later. The rabbinate and local Jewish councils were primarily tax-raising agencies. Only 30 per cent of what was raised went on welfare and official salaries; the rest was handed over to the crown in return for protection.

The need for maintaining religious traditions, which made the Jews different for the rest of the population, propelled them to live in closed communities, although they were not compelled to do so (Grayzel, 1968, p. 393). The preference for living in a Jewish environment had been conditioned above all by a desire to live according to Jewish tradition. Jews were also separated from the Polish population by the language they spoke. Right through their history, Jews usually spoke the language of the country in which they lived. In Hellenic times they spoke Greek; the famous Jewish philosopher Maimonides spoke and wrote in Arabic; the Jewish commentator on the Bible, Rashi, spoke French; and the rabbis of the Middle Ages in Germany spoke German. When the Jews from Germany began to arrive in Poland, they brought with them a language that was a mixture of German, Hebrew and words of any languages they absorbed over centuries of exile. In Poland, however, due to the limited cultural intercourse with the Polish population, the Jews retained and in time refined their own language, known as Yiddish, by the addition of Polish words.

Language was only one of the factors that made Jews different from the people that lived in their proximity – another one was education. The respect for learning which the Jews had retained since the biblical times, was instrumental in the establishment of a simple but widespread system of education accessible to all. Education of a Jewish child began at the age of three. Consequently, almost the entire Jewish community attained a much higher intellectual level than the bulk of the Polish population.

Judaism does not recognise wealth as being of value in itself, but as a means of achieving knowledge and wisdom. A poor but wise man is, according to Jewish tradition, more worthy of respect than a rich but uneducated man. The Jews always considered themselves as people of the Book and thought that their endurance and historical continuity were a result of their adherence to and study of it (Hertz, 1988, p. 78). For a Jew, even for a poor and uneducated one, the highest value was wisdom achieved through learning. Learning was also considered as a way of serving God. The rich man, on the other hand, dreamed of having a son-in-law who would devote his entire life to study of the Holy Books. It was common for a rich Jew to search for a poor but promising young student as a husband for his daughter. After the marriage the student would be supported by his father-in-law for many years. Some rich Jews were also known for their generosity in supporting the building of synagogues and houses of learning (ibid., p. 101).

A most important institution was a kind of school called 'heder', where Jewish boys were taught reading the Scriptures. Any village with a sufficient number of Jewish inhabitants made every possible effort to engage a teacher for the children. It was the only communal institution which was never neglected. The school was usually under communal supervision and the community had to make sure that the teachers were paid either by the parents who could afford it, or by the community for those who were too poor. The so-called 'heder' was a rather successful institution. For this reason that illiteracy was rare among Polish Jews of that time.

The Jews of Poland in the sixteenth century could also boast of having a number of famous Talmudic academies. The so called 'yeshivot' were not only schools for training rabbis, but for the retention and further transmission of the wisdom contained in the Talmud. However, the study of the Talmud was not solely for the purpose of satisfying an abstract need for knowledge, but had also practical applications. The Polish rulers who saw in the Kahal an institution that served their interests granted special charters which gave the Jews the right to apply their own judicial system based on the Talmud. The Jews appointed their own judges who's decisions were enforced by the head of the community. Hence the need for academies where Jews were trained in the Talmudic law.

> Thus the Polish Jews of the sixteenth and seventeenth centuries presented an unusual aspect. A group, whose economic opportunities were limited, learned to disregard economics and emphasise intellect. Surrounded by enemies of their religion, they developed their religious life and clung to it more tenaciously than had Jews of other lands under better conditions. Living under the uncertain protection of the nobles who were interested only in income they could derive from the Jews, they learned to cooperate among themselves and established a stimulating communal life. In the midst of a population almost completely lacking in culture, they engaged in an amazing cultural activity.
>
> (Grayzel, 1968, p. 397)

The yearning for knowledge on the part of the Polish Jews could have diverged into other fields in Poland, as Jewish culture once did in Spain and other European countries, were it not for the fact that the cultural level of the Polish population was such that there was little that the Jews could absorb. It was another reason why there was little cultural intercourse between the small Jewish communities and the surrounding population. The difference in intellectual level and the cultural differences of both societies made such intercourse rather difficult. In addition to the cultural isolation, was the prevailing anti-Jewish attitude of the bulk of the Christian population, which made a closer relationship almost impossible. The only social intercourse which was taking place was through trading and other commercial activities, which brought the Jews into contact with the Polish masses as well as with the nobility – a class on a higher intellectual level.

Since commerce and handicraft were degrading occupations for the Polish nobility and incompatible with their status, they were compelled to have recourse to Jewish merchants and artisans to perform these demeaning tasks and to derive a benefit from them. Thus, the Jews became important at every level of society and administration. Every Polish magnate had a Jewish counsellor in his castle, keeping books, writing letters, running the economic show for the Polish nobility. The nobility were eager to have Jews settle in their towns in order to stimulate the development of commerce and handicraft (Mahler, 1942, p.118). Poland in the sixteenth and seventeenth centuries has often been described as 'heaven for the Jews, paradise for the nobles and hell for the serfs' (Abramsky, et al., 1986, p. 3).

Although the nobleman needed the Jew for his economic abilities, he at the same time despised him and looked upon him as a contemptible being. Moreover, the religion of the Jew, the 'enemy of Christ', reinforced this hatred. In addition, with the emergence of a class of Polish traders, the situation changed to the detriment of Jews. A new kind of economic anti-Semitism began to surface when the Jews started to face competition from the Poles. The early advantage that the Jews possessed by their knowledge and experience in trading was slowly eroded by Polish newcomers who always had the power of the state on their side. They succeeded in convincing their rulers to apply severe restrictions against Jewish traders.

It was the nobility who gave seventeenth-century Polish anti-Semitism its specific character and psychological colouring. Inspiration as well as arguments were supplied to these various groups hostile to the Jews, by the Church and above all by members of the Jesuit order. Poland witnessed a wave of religious fanaticism which began at the close of the sixteenth century and reached its peak in the eighteenth century. The anti-Jewish riots, frequent in the seventeenth century, were arranged by students of the Jesuit colleges and by other elements in the urban population, especially on the occasion of religious processions and festivals. Numerous ritual murder trials were initiated by the Jesuits in order to keep the spirit of religious zeal and intolerance alive. The anti-Jewish pamphlets issued by churchmen to demonstrate the 'errors' of the Talmud also struck at Protestants, 'who are not a whit better than the Jews' (Mahler, 1942, p. 120).

Under the influence of the Counter-Reformation, and especially of the Jesuits, reaction set in under the Polish king Sigismunt III (1587–1632). The growing strength of the Counter-Reformation from the end of the sixteenth century, led by the Jesuits, produced an intensification not only of anti-Protestant but also of anti-Jewish animosity. Its leader was the Jesuit Peter Skarga, who officiated in person as prosecutor in a trial for profanation of the Host. Scholars and students, pupils of the Jesuits, were the chief initiators of slanders and riots that degenerated into pogroms (Poliakov, 1974, p. 256).

This attitude was also manifested in the frequent physical attacks and riots on the Jewish streets in urban areas: there were blood libel and host desecration trials in Bochnia in 1605; in Cracow in 1631 and 1635, in Lublin in 1636; and in Łęczyca in 1639. A rumour was spread in the town of Sochaczew that Jews desecrated a sacred wafer by stabbing it until it bled. Three Jews were burned at the stake.

The Church was not alone in attacking Jews. Polish anti-Semitic literature of the sixteenth and seventeenth centuries reflects the hostility of the Polish nobility. The arguments used in this literature dealt with religious accusations against the Jews, but they also emphasised economic competition. The mere fact that Jews were engaged in commerce was a crime, since 'they take the trade away from the city' – from the Christian merchants (Mahler, 1942, p. 116).

At the beginning of the seventeenth century, the distinguished Polish scholar Sebastian Petrycy, who was extremely hostile to the Jews, wrote that 'they [the Jews] corrupt judges with gifts and the lords with bowing' (Hundert, 1986, p.49). He asserted that the Jews were blasphemers, host desecrators, and users of Christian blood. Jews enticed Christians away from their beliefs. This outline of anti-Jewish motifs reflects as accurately as any other the attitude of Christians toward Jews during the seventeenth century.

The Deluge

The year 1648 is known in Polish history as the Deluge and in Jewish history as the edict of 'takh ve-tat' (years according to the Jewish calendar). It heralded the end of the golden age of the Polish Jews and at the same time the decline of Poland. In that year, the Jews of south-eastern Poland and Ukraine were struck by a disaster, which revealed the fragility of their position.

The catastrophe that befell the Jewish community residing in the south-eastern province of Poland had been caused primarily by the exploitation of the Ukrainian peasants by the Poles. The growing export of wheat to western Europe benefited mainly the Polish landlord at the expense of the Polish and Ukrainian peasantry who saw their crops being sold at huge profit. The absentee and usually spendthrift Polish landlord put persistent pressure on his Jewish leaseholder by raising the price of the lease each time it was renewed. The Jew in turn was forced to apply pressure on the peasants.

The Ukrainian peasantry, led by Bogdan Chmielnicki, rose in the late spring of 1648. The rebellion was caused by the cruel treatment by the Poles of the peasants who lived in the south-eastern province, known as the Ukraine. The conflict also had a religious connotation. The population of this territory was Greek Catholic, while Poland was Roman Catholic. In addition, the Ukrainians considered themselves

Russians and looked upon the Poles as conquerors.

The insurrection was primarily aimed at Polish rule and the Catholic church, but the principal onslaught was directed against the Jews, with whom the peasants had had direct contact. The rebellion resulted in the annihilation of hundreds of Jewish communities and the brutal murder of hundreds of thousands of Jews; only those who accepted baptism were spared. Thousand of Jews from villages fled for safety to the fortified towns. These turned out to be a death trap for them. Often Jews fought side by side with Poles to repulse the attacks of Chmielnicki's hordes, but in many cases the Christians of the town sought to purchase their own safety at the price of the blood of their Jewish neighbours (Grayzel, 1968, p. 442). When it came to a direct confrontation between the Poles and the Ukrainian peasants, the Poles always abandoned their Jewish allies to save themselves (Johnson, 1988, p. 259). At Tulchin the Polish troops handed over the Jews to the Cossacks in exchange for their own lives; at Tarnopol, the garrison refused to let the Jews in at all. At Bar, the fortress fell and all the Jews were massacred.

> The Poles made a pact with the Jews to stand together. And two thousand Jews entrenched themselves in the fortress of Tulchin to fight the Cossacks, but the Polish nobles betrayed their allies and broke their pledge. The Jews were left alone and went on fighting until their strength gave out. And in the city of Uman Jews fought for their lives alone. They stood against the enemy until the morning when they were put to death cruelly.
>
> (From the chronicle *Yeven Metzulah* by the rabbi of Ostrov, Nathan Hannover, published in 1653)

It took the Poles ten years to put down the revolt, but the events of 1648–58 and their consequences accelerated the decline of the Polish-Lithuanian Commonwealth and, with it, the situation of its Jewish inhabitants worsened. The Polish economy went into further decline after the wars with the Cossacks and Swedes (1660), resulting in Poland losing her access to the Baltic sea and in 1719 effectively becoming a Russian protectorate.

Various theories as to the causes of the economic decline began to circulate in Poland, but almost all pointed to the Jew as the main culprit for the existing situation. It was said that the Jews had caused the economic weakness after having 'eaten the marrow of the bones of Poland'. Some enlightened Poles, however, recognised the fallacy of this theory. According to Stanisław Szczepanowski: 'because the Poles lack appropriate economic education and live in a world of illusions and fears, they made of the Jews, whom they see in front of them, a scapegoat for all our failures and our own ineptitude' (Oberlaender, 1935, p. 109).

During this period, the Polish Jewry presented a picture of misery and poverty. The situation of the Jewish community was particularly perilous under the Saxon kings (1697–1763). This period is characterised by violent anti-Semitism and frequent sporadic massacres in the east as well as countless trials for ritual murder. Reports of ritual murder and profanation of the Host increased from the beginning of the eighteenth century. This agitation was even given royal approval: 'The blood of Christian children, shed by the infidel and perfidious Jews, cries out to Heaven!', exclaimed the Polish king August II (1697–1733). As for the dignitaries of the Polish Church, they remained faithful to their traditional role of instigators and anti-Jewish propagandists. The Catholic clergy used the usual methods of inventing cases of ritual murder in order to arouse religious frenzy. 'Never was this inhuman accusation made so frequently as in Poland during the first half of the 18th century' (Grayzel, 1968, p. 452).

In 1764 the Polish Diet (parliament), with a stroke of a pen, suppressed the Jewish autonomous Council of the Four Lands, considering it now to be more advantageous to impose upon Jews an individual poll tax of two zlotys, instead of the former group tax. The abolition of the Vaad basically had been caused by pressure from Poles who saw it as providing too many privileges to the Jews.

While the Polish Sejm (parliament) took a decision regarding the Jews, a much more important debate was taking place. The political system in Poland, operating under the rule of 'liberum veto', came under increasing pressure. This rule gave every member of the parliament the power to veto any new law, which meant that a single vote could completely paralyse political decision-making. There was an attempt to amend the law, but it came too late. Due to internal disunity, Poland was militarily, economically and politically too weak to prevent the complete disintegration of the Polish state. In 1772, on the initiative of Prussia, Poland was partitioned between the three neighbouring powers – Prussia annexed the Danzig maritime region, Austria the southern part, and Russia the eastern part of Poland and Belorussia. The collapse of the Polish state significantly affected the Jewish population depending on where it was located after the partition.

2
Jews in the Struggle for Polish Independence

'Yoine*, go to war!' He went, honourable gentlemen, and he fell
for Poland.

('My Żydzi Polscy', Juljan Tuwim, 1942)
[*A derogatory name for Jews]

An important consequence of the 1772 partition was that the bulk of
Polish Jewry now lived under tsarist rule. Of the three Polish territories under foreign rule after the partition, it was only in the
Russian-controlled areas that Jews were subject to severe legal restrictions. In the area under Austrian control, there were only two
regulations restricting the rights of a Jew as a member of a separate
ethnic group: the use of Yiddish and Hebrew language was outlawed
in all public and legal institutions. Apart from that, Jews living in the
Austrian part of Poland had equal rights with other citizens (Hartglas,
1936). Equality of rights also came into force in the area under
Prussian rule, where the number of Jews was negligible.

Following the partition there were several attempts to reform
Poland's political structure, but they were ultimately frustrated by
Russian, Prussian and Austrian intervention. Poland had, nevertheless, obtained from Russia a certain degree of state autonomy.
Elections to the Polish Sejm (parliament) took place in 1788 and in
1791 a new Constitution, the so-called '3 May Constitution', was
adopted. It was based on French revolutionary ideas. The Constitution
did not, however, result in significant changes in the status of Jews.
The Jews retained their former position as innkeepers and middlemen
who squeezed out the profits from the peasants for the benefit of the
Polish noblemen. Thus, the nobility had a vital interest in sustaining
the existing state of affairs. There was, in fact, a group of the higher

nobility who seemed to have displayed a more tolerant and humane attitude toward the Jews not because of a sincere belief in justice but because of their economic interests (Mahler, 1942, p. 123).

The position of the Jewish community as a seperate entity began to be debated as a special problem. A pamphlet published at that time makes the following points: 'a part of the Jewish population should be settled as tenant farmers, but the Jews in the cities should not be restricted in their trade and handicraft, they should enjoy to some extent the rights of citizenship and should be admitted to limited membership in the merchant and craft guilds'. The authors of the pamphlet were the first in the history of Poland to advocate publicly a policy of mutual understanding between 'two nations on one soil'.

In response to these 'progressive' suggestions, the Polish nobility took advantage of the open discussion on the Jewish question in the period of reform to start a campaign against the Jews. In their political pamphlets the Jews were depicted as the cause of Poland's misery, and particularly of the poor state of Polish commerce and industry. A Polish statesman, the priest Staszyc, applied to the Jews such epithets as 'the plague', 'contagion', 'putridness' and the like. Some extreme anti-Semites demanded the expulsion of Jews from the cities and that the expelled Jews become peasants or be used as labourers on public works. As for cities like Warsaw and many others, which applied the old rule of 'de non tolerandis Judaeis', they should expel all the Jews already settled there. This rule should also apply to Jews who converted to Christianity. In many anti-Semitic pamphlets of that time the converts were attacked with the same vigour as the Jews, for 'taking away the bread from Christians' (ibid., p. 126).

In 1793, the second partition of Poland between Russia and Prussia took place, but the aspirations of the Poles to regain sovereignty remained alive. The return in 1794 of Tadeusz Kościuszko, the Polish fighter in the American War of Independence, heralded a new phase in Poland's struggle for independence. He became the leader of the insurrection, which was, however, of very short duration. After several battles with the Russians, the Poles suffered a final defeat in the battle of Maciejowice and Kościuszko was taken prisoner.

The Jewish population did not remain indifferent. The Jews were already imbued with a spirit of patriotism and many Polish Jews actively participated in that uprising with weapons in their hands. Even the Polish anti-Semitic historian, Tadeusz Czacki, praised the Jews in the Kościuszko insurrection: 'The Jews were not afraid of death, thereby proving that the fate of the motherland was close to their heart' (Orlicki, 1983, p. 21).

Jewish participation in that insurrection is well known in Poland through the story of Berek Joselewicz, who organized a volunteer battalion of Jewish cavalry. In September 1794 a Jewish unit numbering a few hundred fighters under his command fought Suvorov's bloody onslaught against Praga almost to the last man. Berek Joselewicz himself was killed on the battlefield near Kock. He became a Polish folk hero and his death was immortalised in a poem by the famous Polish writer Maria Konopnicka.

Tadeusz Kościuszko, the leader of the uprising, expressed his admiration for Jewish participants in the defence of Warsaw. He awarded the 'Virtuti Military' cross to captain Natkiewicz and major Moshe Junghof. Among other Jewish fighters who received medals was sub-lieutenant of the ulan cavalry Josel Dombrowski. In addition to the names of Berek Joselewicz and Jan Rozenfeld, researchers found three more names of Jewish participants in the fighting on the streets of Warsaw. These were Calek Abrahamowicz, Fiszel Abraham and Josek Ickowicz.

One Jewish historian makes a special comment on the fact that during the insurrection there was a high degree of fraternity between the Jews and the Poles. As evidence of this fraternity he notes an 'extremely characteristic sign' that in the course of the fighting there was not a single case of anti-Jewish excess (Schiper, 1935).

It seemed as if the fraternity of arms which prevailed during the fighting for Warsaw would result in some freedoms that were previously denied to the Jews. However, as soon as the fighting stopped, the old antagonisms surfaced once more. A number of Jews were accused of treachery because they allegedly assisted some Russian inhabitants to leave Warsaw. A significant number of Jews were arrested on suspicion of aiding the enemy.

In June 1794, the Jewish community approached the High National Council with a request to cancel the disgraceful 'ticket' tax which every Jew who came to Warsaw had to pay if he wished to live there. This tax was particularly detrimental for poor Jews who were leaving the neighbouring towns and villages for Warsaw. 'It is not right' – the petitioners claimed – 'that a class of residents, who are as useful as any other and who participated in the defence of Warsaw should be denied this right' (ibid.). But all the arguments in favour of abolishing the 'ticket' tax did not convince the authorities and the tax remained unchanged. Even the personal intervention of the leader of the insurrection, Kościuszko, did not help, despite the fact that the banners of the insurrection bore the inscription 'the fatherland is a mother for everyone'. For the Jews, Poland remained a step-mother (ibid.).

Following the collapse of the insurrection, Poland was partitioned for the third time in January 1795. The third partition signified the removal of Poland from the map of Europe. Prussia was allocated 20 per cent of the Polish territory, including the capital Warsaw, Austria received 18 per cent, while Russia obtained the largest part – 62 per cent of Polish territory and 45 per cent of its population.

New hopes for Poland's independence emerged with the Napoleonic conquests. In November 1806 French troops entered Warsaw, and the Tylza Treaty of 1807 established a new Polish Duchy with Fryderyk August as its king. It only lasted until the defeat of Napoleon in Russia in 1812.

Following Napoleon's defeat, a Congress in Vienna in 1815 decided on new borders in Europe: the Poznan and Bydgoszcz departments were incorporated into Prussia as the Great Poznan Duchy, the greater part of Galicia remained in Austria, the rest of the Warsaw Duchy became the Kingdom of Poland and the Russian Tsar Alexander I was proclaimed its king. Almost all of Poland, including the major cities of Warsaw, Lodz, and Lublin with their large Jewish populations, came under Russian rule, but central Poland was allowed to maintain a quasi-autonomous status. This area became known as Congress Poland.

Russia granted Poland a new constitution, which formally gave the Poles a large degree of autonomy. The Polish constitution of 1815, although a liberal document, excluded the Jews. A commission, while recognising Jewish entitlement to civil rights, demanded that the Jews must first change their present occupations and change their system of education. Novosiltsov, the Tsar's representative on the Administrative Council, proposed Jewish legal emancipation in 1817 provided the Jews change their way of life. But the Polish members of the Council declared: 'Let them first become Poles.' Subsequently, the Council decided against the emancipation and, furthermore, to expel the Jews from towns under the old charter of 'De non tolerandis Judaeis', or at least to confine them to special quarters (Margolis and Marx, 1956, p. 665).

Czartoryski, a Pole, was put in charge of cultural affairs in the territories annexed by Russia. He concerned himself with the education of Jews and drew up a memorandum for Alexander I. In a letter to the Emperor of 24 December 1817 he said:

The Jews are the chief cause of the wretchedness of this country. Your majesty, out of piety and wisdom, has wished to convert them to Christianity. But that notion must be the Government's secret, as I said in a paper I submitted on this subject ... otherwise this fine, holy idea cannot succeed ... a beginning must be made by administrative directives on preparing them for conversion; they must be made Christians culturally.

(Beauvois, 1986, p. 82)

The Poles revolted again in November 1830. During this revolt, as during previous attempts, there were many young Jewish volunteers who wished to participate in the struggle for independence. The Warsaw rabbi Dawidson appealed to the Jewish population to take part in the insurrection. However, when the issue of calling Jews to join was debated, the head of the Polish government, Chlopicki, refused to enlist Jews into the Polish guard, and the war minister, Franciszek Morawski, pleaded not to admit the Jews to military service. 'It would pain a Pole to recollect,' he said, 'that in this struggle we could not dispense with the help of the people of Israel' (Schipper, 1932, p. 169). Morawski objected to the idea of 'Polish and Jewish blood being mixed together', and did not want the outside world to say that 'Poland acquired its freedom with Jewish help'. The motion was upheld by the overwhelming majority of the Diet.

While the decree excluding Jews from serving in the Polish army was issued, Jozef Berkowicz, the son of Berek Joselewicz, began the formation of a voluntary 850-man Jewish unit within the National Guard. The leader of the Guard, Antoni Ostrowski, praised the armed posture of the Jewish fighters: 'Their behaviour was excellent, they acted like experienced and intelligent soldiers' (Orlicki, 1983, p. 22).

In other parts of Poland, Jews were asked to collect money to buy provisions and weapons for the uprising. In Warsaw, Cracow, Lodz and other large cities, the Jews contributed large amounts of money for the 'National Treasury'. All these efforts, however, were of no avail. The Polish revolutionaries were hostile to the Jews and accused them of treason. The Jews found themselves in a precarious situation. Separated by the battle lines between the Russians and the Polish fighters, they were being accused by both sides of treason for the benefit of the opposite side.

The final confrontation with the Russians took place in Warsaw in August 1831. After a two-day battle Warsaw capitulated. The collapse of the insurrection was not the end of the attempts at liberating Poland from foreign rule. In 1846–8, Polish émigrés in Paris began to prepare an uprising against the Russians. One of the active participants in this movement was the great Polish poet Adam Mickiewicz. The Political Declaration of the Polish Legion, proclaimed by Mickiewicz in Rome on 29 March 1848, affirmed in Point Ten: 'To our elder brother, Israel, respect, fraternity and help on his way to eternal and earthly welfare; equal rights in every matter' (Kieniewicz, 1986, p. 74). The plan was uncovered by Russian intelligence and led to further persecutions of Jews under Russian rule.

The last insurrection against the Russians took place in January 1863. The period prior to the insurrection had been a particularly difficult one for Polish Jews. The bulk of the Jewish population, except for a small number of Jewish financiers and industrialists, lived in poverty. In a number of towns the law of 'De non tolerandis Judaeis' was still in force, and even in the towns where they were permitted to reside, they were confined to certain areas. They were allowed to acquire property only in exceptional cases; until 1842, about 120 permissions to buy property were granted (Konic, 1938, p. 4). 1859 witnessed a high point in the campaign of the Poles against the Jews. So violent were the attacks launched by a section of the Polish press that this year has come down in the history of Poland as the year of the 'Jewish War' (Mahler, 1942, p. 133).

The situation underwent a sudden and drastic change in 1863 when the Poles made the last attempt to gain independence. Large demonstrations took place over the entire territory of Poland, particularly in Warsaw. Many Jewish patriots participated in demonstrations together with bishops, priests, nuns and ordinary Poles. The battle cry of the day was 'kochajmy się' – 'let us love each other'. Prayers for Poland's liberation were recited in Jewish schools and synagogues. Earlier, in 1861, many Polish–Jewish demonstrations and patriotic protests were organised, especially in Warsaw. In October 1861 when many Poles were arrested by the Russians during a service in the Saint John cathedral, and the Polish clergy ordered in protest the closure of all churches, the Warsaw rabbi, Ber Maizels, the president of the Jewish community, and a certain Jastrow, ordered the closure of all synagogues as a sign of solidarity. On the order of Russian authorities all three spent three months in jail.

The apogee of Polish–Jewish friendship was reached when the leaders of Polish patriotic movement put emancipation of Jews on their agenda. Warsaw rabbis supported the initiative, inviting their co-religionists to collaborate with the Poles and to support their national claims. Polish anthems were sung in synagogues and Jews were to be addressed, henceforth, as 'Poles of Mosaic denomination'.

On 22 January 1863, the Provisional National Government issued an appeal to the Polish nation calling for a war against the occupiers. For the first time in Polish history, the appeal stated that 'all Poles without distinction of faith, origin and descent will become free and equal citizens of the country'. The appeals launched by the government also called for the 'brother Poles of Jewish faith' to participate *en masse* in the revolt. Jews were accepted in all military formations without any discrimination. The appeal clearly implied that Jews would benefit from equal rights should Poland become independent. The promises contained in the appeal were never tested as the insurrection failed two years later.

The insurrection of January 1863 brought about a standstill in anti-Semitic agitation. The Jewish middle class and Jewish intellectuals displayed such fervent patriotism in supporting the uprising by material aid and personal participation in the struggle, that even the most malignant anti-Semites were compelled to express their admiration. Never before and never since was the friendship, conciliation and brotherhood of 'two nations living on one soil' so enthusiastically celebrated as during these years of armed struggle against the Russian oppressor (Mahler, 1942, p. 134).

Despite all the difficulties and problems that the Jews encountered at the end of the eighteenth century, Jewish emancipation in Poland was already being transformed into patriotism and attachment to the native land. Rabbi Ber Maizels, a participant in the national uprising of 1863, referred to the famous, sixteenth-century Rabbi Moses Isserles in the following words:

> Our greatest religious authority, Moses Isserles, on whose ruling the whole house of Israel is based, showed us in his decisions regarding the relations of Jews to nations of other religions, that we should love the Polish nation more than any other, because the Poles have been our brothers for centuries.
>
> (Lichten, 1986, p. 109)

Jewish patriotism had been revealed in the works of famous Polish writers such as Jadwiga Orzeszkowa and Maria Konopnicka. In the well-known epic by the greatest Polish poet, Adam Mickiewicz, *Pan Tadeusz*, one of the main characters – a Jew, Jankiel – is portrayed as having the 'reputation of a good Pole', a patriot fervently and sincerely devoted to the Polish cause. 'The dear old Jew loved the fatherland like a Pole' (Hertz, 1988, p. 28).

However, the views of these Polish writers did not represent the prevailing mood among the Polish intelligentsia. Jewish participation in the Kościuszko uprising in 1794 and in the uprisings in November 1830 and January 1863 has been ignored by most Polish historians. The eminent Polish historian Kraszewski, for example, in his major work The *History of Poland During the Three Partitions,* did not mention the participation of the Jews in the uprisings. Neither did he mention the heroic combat of the Jewish battalion in the defence of Warsaw during the Kościuszko revolt under the command of Berek Joselewicz. The only reference to the Jews in Kraszewski's work were death sentences for treason carried out on a few Jews (Benet, 1992).

As a result of virulent anti-Semitic propaganda, Poland became the arena of several pogroms. In 1881 a pogrom, which took place in Warsaw, was caused by a rumour spread during the midnight mass in the Church of The Saint Cross on Krakowskie Przedmieście street, that Jews have tried to create panic by calling 'fire!' The mob went out into the streets to attack Jewish passers-by and to loot Jewish shops. Further bloody pogroms took place in Galicia in 1898 influenced by the creator of the Popular Movement of Galicia, the Polish priest Stanisław Stojałowski (Korzec, 1980).

When the revolution broke out in Russia in 1905, there were expectations of the collapse of the tsarist regime and with it of the liberation of Poland. However, the failure of the Russian revolution of that year also meant the end of immediate prospects for Polish freedom. At the same time, anti-Semitism was a factor exploited by many Poles as a rallying force of Polish nationalism. These elements were united into the National Democratic Party (Endeks).

The Narodowa Demokracja (National Democracy) was established in the early 1890s and from the outset adopted an anti-Semitic position. The National Democrats' platform of 1903 stated that the Jews ought to be completely subordinated to the Polish national interest and removed from the key positions in Polish economic life, and that their influence in Polish society and culture must be curtailed. Roman Dmowski, the leader of this party – an advocate of the eventual union of Polish lands under tsarist rule – had been an outspoken anti-Semite since his youth, and his expressly stated anti-Jewish position formed an integral part of his political writings (Gutman et al., 1989, p. 98). According to Dmowski, the Jews formed an alien body in Poland and, with the exception of some individuals, they were neither capable nor deserving of being integrated into the Polish nation. For Dmowski, mass assimilation of the Jews was undesirable, as it would undermine the unique national character of the Polish people. The Jews, according to Dmowski, only took advantage of the political and social weakness of Poland in order to penetrate the country. In times of trial they had always joined forces with Poland's enemies, and they constituted not merely a foreign element but a kind of subversive force (ibid.).

A new period of Polish–Jewish relations may be dated from 1910, when the National Democratic Party began exploiting anti-Semitic feelings among the Polish middle classes. Under the veil of Polish nationalism, an economic boycott against the Jews was instigated in 1909–10. A slogan went forth: 'Do not buy from Jews!' Roman Dmowski also launched the slogan 'stick to your own kind'.

The theories of the Polish anti-Semites were borrowed from central Europe; they included a mixture of all kinds of anti-Semitic and racial 'theoretical' systems. The Jews were accused of greed and avariciousness, of capitalism based on speculation, of a will to dominate the world and of spreading a subversive doctrine of atheism, liberalism, anarchism and the like. This propaganda called all Christian peoples to economic, political and cultural self-defence against the dangerous enemies of Christendom.

In Poland it was not as easy as in western Europe to represent the Jewish people as a nation consisting entirely of rich people. The dire poverty of the Jewish population in the small towns and in the Jewish quarters of the big cities was evident and manifest to everybody. But the Polish anti-Semites found this fact a great danger for Poles. The poverty of the Jewish masses, they said, was evidence that the Jews were able to achieve economic superiority over Poles by their miserly living and by their remarkable endurance under the worst conditions of life. The Polish historian Jeske-Chojenski thus explained the poverty of the Polish Jews:

> For thousands of years the Jews have been living in a northern climate. Such a climate calls for more abundant and essential food than the southern climate. Yet they feed themselves in the same way as they did in Palestine. Amidst cold and frost the Jew lives a whole day on a piece of herring, on a crumb of bread watered with brandy and greased with a head of onion or garlic. A Polish dog would die with such a diet, yet the Jew feels fine and multiplies like sand on the seashore.
>
> (Jeske-Chojenski, 1913, p. 90)

One of the main points in the anti-Semitic propaganda was the

great danger for Polish Christian culture emanating from the assimilation of the Jews. The so-called assimilationist Jews were merely
camouflaging the real aim of their nationalistic fellow-Jews by superficial assimilation to Polish culture, which they infected with a
destructive Jewish virus. As for the Zionists, 'they were not a whit
more sincere; they carried on their propaganda for Palestine as a
Jewish home not because they really desired to emigrate but because
they wished in this way to strengthen the Jewish national spirit in
Poland so as to transform that country into a Jewish national state'
(Mahler, 1942, p. 138).

With the war of 1914 drawing near, hopes for Polish independence
grew. An ardent desire was reborn among the Jews to stand up and
fight side by side with their Polish fellow-citizens. Many Jewish
students studying abroad, some from Galicia and others from the
Russian sector of partitioned Poland, joined the Polish Legions created
by Józef Piłsudski. On 5 October 1915, there appeared the Association of
Polish Youth of Jewish Origin – Żagiew (The Torch). In a special manifesto, addressed to the Polish Jews, Żagiew declared that 'beginning
today they [the Jews] will prove by their behaviour and actions, their
sincere sentiments of gratefulness and attachment to the land which for
centuries fed their forebears and where they are buried' (Lichten, 1986,
p. 117). Żagiew and another group called Zjednoczenie also issued a
proclamation to Jewish youth:

> Standing on guard for a Polish idea among Jews, we Polish youth of
> Jewish religion intend to inculcate in the Jewish masses, to which
> we are tied and to which we will irresolvably be tied (in the future)
> by mutual origin, faith and tradition of our fathers, sincere love
> and affection for Poland and sentiments of real citizenship in the
> Polish Republic.
>
> (ibid., p. 118)

A general congress of Zjedoczenie Polaków Wyznania Mojżeszowego
Wszystkich Ziem Polskich (Association of Poles of Mosaic Faith of All the
Polish Lands) was called in Warsaw. The congress stipulated that:

> Without abandoning the faith of our fathers nor renouncing its
> tradition and history, we take our stand unreservedly in favour of
> Polish nationality; we give ourselves wholeheartedly to the Polish
> homeland and desire to serve it and co-operate in its growth and
> development. At the same time we demand full and real equality of

rights and the elimination of economic or political discrimination. We want to be Polish citizens with full rights and duties, and not second-class citizens.

(ibid., p. 121)

The First World War and the Jews

At the outbreak of the First World War, the European powers had aligned themselves into two opposing sides: the Central Powers (Germany and Austria-Hungary) on the one side and the Allies (France, Russia and Britain) on the other. From the outset of the war, Germany was forced to fight on two fronts: against France in the west and Russia in the east. Thus the major areas of Jewish settlement – Congress Poland, Galicia, and Russia – became the scene of battles on the eastern front.

Before the outbreak of the First World War, most Polish parties and political groups, were divided into two opposing political orientations. One supported the central powers (Austria-Hungary) the other backed tsarist Russia. The Revolutionary Fraction, led by Józef Piłsudski, adopted a position on the side of the Central Powers. From the day the Germans advanced into Poland, they sought to enlist the support of the population in the war against Russia. Germany, like Austria-Hungary, allowed Piłsudski, the leader of the Polish liberation movement, to mobilise the Polish Legions to help fight the Russians. Jews had fought in Piłsudski's Polish Legions from their inception, served as high-ranking officers, and held important posts in their civil branches.

In 1915 the Germans broke the Russian defences on the central and northern fronts, forcing the Russians to abandon Vilna, and helped the Austro-Hungarian army to push the Russians out of Galicia. From this time until the end of the war the Central Powers controlled Congress Poland and Galicia.

Poland regained her independence in 1918. The three powers that ruled Poland for almost 150 years were overthrown: tsarist Russia in the Revolution of 1917, and Germany and Austria-Hungary as a result of their defeat by the Allies. On 11 November 1918, the very day that Germany accepted the terms of armistice, the Polish Legions under Piłsudski disarmed the German troops and proclaimed the independence of Poland.

The emergence of an independent Polish state in 1918 posed new and difficult problems for a Jewish community now numbering three million and making up 10 per cent of the population. Despite the prevailing anti-Semitic atmosphere in Poland at the end of the nineteenth century, Jews played an important role in the Polish economy (Hertz, 1988, p. 107). They were represented in foreign trade, in finance and industry, and in the free professions. A large part of the Jewish population in Poland during the period before the First World War was engaged in commerce. As in previous periods, the commercial activities of the Jews were mainly in petty trade in which they had already an established tradition. The social structure of the Jewish community is considered by some Polish historians as the source of anti-Semitism in Poland.

> The occupational structure of the Jewish petty-bourgeoisie favoured the emergence of conflicts between Jews and Poles. The enormous concentration of the Jewish element in commerce, *where there were often cases of swindle*, resulted in the spread of adverse attitudes towards the Jewish merchant who became identified with exploitation.
>
> (Tomicki, 1982, p. 317; italics mine)

Another excuse for Polish anti-Semitism was the fact that due to special historical circumstances Jewish national life flourished in Poland to an extent unparalleled in western or central Europe. Some Polish intellectuals presented the national character of the Jews in Poland as a kind of negative exclusiveness, as 'separateness' and total cultural 'isolation' (Hertz, 1988, p. 13). One Polish historian interpreted Jewish exclusiveness as being a result of historically excessive privileges:

> The Polish kahals led by rabbis are a phenomenon the like of which has never been seen anywhere else. These were small republics with their own elected presidents, and if one were to look at them applying their ... laws of Moses and the Talmud, if one were to be led blindfolded over the innumerable towns from one kahal to another without seeing the rest of the country, one would think of being in Palestine not in Poland.
>
> (Jeske-Chojenski, 1919)

The reality was quite the opposite. From the end of the eighteenth century on, there was a growing trend among Polish Jews to break out of the cultural isolation. It was the beginning of the emancipation movement within Polish Jewry. The younger generation of Jews steadily became more secular and was freeing itself from the religious influences.

Paradoxically, the situation of Jews in Poland began to deteriorate further precisely at the time when religious tolerance was becoming the norm in western Europe, where Jews were granted full civic rights. Polish intellectuals who are proud to emphasise the westernisation of the Polish nation, fail to mention that while Europe had been moving since the Age of Enlightenment towards a more egalitarian society, the Poles were heading in the opposite direction as far as religious tolerance was concerned (Smolar, 1987, p. 32).

The Jews of western Europe had been subjected to secularisation somewhat earlier. The end of the eighteenth century saw the beginning of a movement among east European Jewry that has gone down in Jewish history under the name of Haskalah. Haskalah (in Hebrew: 'Enlightenment'), a movement for spreading modern European culture among Jews, believed that Jewish emancipation required intellectual and social conformity with the non-Jewish population and that the latter could be achieved by modernised and westernised Jewish religion and customs. It thus attempted to mediate between Orthodoxy and radical assimilation.

The movement spread rapidly to the Jews in Poland. When Jewish life had begun to undergo rapid secularisation and when secular studies had become a means for achieving social advancement, the study of other than religious subjects became increasingly accepted and some young Jews broke away from their traditional environment in search for a world outside of their confined space. They had to change not only their habits but their appearance as well. No longer did they wear the traditional black coat and grow long sidelocks; in time they became indistinguishable from an average Pole. Some achieved important positions within the Polish intelligentsia and contributed to Polish culture and art.

Some succeeded in other areas of secular studies. Medicine, for example, was of particular importance for young Jews. For some Jewish families 'to have a son a doctor was now as prestigious as having a son who was a learned rabbi' (Hertz, 1988, p. 103). There was also much interest in the study of state law because it was thought that such knowledge would be useful in business dealings with the outside world. In time, law took its place beside medicine as a means of achieving social respectability through education.

As early as in the first half of the nineteenth century there had come into existence a new group of Jewish merchants, bankers, industrialists, publishers and professional men who had absorbed Polish culture and who regarded themselves as 'Poles of the Old Testament persuasion'.

They were the forerunners of a new trend within the Jewish community – of total assimilation. It was a desire to merge with the basic elements of Polish culture, including the adoption of Christianity, so as to become indistinguishable from the surrounding population.

The decision to assimilate Polish language, culture and people was not motivated by pragmatism alone. At that time Catholicism was already so linked with Polishness that some Jews hoped to become even better Poles by adopting the majority faith. In the nineteenth and early twentieth centuries conversion meant a final step toward unity with the Polish people. As the Jewish historian Shatzky noted:

> Under the political conditions of the time, assimilation did not mean merely embracing Polish culture. The Roman Catholic Church played too important a role in the preservation of Polish culture to make it possible to separate Catholicism from Polonism.
>
> (Lichten, 1986, p. 112)

Antoni Lange, a prominent poet and literary critic, born a Jew, son of an insurgent in the 1831 uprising, published a pamphlet in which he stated:

> To be a Pole is tied so closely to Catholicism that the two things seem to be inseparable. If you are not a Catholic, you are not a Pole. It is one of the falsehoods which are inculcated so deeply that it is difficult to combat it ...
>
> (ibid., p. 113)

Subsequently, Lange converted.

Another Jew, Julian Klaczko, may be considered the first outstanding Polish writer of Jewish origin. He began his career writing poetry in Hebrew and ended as a prominent writer of Polish poetry. He was an ardent Polish patriot who by converting to Catholicism, publicly demonstrated his Polishness. For him, to become a real Pole meant the adoption of their religion.

The influx of Jews into the ranks of the more enlightened Poles did not always meet with favourable reception. Many Poles began to speak of the 'Jewification' of Polish culture, and the Polish upper classes began to treat the newcomers as intruders. On the one hand, especially after 1863, the mass assimilation of Jews was viewed as the sole solution to the Jewish question in Poland; on the other, a distance was kept from those new Poles of the Jewish faith. Paradoxically, that distance increased as the assimilation of Jews gathered momentum. Many Poles – like Jeske-Chojenski, for example – saw assimilation as the pernicious infiltration of Polish culture by elements that carried alien and hostile values.

As anti-Semitism was growing at the turn of the nineteenth century, the adherents of assimilation often faced the dilemma of how to continue their activities in the face of increasing Polish prejudice and discrimination against Jews. They concluded that assimilation could not depend on the attitudes of the other side. Assimilation was a process that must go on, regardless of adverse conditions. However, despite the expressions of Jewish solidarity with the Polish cause, the attitude of the Polish intelligentsia and the lower middle classes remained hostile on the whole. Polish analysts provide a peculiar interpretation of that period.

In the last 30 years before the outbreak of the First World War, according to one such analyst, Orlicki, the 'young' Polish bourgeoisie and lower middle class entered into a period of sharp competition with any 'non-Polish' economic domination. The only 'non-Polish' competitors mentioned by Orlicki are Jews: Bloch, Epstein, Fajans, Kronenberg, Loevenstein, Natanson and Wawelberg, who, according to Orlicki, established or developed trading banks and insurance companies, the chemical, paper and sugar industries, rail and water transport on the Vistula river (Orlicki, 1983, p. 28). What should have been to the credit of Polish Jews for their initiative in developing the economy, became a question of 'economic domination'. Once the Jews performed their task they were superfluous. The main problem to be solved was how to get rid of them.

The debate of how to solve the Jewish question was already in full swing well before Poland achieved its independence in 1918. There were basically two different and contrasting principles advocated by the adherents of a particular solution.

The conservative, clergy-dominated group suggested that the Jews renounce their religion and their national peculiarity in favour of complete assimilation or that they should leave Poland. The national-democratic camp expressed its scepticism as to the possibility of Polonising such a large mass of Jews and saw the solution of the Jewish question in their migration from Poland. To stimulate such mass migration, they advocated economic warfare, which would force the Jews to leave and at the same time provide economic opportunities for Polish elements.

The Polish socialists saw the solution in the removal of religious superstitions, which, they claimed, would gradually remove the wall separating Christian Poles from Poles of Mosaic faith. 'In a situation in which complete emigration of Jews from Poland is impossible, and their assimilation improbable, Jews should be emancipated and their rights as a minority should be recognised' (Orlicki, 1983, p. 29).

As subsequent events in Poland have shown, it was the first alternative that finally prevailed in independent Poland.

Part II

Before the Great Catastrophe (1918–39)

3
The Polish Eagle Spreads its Wings (1918–35)

This is the day of blood and glory,
Let it be the day of resurrection.
In the rainbow of the French sky,
The white eagle spreads his wings,
He calls us from high above,
Free Poland, throw off your chains!

(A popular Polish song)

On the day Germany accepted the terms of armistice, the Polish Legions under the command of Piłsudski marched into Warsaw and the independence of Poland was proclaimed. The newly acquired freedom was met by a wave of patriotism and national pride. A popular song spoke of Polish fighters who began in France their march toward Polish liberation.

But while the general mood of the population of Poland was one of immense exhilaration and the white eagle, the Polish national symbol, flew high in the Polish sky, the dark shadow of its wings began to spread over Polish Jewry. No sooner had Poland regained her freedom when there appeared clear signs of Polish hostility towards the Jewish population. The new Poland was born in an anti-Jewish atmosphere (Rudawski, 1987).

As soon as the Germans withdrew from Warsaw, signs appeared throughout the capital of free Poland calling for a boycott of Jewish stores, and only a month after the establishment of the assembly of the Sejm Ustawodawczy (Constituent Parliament) – on 19 March 1919 – the Związek Ludowo-Narodowy tabled a motion which resulted in a Commission for Jewish Affairs being set up. Its task was 'the comprehensive examination of the Jewish question ... with a view to resolving the problem'.

Anti-Semitism had been spreading in Poland long before the country became independent. The National Democratic party (Endeks) established in 1897 contained in its programme a demand to de-Judaeise the Polish economy, while the Christian Democrats and, to a lesser extent, the largest peasant party, 'Piast', had also in their programmes anti-Jewish paragraphs. Anti-Jewish messages were also preached from the pulpits in the churches by a significant part of the Catholic clergy. The declaration of Polish independence in 1918 was followed by a wave of pogroms in many places. They were perpetrated not only by the Polish population at large, but also by the liberating armed forces under the command of general Haller. Whenever Haller's units were approaching, the Jews were in fear of pogroms at the hand of the 'Hallerczyki' – the name given to his troops.

As the Polish units continued their advance, they left a trail of violence, destruction and death. In every liberated village taken over by the Poles, it was the defenceless Jewish population that became the principal victim. A pogrom in the town of Kielce on 5 November 1918 occurred six days before the official date of Polish independence. In Lida near Vilno, after the city was taken by the Poles a pogrom resulted in 37 deaths and 150 wounded. The arrival of the Polish army in Vilna was followed by a pogrom that lasted three days and took over 60 victims (including a number of old men in the synagogue). The liberation of Cracow and Lvov on the 28 October was accompanied by pogroms in both towns. Within months of gaining independence a few hundred Jews were murdered either by the mob or by Polish soldiers, and scores of hundreds were wounded. A dramatic event occurred in the town of Pinsk on 5 April 1919, when the local Jews gathered in order to discuss the distribution of flour sent from America to make bread for Passover. While the meeting was taking place in the 'House of the People' – a Zionist club – it was surrounded by a unit of the Polish army which went on a shooting spree, killing between 50 and 100 of those who attended the meeting.

The Polish Minister of Military Affairs, General Leśniewski, presented his version of what happened:

> On the morning of Saturday 5 April a secret meeting of the Bolshevik organisation took place, despite notices put up on street corners 'forbidding all gatherings' and announcing a state of martial law ... Major Łuczyński, the military commandant, was warned that the meeting would discuss in detail the plan to kill the Pinsk garrison on the night of 5 April. Łuczyński sent out a small

detachment of soldiers ... Of the 80 participants of the Bolshevik
meeting, 33 were shot on the spot.

(Lewandowski, 1987, pp. 55–6)

The events of 1918–19 prompted the US government to send a
commission under the chairmanship of Henry Morgenthau to carry
out an investigation. A British mission also was sent to inquire into
the situation of the Jews in Poland. The international reaction to the
Polish pogroms was expressed by the future American President
Hoover (he was representing the US at the peace conference), who said
at the time: 'the fact that the perpetrator of these crimes is the Polish
nation, which for over a century had evoked the sympathy of the
whole democratic world, created a profound disappointment and
brought out some doubts about the maturity of the Polish nation.
There is even a question whether Poland deserves its independence'
(Korzec, 1980, p. 67).

The history of the Polish Jews since the day Poland became independent is an unbroken record of persecutions and murder. Any
internal or international political event involving Poland invariably
brought in its wake severe consequences for the Jewish population.

In the spring of 1920, a conflict between Poland and Soviet Russia
erupted into a full-scale war. The Jewish population supported the
Polish war effort and tens of thousands of Jewish men and women
served in regular military units on the front lines. Wherever the
Bolsheviks were driven out, the Jewish community greeted the Polish
army with bread and salt. But in many places, as soon as the Russian
army withdrew, Polish soldiers aided by Polish civilians turned against
the Jews, accusing them of treachery and collaboration with the
Bolsheviks (*Images*, 1977).

The conflict created a genuine 'Bolshevik' psychosis among the
Polish population. It was reinforced by propaganda emanating from
the Church which constantly proclaimed that bolshevism was a
creation of the Jews and that its aim was to conquer the world beginning with Poland. Some posters depicted soldiers of the Red Army
carrying white and blue flags with the star of David. The propaganda
was accompanied with a wave of pogroms – in Minsk Mazowiecki,
Siedlce, Lukow, Białystok and Włodawa. Military tribunals kept
pronouncing death sentences and executing a great number of Jewish
'spies'. In Płock, Rabbi Shapiro was killed under the pretext of sending
signals to the enemy after being seen in a prayer shawl on the balcony
of his house.

N., a native of Vilna and a witness of the liberation of his home town by the Polish army, describes thus what happened in October 1920, on the day the Polish General Żeligowski and his army units occupied the city:

> I was only a child, but I still have before my eyes an image I will never forget. Among the many Jewish synagogues in Vilna there was one in our little street where my father was the treasurer. On this Saturday, about midday, the church bells began to ring to announce the arrival of the Polish army under the command of Żeligowski who had driven out the Russians from Vilna. Riding a horse with a drawn sword in his hand he was approaching the Ostro-Bramska Cathedral. Suddenly, I heard loud, piercing screams. As the Jews came out of the synagogue they were attacked by the soldiers and the Polish mob and a pogrom began. Soon, in the middle of the roadway and on the pavements, lay scores of Jews dead or wounded. My father was among the killed. This was the way in which the Poles had celebrated the liberation of Vilna.
>
> (Interview with the author)

The Minority Treaty

The emergence of a Polish state within the borders fixed by the Treaty of Versailles was a kind of an anachronism. In a state in which every third citizen was not considered a Pole, the concept of a nation-state was rather misleading. The 1931 census shows that out of a total population of 31,916,000, only 21,993,000 (68.9 per cent) were Poles. Of the largest minorities, 4,442,000 (13.9 per cent) were Ukrainians and 2,733,000 (8.6 per cent) were Jews (Tomicki, 1982, p. 310).

Polish analysts Piotr Dunin-Borkowski and Tadeusz Holowko agree that of all national minorities in Poland the Jews were the only one that accepted Polish statehood as the framework for their life and actions. Such was not the case with the Ukrainians, the Belorussians, the ethnic Germans, and the Lithuanians, among all whom strong nationalistic tendencies existed. The 'Institute for the Study of the National Minority Problem', stated that it was unwise to antagonise the Jewish population – the only minority without either territorial claims or any other demands affecting the status or frontiers of the Polish Republic (*The Jewish Chronicle*, 9 January 1931). Yet it was only the Jewish minority that was singled out as being alien.

The situation of the Jews in Poland surfaced on the international scene after the end of the First World War when the question of protection of national minorities, including the Jews, arose. Following negotiations in Paris, the Polish Minority Rights clause was inserted as part of the Paris Peace Conference. The Minority Treaty as it applied to Poland was a special case because it contained a special mention of Jewish minorities.

Despite opposition by the extreme nationalistic elements in the Sejm (Polish parliament) 'on the ground that it is an intolerable interference with the sovereign rights of Poland' (Black, 1987, p. 27), the Minority Treaty was signed by the Poles on 28 June 1919 and ratified on 31 July 1919. In addition, the Polish Constitution of 17 March 1921 in its Article 95 stated that 'the Polish Republic assures full protection of life, freedom and assets of all regardless of origin, nationality, language, race and religion'.

The Minority Treaty which imposed upon the Polish state the duty to protect the rights of national minorities, including Jews, was often broken, and a number of petitions protesting the treatment of national minorities were presented to the League of Nations. During the period 1920 to 1931, 155 complaints against the Polish state were lodged with the League.

Article 12 of the Minority Treaty, which gave the League of Nations the right to supervise the execution of the Treaty, was abrogated by Poland in August 1934, and on 13 September the Polish Government announced that it would refuse to cooperate with the League of Nations in matters pertaining to the question of minorities protection (*Unity in Dispersion*, 1996).

Symptomatic of the anti-Jewish bias of the first parliament was the retention of some of the pre-First World War laws which restricted the rights of Jews. On 12 June 1919, Jewish deputies – Grunbaum, Thon, Hartglas and others – introduced a motion in the Sejm for the removal of the regulations of the Polish Kingdom, going back to November 1841, which restricted certain rights of the Jewish population. The debate regarding the removal of all restrictive laws, which were still in force after Poland gained her independence, lasted until the summer of 1925.

A few examples will illustrate the situation. A letter addressed to the leaseholders of a mine in the Dombrowski region stated the following: 'The Office of the Mines informs you that the partnership agreement concluded on 4 July 1923 is illegal, because Maurycy alias Moryc Meitlis, as a Jew has no right to engage in mining according to art. 495 of mining legislation of 1912' (Hartglas, 1936).

The regional Land Department in Warsaw wrote to Jankiel Szarfszechter in Falenice on 26 January 1928: 'The regional Land Department informs you that in conformity with the regulations of 1891, according to which any person of Mosaic faith may not acquire land, the permission to buy land from Marcin Jaroszewicz of Zagozd is thereby denied' (ibid.).

The Municipality of Siennice of the Minsk Mazowiecki region of the Warsaw district wrote to Dawid Jablonka on 7 February 1929: 'The municipality of Siennice informs you that according to art. 295 of the regional law of 1864, the starosta [county head] of the region of Minsk Mazowiecki has rejected the resolution of the general meeting of Siennice in the matter of electing a soltys [village head], because the elected candidate Szlama Chorowicz is of Mosaic faith' (ibid.).

Piłsudski's government made strenuous attempts at restraining the anti-Semitic trends in the country, but when Piłsudski withdrew from political life in 1922, the anti-Semites took advantage of his absence from the government to unleash a wave of anti-Jewish propaganda in the parliament and outside. The most uncompromising position was adopted by Stronnictwo Narodowe and other organisations under its influence. Its economic, cultural and social anti-Semitism had been the cause of numerous, sometimes violent, anti-Jewish actions by the extreme wings of the nationalistic Obóz Narodowo-Radykalny (National-Radical Camp), Falanga, and Związek Młodych Narodowców (the Union of Young Nationalists).

Piłsudski – the Protector of the Jews

Political life in independent Poland in the early 1920s was, to a great extent, dominated by the conflict between Józef Piłsudski and Roman Dmowski – the founder of the National Democratic party, whose members were popularly known as Endeks. Anti-Semitism formed an important element of this party's ideology. Only those of the 'Polish race', asserted the National Democrats, qualified for citizenship, and a 'Pole' had to prove that he had not been Jewish for three generations. It was one of the first applications of racial discrimination, years before the advent of National Socialism in Germany (Black, 1987, p. 15).

In the struggle for power, the National Democrats employed anti-Semitic slogans, counting both on their universality and that they would be readily taken up by the voters. The Endeks enjoyed the support of the Catholic Church and many members of the Church hierarchy were National Democrats. Edmund Dalbor, the first primate of independent Poland, was an ardent supporter of the National Democrats and their anti-Semitic ideology.

In 1926, supported by the armed forces and some political groups, Piłsudski affected a *coup d'état*. The coup came as a result of political and economic instability in post-war Poland and was welcomed by the vast majority of the Polish population, for whom Piłsudski was a national hero and the liberator of Poland. The Jews strongly backed Piłsudski not only because they hoped he would remedy the ills of the previous regime, but because of his stand regarding the problem of minorities in Poland, including the Jewish minority.

Indeed, the anti-Jewish trend was significantly moderated in the first years after the Piłsudski coup and particularly during the term of Kazimierz Bartel as head of the government. On 19 July 1926, the Prime Minister, Professor Bartel, made the following statement in the Sejm: 'The Government will announce in the proper manner that all restrictions applicable to Jews introduced by the former occupying powers are abolished and no longer applicable to the Jewish population' (Hartglas, 1936, p. 160).

Although the activities of Polish political groups whose ideology contained a great amount of anti-Semitism were more restricted after Piłsudski's coup, they nevertheless relentlessly pursued an intensive anti-Jewish propaganda campaign within the parliament and among Polish students at the universities, intelligentsia, and peasants in the villages. By exploiting the religious elements and with the help of the clergy, who gave them a great deal of sympathy and support, they were able to exert great influence upon the uneducated masses. As for the intelligentsia, they kept pointing out the alleged competition from Jewish students. As a result of this campaign, disturbances directed against Jewish students erupted at some universities. At the same time the National Democrats kept attacking the government for its liberal policies toward the Jews. They were helped by a pastoral letter issued by the Polish bishops on 5 December 1927 calling for united action by Catholics to support the anti-Semitic National Democrats in the coming elections.

Influenced by an endemic anti-Semitism rooted in religious beliefs, Christian Poles came to see the Jews as an alien element that had no place in independent Poland. There was, in their eyes, a clear distinction between Christian Poles and Jews, with the result that in independent Poland Jews could not call themselves Poles in the same way as Jews in France or America, for example, called themselves

French or American. In Poland, a Pole was meant to be a Christian, and a Jew something distinct from a Pole.

The distinction between a Christian Pole and a Jew had already been ingrained in the minds of Poles from the early childhood. The image of a Jew as synonymous with a killer of Christ had been transmitted not only by the clergy but by the older generation of Poles.

> A creek was flowing nearby and as it was in the middle of a hot summer day I went to play in the shade of the trees lining the creek. A few boys of my age were splashing in the water and soon I joined them, got undressed, and plunged into the creek. They were a friendly bunch and were rather curious to meet a city boy.
>
> I don't know whether all 9-year-old children have an acute sense of observation but this bunch was certainly very perceptive, for as soon as I took off my clothes they began to look at me or, to put it more precisely, at a certain part of my anatomy that appeared to them somehow peculiar. They immediately noticed that I was circumcised.
>
> 'You are a Jew! You are a Jew!' – one of the boys exclaimed. There was no real animosity in his voice – rather curiosity. Another boy was less friendly: 'We must not play with him. My mum told me not to get near a Jew.'
>
> 'Why not?' – I asked.
>
> 'My mum said the Jews killed Jesus.'
>
> 'Who is this Jesus?' – I asked.
>
> There was silence. Nobody seemed to know. One boy attempted to explain:
>
> 'They nailed him to a cross; I mean the Jews did. This is why we must make the sign of the cross ourselves.'
>
> They began to argue. Finally, one of the boys suggested that if I made the sign of the cross I could play with them.
>
> (Author's recollections)

Despite the open hostility emanating from anti-Semitic groups and from the population at large, the Jews constantly declared their loyalty to the Polish state. In 1928, during preparations for the commemoration of the tenth anniversary of Polish independence, the Jews were the only minority to announce their participation – all others declined to take part. Dmitry Levitsky, a Ukrainian nationalist, stated in an interview that 'we Ukrainians are not loyal to the Polish state, and we do not want to be'.

There was the trial of Steiger, who was charged with trying to assassinate the Polish president by throwing a bomb at him. The anti-Semites made much out of it because he happened to be Jewish. It was a Polish 'Dreyfus' affair. Steiger was subsequently acquitted when it was found that a Ukrainian nationalist was responsible. Yet the Poles did not show any appreciable signs of anti-Ukrainian sentiment at the same time as they were attacking Jews and accusing them of a lack of loyalty.

Polonisation of the Jews

According to the Minority Treaty, Poland was obliged to respect the rights of minorities in the area of schooling. Minorities were entitled to establish and maintain their own private schools and to teach in their native language. The Jewish community had established a wide net of private schools giving various degrees of religious instruction, ranging from strictly orthodox to the entirely secular. They were financed by Jewish organisations and did not benefit from state subsidies. It must also be said that the state did establish a number of state schools especially for children of 'Mosaic faith' in which Jewish religious festive days were observed, but instruction was in the Polish language.

By the 1930s there occurred a distinctive evolution in Jewish schools. Jewish primary and high schools in which Yiddish and Hebrew were taught, gradually introduced bilingual education, in Yiddish and Polish, and Hebrew and Polish. Statistics show that while in the 1925/6 school year, only 3 per cent of all Jewish schools were bilingual, the proportion rose to 50 per cent in 1937/8, and showed an upward trend.

The process of Polonisation which had begun at the end of the nineteenth century became much stronger after Poland regained her independence. By the early thirties the class specified in Poland as intelligentsia contained a large Jewish element. In 1931, Jews and those of Jewish origin constituted about 16 per cent of the total intelligentsia in Poland. Jews comprised almost 50 per cent of free professionals and about 55 per cent of the medical profession. They also constituted a high percentage in literature and arts (Tomicki, 1982, p. 318).

Jewish contributions to Polish culture are beyond dispute. The most popular Polish poet before the war was undoubtedly Julian Tuwim, but the list of Jewish contributors to Polish literature includes names such as Antoni Słonimski, Bolesław Leśmian, Józef Witlin, Adam Ważyk and Mieczysław Jastrun. Jews were also among the great musical performers. Names such as Henryk Wieniawski, Wanda Landowska, Arthur Rubinstein and many others are well known not only in Poland, but in the world. There were also outstanding Jews in Polish art, ranging from Maurycy Gotlieb to Henryk Kuna, Eugeniusz Zak, Mela Mutermilch and Roman Kramsztyk. People of Jewish origin also left their mark in the Polish theatre. Among Polish actors, Stanisław Stanisławski was considered brilliant at portraying Polish characters, and his mastery of the Polish language was thought unsurpassed.

The assertion by Polish anti-Semites that Polish culture was being 'Jewified' may not have been misplaced, for the contribution of people of Jewish origin to Polish culture was indeed very significant. That, however, did not mean that Polish culture acquired Jewish features. What most Jewish contributors had in common was a strong desire to become part of the Polish nation, and there was nothing 'Jewish' in their creativity. Although some of these people were actually Jewish or of Jewish origin, they did not consider themselves as such. They had entirely broken away from their Jewishness and had fully identified with things Polish. 'They all lived in the world of Polish values and attempted to represent those values in their creations that had little to do with the tradition of Jewish culture' (Hertz, 1988, p. 237).

Yet the assimilationist trend among Jewish contributors was looked upon by Polish intellectuals as an invasion. In prewar Poland considerable effort was made to prove that Julian Tuwim was a Jewish poet who wrote (badly!) in Polish (Hertz, 1988). Similar assertion was made in Poland as recently as 1998 about the greatest Polish poet, Adam Mickiewicz (see Chapter 11). Polish Jews were in a no-win situation: accused of separateness on the one hand and of intrusion into Polish culture on the other.

The Great Depression and its aftermath

The economic crisis of the 1920s gave the anti-Semites a new propaganda weapon. Appealing to the general mood of the Polish population, Polish anti-Semites classified the Jew as a competitor and as an exploiter. By the late 1920s anti-Jewish tendencies became more prevalent, for in addition to the inherent religious anti-Semitism among the Polish population, economic difficulties began to play their role in creating increased animosity. Rising unemployment attracted the attention of political groups who began to exploit the situation by blaming the presence of the Jews in Poland as the root cause of all ills. If only one could get rid of the Jews, they claimed, there would be work for everybody. The reality of the situation was that the hardest hit by the economic crisis were the Jews. The overwhelming majority of Jews in the cities and small towns in central and eastern Poland lived under conditions of dire and deepening poverty, and their income lagged behind the average income of a Polish industrial worker (Gutman et al., 1989, p. 102).

Employment opportunities, which were already quite restricted for the Jews on account of discrimination on the part of Christian employers, became even more restricted during the depression; scarcely any Jews were accepted into government services. While the Jews constituted about 10 per cent of the population they accounted in 1923 for only 2.23 per cent of government employees, and that proportion fell to 1 per cent in 1930. Jews constituted 30 per cent of the urban population, but accounted for only 2–3 per cent of municipal employees (Ben-Sasson, 1976, pp. 955–6). In some cases, employment opportunities were denied to Jews even in Jewish enterprises. A Jewish newspaper reported at the time that a strike erupted at a textile factory owned by Ettington, a Jew, because Christian workers numbering several hundred objected to the employment of the one and only Jewish worker (*The Jewish Chronicle*, 16 Nov. 1928).

At the same time, the governing council of the Stronnictwo Narodowe (Nationalist Party) organised a boycott of Jewish businesses. Similar activities were adopted by the Ruch Młodych Obozu Wielkiej Polski (Youth Movement of the Camp for a Great Poland). Signs in front of some shops located outside the Jewish quarter indicating a Christian owner began to appear here and there. This period saw also the beginning of physical harassment of Jews who ventured into the Christian neighbourhood. For a religious Jew who retained a distinctive way of dress and hairstyle, this was forbidden territory, but even for those who adopted a European style of life but could be recognised as Jews on account of facial features, parts of towns had become unsafe.

Some Jews, certainly a small minority, lived outside the Jewish quarter amongst Christian Poles. They did their utmost to hide their Jewishness, at least in appearance, so as not to attract special attention from their Christian neighbours. It was a kind of social mimesis – an attempt to blend in to the environment in which they lived. They did not speak Yiddish and generally had assimilationist tendencies, including conversion to Christianity.

Anti-Semitic incident often acquired religious connotations. In June 1929 such an incident occurred in the city of Lvov. On 2 June a

Catholic procession in honour of the celebration of Corpus Christi passed in front of a Jewish college on Zygmuntowska street. Some of the participants in the procession claimed that they saw Jewish girls making obscene gestures during the passing of the procession. This was sufficient to provoke a violent reaction among the faithful, resulting in the almost total destruction of the college by the mob. The Church, which at first declared the rumours false, did nothing to calm the mob. On the contrary, it organised religious processions at the same place for the next seven days in defiance of the Jewish 'heretics'.

Beginning in June 1931, anti-Jewish incidents took place in a number of other cities and villages: in Złoczów, Michalin, Konskie, Radom, Lublin, Jeziorna and Grodzisk. Serious incidents took place in Cracow on 14 and 15 November when windows in the Saint Bernardine church were broken. The Cracow cardinal Sapieha supported on this occasion the theory that it was a deliberate provocation on the part of the Jews.

In March 1933, only a few weeks after the Nazis came to power in Germany, the Endeks staged their first large-scale anti-Jewish riots in many towns and villages. In November 1933, a well-known lecturer at Warsaw University, Professor Rybarski, stated in the Sejm on behalf of the Endeks that 'there is no room for the Jews in Poland'. 'Poland without Jews' became the official slogan of the Endeks (Marcus, 1983, p. 346).

Following the Nazi accession to power in Germany, a number of organisations based on the Nazi model sprang up all over Poland. In April 1934 the National Democrats merged with other groups to form a National Radical Camp, generally known as ONR or Nara. Its official organ, *Sztafeta*, had a wide distribution and faithfully copied Nazi publications concerning Jews.

There was also a call not only for an economic boycott but for a 'kulturkamf' as well: the elimination of Jewish presence in art, literature and social life. *Gazeta Warszawska* – a leading Warsaw daily – began to publish lists of Jewish writers, poets, actors, professors and lawyers, some of whom had been Christian converts for generations.

On 7 June 1934, a delegation of rabbis obtained an audience with the Cardinal Krakowski of Warsaw in order to try and invoke his influence to curb anti-Jewish excesses. The cardinal did not miss this opportunity to declare his animosity toward the Jews. Even if he condemned violence as contrary to Christian ethics, he insisted that the Jews had brought it upon themselves, for they were hurting Christian feelings by propagating atheism and publishing pornographic literature.

The signing of the Polish–German non-aggression treaty on 26 January 1934 signalled a further move against the Jews. The events taking place in Germany spilled over the border and reinforced the current of anti-Semitism among the Polish population. For not only did attacks against Jews become a daily occurrence, but the search for a solution to the Jewish question in Poland acquired a form not dissimilar to that adopted by the Nazis in Germany.

Government authorities began introducing rules and regulations that discriminated against Jews in the economic and educational areas. The official government news agency PAT reported in April 1935 that the Ministry of Education had launched a competition for 22 stipends for students of state-run gymnasiums. The condition of entry was that the applicant must be of Catholic ancestry. Similar measures were taken elsewhere. The Lodz City Council adopted an 'Aryan' resolution giving the right to a subsidy for literature and art only to those who could prove Christian roots.

Gazeta Warszawska – the official organ of Polish anti-Semites – constantly stressed the results of anti-Jewish policies of the Third Reich as an invaluable example for all nations that had a Jewish problem. 'They teach us that the Jewish question can only be resolved by strong decisive action. The country will consider the problem solved only when not a single Jew will remain' (*Unzer ekspres*, 10 April 1935). Another daily, the *Dziennik Narodowy*, whose editor was Professor Rybarski, praised the Nuremberg laws just passed in Germany: 'anyone who understands the Jewish question and has a feeling of national pride, must admit that this way of solving the Jewish problem is wise and correct'.

The virulent anti-Jewish propaganda was accompanied by a wave of attacks on individual Jews on the streets, as well as in the universities and other institutions where there was a Jewish presence. Jews were attacked in Vilna, and in the town of Kielce there was a pogrom with many Jewish casualties. The authorities attempted to suppress the news about the disturbances and resorted to severe censorship. The Jewish newspaper in Kielce, the *Kieltzer Zeitung*, was confiscated by the censor for reporting news which could 'create communal tension'. The editor was taken to court for publishing an article about the pogrom and for spreading 'false rumours'.

The attacks had by now become less discriminating; not even women, old men or children were spared. The Jewish press reported several cases of assault against children: 'there are constant bloody attacks against Jewish children attending Public School no. 108 at

Wolność street no. 16. The children are being attacked with stones, sticks and even knives' (*Unzer ekspres,* 1 April 1935).

> In 1935 my parents enrolled me at Public school no. 108 located on Wolność street no. 16. Ironically, Wolność – meaning freedom – did not stand up to its name. It was located on the border between the Jewish and Polish areas of Warsaw. What I dreaded most, happened. From the very first day on my way to school, I was subjected to attacks by the Poles who lived nearby. They would called me 'dirty Jew' and all kinds of other insulting names. It was not only the young Polish boys who abused me, but even grownup men and women sometimes participated in this behaviour. I felt terribly humiliated and defenceless, but what could I do? And so on my way to school and back I would skirt the walls or make a detour in order to avoid the insults thrown at me and the danger of being beaten. It was a harrowing experience which I thought I would have to endure for a whole year.
>
> (Author's recollections)

The press also quoted examples of positive action by some government authorities or the judiciary aimed at preventing anti-Jewish acts or to punishing those responsible of outrages against the Jews. For example, two Poles were sent to jail for refusing to render assistance to a Jew who was drowning in a river near Troki. The accused defended themselves by saying they thought there would be 'one Jew less'. In Lublin, the court issued an order prohibiting the distribution of anti-Jewish tracts.

'Ghetto benches' at universities

The Polish intelligentsia, especially those represented by university students, became the most vehement propagators of anti-Semitism. They not only asserted their attitudes in words, but more often than not had recourse to violence against their Jewish fellow students under the guise of Polish honour and patriotism. A rallying call of the nationalist youth was the campaign against what they believed was the excessively high number of Jews entering higher education. As early as 1919, Poznan university introduced a discriminatory quota system for students admitted to the university. A Jewish deputy, Itzhak Grunbaum, complained in the Sejm about the introduction of a percentage quota system, but to no avail.

The 1922–3 academic year began with a series of rallies at various universities. In September 1922 a memorandum was addressed to the senates of all universities demanding the introduction of a *numerus clausus*. To back up the demand, a rally was called for 1 October 1922, and the demand was renewed in February 1923. In Cracow, rallies were held on 23 October 1922 and on 19 March 1923. The situation was much the same in Warsaw. A rally on 23 November 1923 passed a motion calling for imposition of a *numerus clausus*. It was handed over to the Vice-Minister for Religious Affairs and Public Education.

The Parliamentary Club of the Popular National Union in the Sejm supported these demands. A motion was proposed for changes in articles 85 and 86 of the Universities Act of 13 July 1920. The motion proposed the addition to article 85 of a stipulation that 'in Polish institutions of higher education, the number of students admitted to any given department who are of non-Polish nationality or of Jewish faith, must not exceed the percentage of the said national group, or Jewish faith within the total population of the Polish State' (Rudnicki, 1987, p. 250).

The motion was debated in the Sejm and distributed to faculty boards for comments. Out of 42 faculty boards, only 9 rejected the proposal, and 27 supported the proposal in its entirety. The medical faculty was unanimously in favour of percentage quotas. Seventy-five per cent of professors approved limits on Jewish student numbers and about half were in favour of a percentage quota. Among the few exceptions were the professors of the philosophy faculty, who considered the proposal as being 'against the dignity of the academic community' (ibid., p. 251).

The government formed after the May 1926 coup embarked on several initiatives aimed at reaching a solution to the quota system. In July 1927, minister Gustaw Dobrucki issued a reminder that the law did not allow the introduction of limits based on nationality or religion. He stated that 'the government of Marshal Pilsudski is absolutely opposed to the *numerus clausus*. These measures, however, were not matched by appropriate action in the universities, and students continued to demand the introduction of a quota system. In February 1928, disturbances broke out at Cracow university when Polish students demanded complete segregation of Jews at the university. They finally agreed to stop their campaign after the Jewish students consented to wearing student caps of a different colour to those of the Christians.

At Warsaw University unrest broke out in the law faculty during which several Jewish students were severely beaten up. Incidents also took place in Vilno. Here an anti-Jewish demonstration ended in tragedy. A Polish student of the law faculty, Stanisław Wacławski, was struck on the head by a stone during a brawl and died later in hospital. A wave of strikes and rallies organised by the student organisation Młodzież Wszechpolska ('All-Polish Youth') spread over many academic centres in Poland. Motions demanding the introduction of a *numerus clausus* were passed and, for the first time, the call for a *numerus nullus* was heard.

In the autumn of 1931, the Endeks attempted to physically prevent Jewish students from attending classes, causing many Jewish injuries, including a number of deaths. *The Jewish Chronicle*, published in London, contained reports about incidents at Polish universities which the local press was forbidden to publish by the Polish censor. This is what a correspondent of the English newspaper reported:

> I could never have believed that such hatred could exist in the hearts of men and women and continue to last for such a long time unbroken by even a look at the object of hatred. But I saw it at the University of Warsaw where Poland's future citizens are reared. What struck me most was that Christian girl students should show such bitter hatred as I witnessed. They did not even look at their Jewish girl friends of yesterday and many of them made a gesture of spitting when they passed a Jewish student. Of course, there are a good few Christian students who are far from agreeing with such ways. Yet the majority have adopted these methods.
>
> (*The Jewish Chronicle*, 4 Dec. 1931)

On 5 January 1931 the Polish universities reopened their doors after the closure caused by the incidents of the previous autumn. The Endeks became bolder in their demands. They no longer insisted on a *numerus clausus* but strove for the total elimination of the Jewish presence at universities. Leaflets were distributed openly calling for students 'to break the teeth of the Jews with an iron bar wherever they are encountered'. Bloody incidents also took place at Lvov University, where there were some dead amongst the Jews.

Artur Sandauer, in his *Book of Reminiscences 1919–1939* (Warsaw, 1960), writes:

> The University of Lvov in 1932–6, as I experienced it, resembled to a certain degree a jungle. We used to walk around with eyes wide open and ears strained: an attack might come any moment, from

any corner. From time to time during seminars students would raise their heads from above the textbooks: a stampede, a scuffle and cries would come from the corridors.

(quoted in Banas, 1979, p. 43)

The student anti-Jewish campaign enjoyed the full support of the Catholic Church. Two Catholic priests, Seweryn Popławski and Marceli Nowakowski, in an open letter supported the stand taken by nationalist students. They wrote: 'Because those comments may cause some mental anguish among the young, we the undersigned, experienced teachers of young people, wish to assert that the positive attempts of the faithful in choosing to separate themselves from Jews, does not conflict with the aims, the teaching and dictates of the Church' (*Czas*, 24 Oct. 1937).

Toward the end of 1936 the nationalist students, under the patronage of the Polish episcopate and the primate of Poland, organised a pilgrimage to the town of Częstochowa – the holiest Catholic shrine in Poland. The students vowed 'to build a Catholic state of the Polish nation', and a declaration issued by the students stated: 'We will not rest until the last Jew, alive or dead, has left the Polish soil.'

It was a demonstration of unprecedented amplitude. About 60,000 students or 60 per cent of all Polish students took part in these pilgrimages. This fact refutes the assertion of many Polish analysts that anti-Semitic riots at Polish universities had the backing of only a small minority of students (Marcus, 1983, p. 356).

The anti-Jewish campaign by Polish students was summed up in an ONR leaflet dated 26 January 1937:

Progress, learning, democracy – they all sound wonderful. But what is hidden under this façade? The repulsive Jewish spirit. And this disgusting use of clubs which makes you recoil, is in fact a glorious struggle to free the nation from its Jewish fetters. Just think: you meet a Jew or a Communist in some dark place. And you set about him! You lay into him, driving the metal into his teeth! Just don't back away!

The exact number of bloody incidents at Polish universities is not known, as Polish censorship did not allow articles on anti-Jewish excesses to appear. What is known is that in 1938 three Jewish students were murdered at the Lvov Polytechnik. A year later two university students were murdered, and in May 1939 seven were severely beaten up – one, a first-year student, Markus Landsberg, dying in hospital (*Kurier Warszawski*, 28 May 1939).

As a result of continued harassment, the number of Jews at the universities fell rapidly. No Jews were admitted to Poznan University, to the medical faculty of the Jagiellonian University, nor to a number of other universities. The percentage of Jewish students fell from 20.4 in 1928 to only 7.5 per cent in 1937–8.

Succumbing to the pressure from many student organisations, rectors and deans of Polish universities allowed the introduction of special benches (nicknamed 'ghetto benches') for Jewish students. By the spring of 1937, the rectors of virtually all higher education institutions ordered the introduction of the ghetto benches. In July 1937 the Universities Act was amended, allowing rectors to introduce segregated seating for Polish and Jewish students. Jewish students, unable to actively oppose this rule, refused to sit on separate benches and decided to stand during the lectures. To attend lectures and continue studies in an atmosphere of constant harassment called for a lot of courage and determination on the part of a Jewish student.

There were a few exceptions to the general acquiescence to the anti-Jewish campaign. The group of Poles endowed with real humanism at the time included the well-known Polish professor of philosophy, Tadeusz Kotarbiński. He, together with a small group of university professors and scientists, protested the introduction of ghetto benches at the universities. The rector of Lvov University, Stanisław Kulczyński, refused to allow a ghetto bench to be introduced, and on 7 January 1937 offered his resignation. However, his successor, Longchamps, issued an order on 12 January, the day lectures were due to begin, that the segregated seating scheme should be imposed. In a similar manner, 26 professors, led by Professor Bartel, protested against the introduction of an official ghetto at the Warsaw Polytechnik, but the proposal was approved by the board (*Epoka*, 5 Feb. 1938).

By 1938, the students' anti-Jewish campaign acquired racial overtones not dissimilar to the Nazi campaign in Germany. On 16 January 1938, at an open meeting of students, it was agreed that individuals of Jewish origin could not become members of the student organisation. A few days after an incident in which Father Puder, a baptised Jew, was struck by an assailant in Church, a certain Stanisław Mackiewicz wrote that 'the one logical, clear criterion is, in fact, that adopted by Hitler. A Jew is a person who is of Jewish descent' (*Słowo*, 6 Feb. 1938).

It is beyond doubt that the Nazi anti-Jewish policies gained much support in Poland especially among the students. Voices were raised demanding the enactment in Poland of anti-Jewish legislation along the lines of the Nuremberg Laws (Rudnicki, 1987, p. 264). The so-called 'Aryan paragraph' – excluding Jews from certain organisations – was approved in 1937 by the Union of Non-professorial Staff in State Institutions of Higher Education. Jews previously belonging to these organisations were immediately struck off the membership list (*Wszechpolak*, 4 Feb. 1937). Similar resolutions were adopted by a number of associations and organisations, and other social and professional groupings including engineers, architects, doctors, etc.

The death of the 'protector' of the Jews

From a historical perspective it is clear that Piłsudski at first realised that the economic health of Poland depended on political and social stability. Jews were an active element and their contribution to the economy was very substantial indeed, and it was for this reason that it became imperative to retain a semblance of democracy. However, the anti-Jewish sentiment amongst the Polish population, spurred by nationalistic elements in Polish society and to a large extent by the Catholic Church, made it impossible for Piłsudski and his government to pursue liberal policies. Gradually, the attitude of his government towards the Jewish problem acquired almost identical features to that of the anti-Semitic National Democrats. A close associate of Piłsudski, Bogusław Miedziński, affirmed in the parliament that 'the presence of over three million Jews in Poland is rather embarrassing. Each one of us would prefer if it were not so.' 'But,' he added, 'we have to accommodate them somehow because we cannot expel them from Poland, since nobody else would wants them.'

The death of Piłsudski, the 'protector' of the Jews, in May 1935 sent shock waves through the Jewish community. It was felt that with the passing of the liberator of Poland and the perceived defender of the rights of the Jews, the situation would worsen. For Jews it was not only the passing of a national hero but the death of a man who had been considered a proponent of equal rights for everyone, including Jews. As for the Poles, it was the death of their liberator. The grief after his death was shared by Poles and Jews alike, and for awhile there reigned in Poland an atmosphere of, if not brotherhood, at least solidarity.

> People were seen openly weeping in the streets and an atmosphere of gloom descended upon the Jewish quarter of Warsaw. We talked of nothing else but of the good deeds of Piłsudski while he was alive and his friendliness towards the Jews. Prayers for the memory of our beloved protector were offered in all synagogues. I must say that the

sentiments of the loss of the liberator of Poland were shared by the whole population – Christian and Jews alike. There was, for a very short while, a sense of common bond between the Jews and the Poles. On this rare occasion grief united us all.

(Author's recollections)

But as subsequent events have shown, that brotherhood did not last. The situation had become more precarious because the government, which in the past had attempted to curb the activities of Polish ultra-nationalists on account of world opinion and national interests, saw a danger to its political power in their increasing influence. The end result of this trend was that the Jewish population found itself squeezed between the anti-Semitic camp and a government which had to make concessions to the National Democrats lest it be accused of protecting the Jews. By and large the Polish population supported the policy of the government and shared similar sentiments. The government's policies concerning the Jewish question reflected, therefore, Polish public opinion.

The trend which began before Piłsudski's death, continued to accelerate at an alarming pace when he died. Those Polish circles that previously may have had some misgivings about launching a full-scale attack on Polish Jewry, now openly came out with their various programmes of how to rid Poland of the Jewish presence. 'The Endecja [National Democrats] understood,' wrote Ludwik Krzywicki, 'that anti-Semitic slogans were a useful means of controlling crowds and igniting passions.'

The most extreme step was taken by the local branch of the Stronnictwo Narodowe at Częstochowa, which proposed that Jews be banned from the town. A similar campaign was launched in Brest Litovsk. The Stronnictwo Narodowe (National Party) officially launched a campaign for residential ghettoes (*Wszechpolak*, 17 Oct. and 10 Nov. 1937). All this was done in accordance with the call to create a Catholic state from the Polish nation. Kazimierz Kowalski, chairman of the Stronnictwo Narodowe, wrote that 'the one basic obstacle in achieving this goal is the Jew' (Giertych, 1938, p. 8). In the same year, the Catholic press began to emphasise the religious feature of the Jewish question by publishing articles on the immorality of the Talmud and on the destructive role and character of Jewish ethics and culture. Bishop Pradzynski called for 'an accelerating deportation of this tribe of an alien race'.

The reaction of Polish society to the anti-Semitic excesses was on the whole one of indifference or plain hostility toward the Jews. Of all political parties in Poland, it was only the PPS (Polish Socialist Party),

NPR (National Worker's Party), and PSL 'Piast' (Polish People's Party 'Piast'), who adopted a liberal platform regarding national minorities (Tomicki, 1982, p. 327). The largest of these parties, the PPS, very often came out in defence of the rights of the Jews. However, their political leverage and their influence over public opinion was much less significant than that of the anti-Jewish groups.

While the situation of the Jewish population had been deteriorating and the general anti-Jewish atmosphere increasingly tense, the Jewish press, no doubt in order to lift the spirit of the Jews, attempted to find and publicise cases of the humane behaviour of some Poles. However, such cases were few and far between. Here are a couple of examples quoted in a Warsaw Jewish daily:

> Christian workers collect money to help a poor Jewish family that has been evicted for non-payment of rent on Mala Street no. 9 in Praga [a suburb of Warsaw].
>
> (*Unzer ekspres*, 3 June 1935)

> A Christian lady, Stanisława Gurnicka, looks after the 73-year-old and sick Nachum Starygrod at Gęsia Street no. 71.
>
> (ibid., 16 Aug. 1936)

> An extraordinary event occurred this week. Because of heavy snow falls, the Warsaw City Council employed for a few days some Jews, including some bearded ones, to clean the streets of snow.
>
> (ibid., 8 Dec. 1936)

And *The Jewish Chronicle* of 26 August 1935 reported a friendly speech by the Bishop of Luck, Szelazek, who, while on a visit to Klewan (a small village), in answer to a welcoming speech by a rabbi, said: 'We are all creatures of the same God.' His speech was reported as having left a deep impression.

4
Signs of Impending Disaster (1935–9)

> 'It is possible to murder a great number of Jews but it is impossible to massacre the entire Jewish population.'
> (From a speech in the Polish Sejm by Jewish deputy Minzberg in Dec. 1936)

After Piłsudski's death in 1935, anti-Semitism in Poland once more entered a dynamic stage. It was again used by the opposition as a supplement to its so-called 'national policy', which called for the economic expropriation of the Jews while assuring the Polish nation that this would provide bread for the hungry. At the same time, the government camp – the National Unification (OZON) bloc created in 1936 under the auspices of the government – in its search for ways of extending its base within Polish society, began to use anti-Semitism as an instrument of state policy (Oberlaender, 1935).

The regime came to look upon anti-Semitism as a way of deflecting public attention from the essential social issues. It also had to match the anti-Jewish programme of the National Democrats in order to win greater support. In its propaganda campaign, the government told the peasants that a solution to their economic plight could be found in their replacement of Jewish hawkers in the towns and in the 'polonisation' of commerce. It proclaimed the necessity of ousting Jews from the positions they held in the economy, and the necessity for the emigration of a great part of Polish Jewry was expressed officially by Polish ministers on many occasions (Mahler, 1942, p. 140).

In 1935, under the government of Prime Minister Kościałkowski, anti-Jewish propaganda sharply increased. Government circles were keen to make apologetic statements in the official press denying allegations that the government was friendly toward the Jews. In collusion with the government, new extremist organisations which demanded the radical solution of the Jewish question, came into being. The Jews, they said, should be expelled from Poland and their property confiscated without indemnity. One of the representatives of this trend, Mosdorf, proposed the following solution to the agrarian problem: large land-holdings would be distributed to peasants and the landowners indemnified from the proceeds of the confiscated estates of the Jews expelled from the cities.

The radicalisation of anti-Semitism in Poland was to a great extend affected by the German model and in many cases was patterned on Nazi ideology and practice. The Aryanisation in different forms of various organisations and professional unions continued in the late 1930s and almost up to the day of the outbreak of the war. The anti-Semitic programme of the extreme wing was a mixture of all prevailing anti-Semitic doctrines, including some borrowed from the Nazi movement in Germany. The popular *Dziennik Narodowy* and other Polish newspapers began to praise the Nuremberg laws: 'Anyone who understands the Jewish question and has a feeling of national pride, must admit that this [German] way of solving the [Jewish] problem is wise and correct' (*Dziennik Narodowy*, 20 Sep. 1935).

One of the founders of the ONR (Obóz Narodowo Radykalny – National Radical Camp), the well-known Polish admirer of Hitler, Bolesław Piasecki, who was also the editor-in-chief of the anti-Semitic *Akademik Polski*, very often praised Hitler and his anti-Jewish policies on the pages of his paper. It is worthwhile noting that the same Piasecki, who collaborated with the Germans during the war, was one of the 'builders' of 'socialist' Poland and later became a member of the Polish State Council.

In 1937, the youth of the Stronnictwo Narodowe (NS) and the National Radical Camp (ONR) were screaming nationalistic slogans and committing acts of physical violence against Jews. The 'young' of the National Democratic Party (Endek), who as a group were begin-ning to take over the leadership of the party, did not hide their admiration for fascism. 'Fight with Germany but not with Hitlerism' was one of the slogans, and a resolution of the Supreme Council adopted in February 1936 called for using the same method which led National Socialism to power in Germany (Terej, 1971, pp. 72–3). In its attitude toward the Jews the ONR did not differ much from Nazi ideology, and very often expressed its spiritual identification with Nazism. This is what the central organ of the ONR, *Szczerbiec*, wrote on 25 April 1933:

> What is happening in Germany is a wonderful and cheerful trend. It is a cleansing of German life from the centuries-old contamination by a poison of disintegration introduced by Jewry into the blood of the hostile to us but nevertheless great [German] nation. We are watching what is happening in Germany not only without condemnation but with envy.

Some Polish high-schools, arranged friendly receptions for Nazi 'scientists' who came to lecture on racism. The future German governor of Poland, Dr Frank, was a frequent guest of Warsaw University, where he lectured on the German racial theories.

An increasing number of professional organisations in Poland took formal anti-Semitic action by inserting restrictive paragraphs in their membership statutes, using such terms as 'Aryan', 'Christian by birth', and 'of Jewish descent' (Gutman et al., 1989, p. 135). In November 1935 the Association of Polish lawyers proposed the exclusion of Jews from the profession, including those having third-generation Jewish ancestors (*The Jewish Chronicle*, 19 Nov. 1935).

A resolution adopted at the Kongres Kupiectwa Chrześcijańskiego (General Congress of, Christian Merchants) convened in Warsaw in November 1937 under the patronage of Polish government authorities and in the presence of Polish President Mościcki, stressed the importance of the 'Polonisation of commerce in the country for economic and security reasons' (*Nasz Przeglad*, 16 Nov. 1937).

Some Polish writers, such as Lypkiewicz and Kierski, urged the expulsion of the Jews and the confiscation of Jewish property. A Polish professor, W. Studnicki, was preparing a Polish edition of Hitler's *Mein Kampf*; while in July 1939, barely two months before the outbreak of the war, another eminent writer, Adolf Nowaczyński, called for burning of all books written by Jews. Nowaczyński, Studnicki and Cat-Mackiewicz, another well-known Polish writer, asked their readers: 'if Hitler is so bitterly opposed by the Jews, can he be so bad for the Poles?' (*Haint*, 9 July 1939).

Pogroms in Poland: 1935–9

From economic cold war Polish anti-Semites soon passed to direct action. Worse, however, than the excesses themselves was the permanent pogrom atmosphere, clearly intended to create an emigration panic among Jews. During the 1930s dozens of townships witnessed attacks upon Jews for months on end, with many killed and many more wounded. From 1934 to 1938 more than 500 Jews were murdered, among them 30 university students, and about 5,000 were wounded – 1,000 of them seriously. Simultaneously, a relentless economic war against Jewish merchants has been conducted by the Polish population at large. Jewish traders were forcibly expelled from fairs and market-places and Jewish shops were picketed in hundreds of townships.

The Endek objective to eliminate the Jewish presence wherever possible, bore fruit. Assassinations of whole families in isolated Jewish enclaves among the Christian population, and the murder of Jewish pedlars in villages, became more prevalent in that period. A great number of families who lived for generations among the Poles fled in panic into the relative security of large towns, only to increase the number of destitute Jews in need of help. The anti-Semitic press published almost every day reports of the successful expulsion of Jews from certain localities – in such-and-such a village the last Jew has left, the last Jewish shop closed down leaving the village free of Jews.

Pogroms in pre-war Poland were not a rare occurrence. However, the anti-Jewish excesses and pogroms in the years 1935–7 had their specific characteristics and dynamics. In some instances there were attempts by the Jewish population to put up resistance against physi-cal attacks, but they became futile, for to cause one Christian casualty was to make the whole Jewish community responsible and to provoke violent retributions. By and large the Jewish population endured passively the systematic campaign of violence for fear of reprisals. There always was a sense of collective responsibility, but this attitude only encouraged Polish anti-Semites to further acts of violence, while at the same time accusing Jews of 'inherent cowardice'.

The pogroms in Grodno (1935), Przytyk (1936), Minsk Mazowiecki (1936) Brest Litovsk (1937), and Częstochowa (June 1937) all followed this pattern (Gutman et al., 1989, p. 129). The pogrom in Tykoczyn, the result of a quarrel between Jews and Poles when one Pole died, left two Jews killed and many injured. The official report spoke of drunken hooli-gans, of whom 93 were arrested.

The question of self-defence or passive acceptance of the situation came into the open in March 1936. It began with a short announce-ment by PAT (the Polish Telegraphic Agency) about some disturbances in the small town of Przytyk. The disturbances occurred on the market-place, and at first it was thought that this was a matter of a personal quarrel.

The full horror of this particular pogrom came out into the open during the trial and, at the same time, dilemma which Jews had to face was revealed: should they defend themselves or accept death or injury without resistance? In the course of the pogrom one Christian was killed by a Jew who shot him in self-defence. Witnesses told the court how the Polish mob spread all over the Jewish quarter, how they entered the house of Yosef and Chaya Minkowski and, in view of their five children aged between 6 and 14, clubbed the couple to death.

Polish justice took the side of the attackers. Scores of Jews were arrested and put on trial for defending themselves. Some Christians were also among those tried, but from the onset of the trial it was evident that the judges were biased against the Jews. The defence for the Poles, accused of murdering the Jewish couple, challenged the truthfulness of the Jewish witnesses by claiming that according to the Law in the Talmud Jews were allowed to lie in court.

The outcome of the trial was never in doubt, but it still shocked the Jewish community. Three of the accused Jews were sentenced to be jailed for between three and five years, others to lesser terms. All Poles on trial were acquitted. The perpetrators of the pogrom in Przytyk who, after being acquitted, returned from prison, were greeted by the Polish population as national heroes. The 'victory' over the Jews was celebrated in the church by a Te Deum.

The Jewish population vigorously protested the Przytyk trial verdict by calling a general strike in Jewish Warsaw. It made no impact whatsoever on Polish public opinion. On the contrary: while the trial was still proceeding another pogrom took place in Minsk Mazowiecki, resulting in many victims. The whole Jewish quarter of the town was set on fire, forcing thousands of Jews to flee and seek refuge in the relative safety of Warsaw.

The overtly anti-Semitic trend became clear during and after the trials of those who participated in pogroms; they usually received light sentences. The participants in the pogroms were included in the category of political fighters and escaped imprisonment through special amnesties for political crimes. The murderers of five Jews in the village of Stawy were found not guilty and released. Five prime suspects accused of attacking Jews, of arson and robbery during the Minsk Mazowiecki pogrom, received six months' imprisonment, but were released immediately after the end of the trial. Among the accused also were 14 Jews who tried to defend themselves during the pogrom.

The well-known Jewish economist and sociologist Jacob Leszczynski identified in the period May 1935 to August 1936, 1,289 Jews injured during anti-Jewish upheavals. This number included only those who sought medical help and were registered as such. As many did not, their number is unknown. It was estimated that hundreds of Jews were killed during the disturbances or died later of the injuries they sustained. Leszczynski concluded that since Polish censorship did not allow the publishing of news about the pogroms, the number of killed and injured must have been much higher, and the number of pogroms far exceeded the reported 150. A conservative estimate puts their number as high as 3,000. In addition, there were 194 bombs or incendiary devices thrown at Jewish enterprises in 46 locations. In the course of a debate in the Sejm in June 1936, the then Prime Minister Sławoj Składkowski admitted that in the Lubomirski diocese alone there were 348 anti-Jewish incidents in that year (Rudawski, 1986).

The wave of pogroms spread all over Poland, and Jewish communities in the affected towns and villages were sending pleas for help to Warsaw. At the end of June 1936, Jewish representatives in the Sejm addressed a message to the Jewish population which said: 'We are caught in the fire of an unequal struggle that has no parallel. There is no security of life, health and possessions of the Jewish population. We do not even have the right to defend ourselves. The economic boycott is being waged with extreme brutality, which leads to the complete destitution of the Jewish population.' The Jewish deputy of the Sejm, Minzberg, addressing the Polish parliament in December 1936 with reference to the killing of Jews, said:

It is possible to murder a great number of Jews but it is impossible to massacre the entire Jewish population.

(*The Jewish Chronicle*, 23 Dec. 1936)

His words proved to be prophetic, but the massacre was perpetrated by the Germans, not by the Poles.

Six months later, on 13 May 1937, another bloody pogrom took place in the city of Brest Litovsk. The official Polish Telegraphic Agency (PAT) report of this tragic event was rather brief and clearly placed on the Jews the responsibility for the pogrom:

On 13 May, in Brest Litovsk, at about 7.30 AM during a police raid on illegal meat slaughter, an officer, Stefan Kędzior, was seriously wounded by an attacker with a knife. The injured man pointed to Ajzyk Szczerbowski, a slaughterer, as the assailant. During the transfer to a hospital Kiędzior died.

The murder committed on the person of the policeman Kędzior, caused an anti-Jewish reaction by the Polish community in Brest. In a few places windows in Jewish shops were broken. On the market, some Jewish stalls were destroyed.

(Ster, 25 May 1937)

A Polish journalist who visited Brest immediately after the pogrom described the scene he saw:

> A house attracts my attention. It has a crucifix displayed in the window. Behind another window I see a few holy pictures. Then I see a shop. A handwritten note 'a Christian shop' is displayed in the window. On the sign in front of the shop, on a background of bread and sausages, a large cross has been overpainted. Brest has become religious. Every window, every shop window displays holy pictures and crosses. One shop has no such signs – it also has now window nor window frames. Clearly a Jewish shop. I enter a side street. It looks as if a hurricane had passed through here. But a hurricane which missed shops and windows showing a sign 'Christian shop' or 'Christian apartment.'

(ibid.)

As in previous pogroms, the fact that one of the victims was a Christian made the entire Jewish community collectively responsible. The principle of collective responsibility was strongly emphasised by most Polish newspapers. The Polish daily *Kurier Poranny* pointed an accusing finger at the Polish Jewry:

> It was the atmosphere, continuously induced by them [the Jews] that brought about the crime in Brest, a crime that deserves condemnation. A guardian of security of the state and the executor of justice, whom the Jews above all should honour, had been targeted. While bowing our heads before the body of Kędzior, we do not intend to assign to this event any particular importance. We wish nevertheless to warn the Jews that the consequences of their methods of provocation are bound to fall on them.

Warszawski Dziennik Narodowy, the organ of the Stronnictwo Narodowe, wrote: 'The events in Brest and other localities, force us to adopt the most energetic measures to colonise [by Poles] towns and villages [by Poles], to expel the Jews, and to give the towns a purely Polish character. Time is pressing!'

From among the leading organs of Polish public opinion, it was only the socialist *Robotnik* who was against assigning collective responsibility to Jews for the crime of an individual. 'It is a question of defending Poland from the influence of the ethics and psychology of the Third Reich', *Robotnik* concluded. 'Regrettably, the ethics and psychology of which *Robotnik* is warning, already managed to be injected into the consciousness of a certain part of the Polish society', commented the weekly *Ster* (23 May 1937).

It was clear that the government could do little to change the situation. The Polish Interior Minister, when asked by the Jewish parliamentarians to intervene, admitted that 'everybody in Poland today is an anti-Semite. We cannot put a policeman behind every Jew to protect him and we do not intend to hang our young people because they are anti-Semites'.

Between 1935 and 1937 there were, according to Jewish sources, 16 pogroms in which 118 Jews lost their lives. Present-day Polish apologists have a ready answer to this fact: 'admittedly, the pogroms were quite regrettable, but they do not compare with the death of 2,000 Jews who lost their lives in a single pogrom in the city of Strasbourg in the Middle Ages, or the millions who lost their lives during the German occupation (Lukas, 1986, p. 125).

Emigration or expulsion

The last years of the Polish Republic, from the mid-1930s on, were marked by grave escalation in the anti-Semitic public mood and of anti-Jewish government policies. Even a cursory examination of the Polish press from those years gives the impression that the Jewish question stood among the central problems preoccupying Polish society and the government. The objective of reducing the Jewish population in Poland by immediate mass emigration became something of a national consensus.

An illustration of the prevailing tendencies in government circles in those years is an excerpt of a diary kept by the former Polish ambassador to the Third Reich, Lipski, published in the 1960s (Lipski, *Diplomat in Berlin*). The author reports an audience with Hitler in the course of which he attempted to obtain Hiler's cooperation with Poland in the resolution of the Jewish question. 'When Hitler said that he is considering the problem, I said: if this comes to a conclusion, we will place a monument for you in Warsaw.'

Responding to the public clamour, the government finally officially suggested solving the Jewish problem through emigration. In

September 1936, the Polish government at the annual meeting of the League of Nations submitted a scheme demanding the allocation of colonies where the Jewish population of Poland could be resettled. A month later, the Minister of Foreign Affairs, Colonel Beck, made an official request to international banks for financial help for mass emigration of Jews. On 20 December 1936, Beck declared in the parliament that 'Jews must emigrate because they cannot sustain themselves'. This meant that after being deprived of their livelihood and becoming paupers they must leave the country.

Lupacewicz, a Polish parliamentarian, proposed political and economic pressure through discriminatory laws, which would create conditions that would force Jews to leave Poland. They included depriving Jews of civil rights, confiscation or freezing of assets, and the incarceration of about 600,000 Jews in concentration camps. Lupacewicz went as far as to envisage a preliminary budget of 1 zloty per day for the maintenance of one Jew in a camp – 60 groszy for food, 20 groszy for clothing and 20 groszy for other expenses (Ros, p. 17). Leon Petrzycki, a well-known lawyer, declared in the senate that, although he was not guided by any anti-Semitic sentiments, he could foresee that the situation of Jews in Poland would further deteriorate. The only solution, he asserted, was emigration.

Such theories provoked a reaction among Jews, who saw that even the government itself had adopted an official programme aimed at depriving them of civic and economic rights guaranteed by the constitution, and foresaw their own deportation. Not since Poland had become independent, only twenty years before, had the anti-Jewish movement taken on such a ferocity. It finally convinced all but the staunchest proponents of a struggle against the wave of discrimination, that an internal solution to the Jewish problem in Poland was impossible.

This was perceived by those Jews who saw the solution of the Jewish problem in the creation of a Jewish state in Palestine. The Zionist movement which already had a mass following within Jewish society in Poland, made significant gains in that period. Thousands of young Jews were leaving Poland to built a new existence in Palestine. The eagerness of young Jews to leave can be judged by the bizarre plan of a Jewish lawyer, Rypel, to organise a march from Warsaw to Palestine. On the eve of the march, on 16 November 1936, about 1,000 participants took an oath: 'If I Forget Thee Jerusalem ... ' The next day, after reaching the village of Piaseczno – about 20 kilometres from Warsaw – the marchers were dispersed by the Polish police, apparently under pressure from the British government.

Since the British had proclaimed a White Paper that virtually closed the gates of Palestine to all but 15,000 Jewish emigrants annually, there appeared in the Polish parliament a plethora of suggestions of places to which Jews could be sent. Exotic locations such as Madagascar, Uganda or San-Domingo were often mentioned. Earlier, a Polish daily published an article by Frondziński – a Catholic priest – who suggested the resettlement of all Polish Jews in Abyssinia. 'Once the majority of Jews would had left Poland, the reason to hate them had disappeared and they will be welcomed into the fold of the Church' (*Kurjer Poznański*, 2 Oct. 1935).

Replying to a question in the Sejm by general Skwarczyński and 116 other parliamentarians of OZON, the then Prime Minister, Składkowski, said: 'The Polish government agrees that in order to solve the Jewish question, one of the most important tasks is a significant reduction in the number of Jews through emigration' (Ros, p. 15).

In 1938, the delegation of the Polish Federation of the League of Nations Societies presented a memorandum to the International Congress of the Union of the League of Nations Societies in Copenhagen in which it not only claimed that the Jewish question was an international problem, but accused other nations of creating the Jewish problem in Poland. It asserted that this problem was 'a result of crimes against Jews committed by almost the whole of Europe'. The memorandum claimed that 'Poland has the right to demand assistance in the solution of the Jewish question from those Western nations which caused the excessive concentration of Jews on Polish territory. This would entail the allocation of colonies to Poland, the allocation of the whole of Palestine to the Jews or the opening of the gates of Western countries to Jews who were previously expelled from them in a cruel fashion' (Arczyński and Balcerak, 1983, pp. 42–3).

Even the Polish left – the Polish Socialist Party (PPS) – admitted the necessity of solving the Jewish question in Poland by a reduction in their numbers. A booklet published by the socialist *Robotnik* contained an article by J. Barski in which he agreed that 'a considerable part of Jews must emigrate ... The idea of emigration has taken root in Polish society and nothing better can be invented'. The programme of the People's (Peasant) Party, also proposed a resolution of the Jewish question through emigration (Banas, 1979, p. 42).

In 1938, anticipating the expulsion by the Nazis of Polish Jews living in Germany, the Polish government proclaimed a law which provided that persons who had spent a minimum of five years in continuous residence abroad after the restoration of the Polish state, would be deprived of their Polish citizenship and forbidden to return to Poland. It also announced a control on Polish passports issued abroad. German reaction was characteristically ruthless. On the night of 28 October 1938 (the law was to come into effect the next day), 15,000 Jews holding Polish passports, many born in Germany, were expelled by Germany. Only some of these deportees were permitted to enter Poland. Eight thousand were interned by the Polish authorities in a hastily set up camp at Zbąszyń on the border's no-man's land (*Unity in Dispersion*, 1998, p. 97). They remained there until the outbreak of the Second World War.

As late as February 1939, when the danger of Hitler's war plans were all but clear, Poland was considering a law on Jewish emigration. According to this law a list of 50,000 to 100,000 Jews that would be forced to leave Poland was to be compiled annually. The financing of this scheme would be entirely the responsibility of the Jewish community. Due to the political situation, particularly the invasion of Czechoslovakia, the law was shelved.

The economic war against the Jews

The new independent Poland, restored after the First World War, had to solve economic and social problems inherited from before the war. The vital agrarian question made no headway after the restoration of national sovereignty. More than half of all land was owned by Polish magnates, whereas the peasantry, constituting 73 per cent of the population, lived on small holdings which were not sufficient even for the most modest livelihood.

Poland lost the pre-war Russian markets for its textile and clothing industries and compensation in new markets was not sufficient to make up for the loss. This accounts for the fact that Poland, in contrast to the developed capitalist countries, could not recover after the world crisis in 1929. The standard of living in Poland became the lowest in Europe as measured by consumption of the main commodities and the number of unemployed. The deepening of the economic crisis in the country brought about a significant increase in anti-Semitic activities. The propaganda of 'Polonisation' of the economy by ousting the Jews from their positions acquired a new impetus. Until now, it was argued, 'we have been engaged in the struggle for our political freedom, now that we have obtained political power, we have to take up the task of economic liberation from the Jews' (Mahler, 1942, p. 139).

A factor that had important consequences was the strong concentration of Jews in urban areas. In some towns in eastern Poland, over 75 per cent of the total of city-dwellers were of Jewish origin, and 61.9 per cent of people engaged in commerce were Jewish. In some localities in eastern Poland almost all commerce was in Jewish hands. It must be noted, however, that the term 'commerce' includes small trade and peddling, which constituted 80 per cent of the Jews' total commercial activities (Tomicki, 1982, p. 316).

The economic boycott proclaimed by the anti-Semites acquired a certain legitimacy when the then Polish prime minister, General Sławoj-Składkowski, declared in parliament on 4 June 1936 that 'there must be no violence, but an economic boycott of Jews is welcome'. Thus the anti-Jewish economic boycott was officially sanctioned.

In order to facilitate the application of the boycott, a law proclaimed by the government and approved by the Polish parliament required every owner of a building, store or business to display in a prominent place his original full name as it appeared in the register of the population. The objective of this regulation was to make it easier for a Pole to determine whether a business or a building belonged to a Jew. Although a number of Jews bore Polish family names, as a rule Jews had a Yiddish or biblical sounding given name. It served the anti-Semites as a means of identifying Jewish businesses. They placed pickets in front of Jewish shops located in Christian areas and prevented Polish customers from entering.

At the same time, according to instructions issued by the government, all Jewish employees of large Polish enterprises were to be sacked. Officers of the Polish police began visiting a number of textile factories and taking an accurate list of all employees with details of their ethnic origin and religion. This rule practically excluded Jews from Polish enterprises. But even Jewish entrepreneurs were limited in their ability to employ Jews because of objections raised by other Polish employees. It was not rare for a strike to take place because a Jewish owner had engaged a Jewish worker, and sometimes the Polish workers would go on strike in order to force the sacking of a Jewish employee by the Jewish owner. There was a case when Polish students picketed a well-known cafe because it employed one Jewish musician in the band. They forced the owner to dismiss him.

Not satisfied with the call for an economic and cultural boycott against the Jewish population, the Polish anti-Semites brought up once more in the Polish Senate the question of ritual slaughter. The justification of the attempt to outlaw ritual slaughter was that it was a cruel way of killing animals, but the real reason was to remove the meat trade from Jewish hands. The new law gave the government the right to take over the slaughter and marketing of kosher meat, and to use the revenue to support Christian trade in this commodity. It was to be introduced in stages and to be completed by the end of 1943. It was a disturbing step for the Jewish population and it provoked a strong reaction not only amongst religious Jews but amongst the Jewish population at large, including the Jewish socialist anti-religious party, Bund, who saw in this law another attempt to deprive Jews of their rights. The rabbis declared a day of fasting and forbade the sale and consumption of meat for two weeks between 14 and 31 March 1939.

It was, however, difficult to spread this message to the Jewish population because of strict censorship imposed by the government. On the first day of the meat strike half of the front page of all Jewish newspapers was blanked out. But on the following day a column on 'What do we eat today' with a suggested menu consisting of dairy products appeared. The message was clear, and the vast majority of Jews abstained from consuming meat. Meatless days went on for two weeks. There was an ironic twist to the situation. While the anti-Jewish campaign was raging all over the country, the Nazis were waging an anti-Polish campaign in Germany and especially in Danzig. In German Silezia and East Prussia, Polish shop windows were broken by Germans.

The Church and Polish nationalism – a sinister combination

The Catholic Church had a powerful influence upon the Polish masses. It had the forum from which to appeal to Poles, who were in the great majority regular church-goers. The church, however, instead of preaching love, disseminated vicious propaganda depicting Jews as killers of Christ and as atheistic communists. The Poles were led to believe that all communists were Jews and that all Jews were communists. A periodical, *Samoobrona Narodu* (Self-defence of the Nation), published by the diocese of Poznan with a circulation of one million copies in the late 1930s, usually contained articles expressing such views. 'Probably in no other country was there such a massive Catholic, Jew-devouring literature as in Poland' (Myślek, 1966, p. 265).

In June 1934, a delegation of rabbis in an audience with Cardinal Krakowski asked him to intervene on their behalf with the nationalistic youth to stop the anti-Jewish violence. In response, the Cardinal reminded the rabbis that Jews offend Christian feelings by leading 'the godless movement' in Poland. He did nevertheless condemn all acts of violence, but at the same time asked the rabbis to influence the Jews to give money to the state rather than use it for communist propaganda (Marcus, 1983, p. 363).

The anti-Semitic propaganda by the Endeks enjoyed full support of the Catholic church. A pastoral letter by the Polish primate, Cardinal Hlond, published in a Catholic monthly and read in all churches, indicated his support of the Endeks (*Unzer ekspres*, 23 March 1936). The cardinal defended the economic boycott against Jews by saying that a Pole was justified to give preference and to show more love for his own kind than for Jews. The Cardinal added that the Jewish influence on the Polish way of life was poison. Jews were spreading pornography, cheating in commercial dealings, charging high interest and engaging in white slave trading. 'We must safeguard ourselves against the bad moral influence of the Jews. We must insulate ourselves from the anti-Christian culture and, above all, from the Jewish press and the demoralising Jewish publications' (Heller, 1977, pp. 112–14). At the same time, the Cardinal suggested that Catholics should be fair because even among Jews there were honest people, philanthropists, respectable people, intelligent people with high ideals. Anti-Semitism was justified within the limits of defence against Jewish influence. But 'beating them is not allowed as it is contrary to Catholic ethics' (*Unzer ekspres*, 23 March 1936).

Not all Polish newspapers printed the letter. Even papers that were said to be Catholic failed to publish it. The anti-Semitic press reported only those parts of the letter which spoke negatively about Jews, and in particular that it was allowed to boycott Jewish shops. The conservative journal *Czas*, commenting on the letter, noted the following: 'Jew-hatred has become a kind of programme of many post-war political parties. Such hatred has already penetrated the Polish population to such an extent that even respectable Catholics are nursing this hatred.'

A statement similar in spirit to that of Cardinal Hlond was made by the Archbishop of Cracow (later Cardinal), Adam Stanisław Sapieha, in April 1936. In it he advocated an anti-Jewish boycott and accused the Jews of spreading communism in Poland (*Tygodnik Polski*, 5 April 1936). Another popular individual spreading anti-Semitic propaganda was a catholic priest named Trzeciak. He was 'nominated' by the Polish anti-Semites as their spiritual leader. Trzeciak's method consisted of falsely quoting from the Bible and the Talmud, in both of which he claimed he was an expert, and he was called upon to testify as such in the Polish parliament.

In a speech for a large Polish audience on the theme *'The Jewish Problem in the Light of Christian Ethics'*, he branded the Jews not only Poland's enemies, but as Christ said, the sons of the Devil. 'Saint Jerome hated the Jews and Pope Pius V expelled all Jews from the papal domain. Poland should follow this example: Jews should be destroyed, exterminated and expelled from Poland ... Noble are those Christians who refuse to sit with Jews on the same bench at university.' He furthermore offered credence to the ritual murder libel by referring to the grave of a Christian child in the city of Ostrołęka who – he said – was murdered by Jews for ritual purposes. 'Every Polish woman who buys from Jews is a traitor. The Christian religion imposes a penalty for dealing with Jews.' The audience applauded the speaker (*Unzer ekspres*, 17 Nov. 1936).

It should have been clear for an average intelligent person that Trzeciak was trying to propagate virulent anti-Semitism, but there was little opposition within Polish society. No member of the Polish government nor member of the parliament found it necessary to counteract Trzeciak's propaganda. Not a single word of criticism of the patently false assertions by Trzeciak was pronounced by Catholic circles, among whom were many knowledgeable members. The institution of the Catholic Church in Poland – even the Vatican – remained silent. It appears there was tacit approval by the Church of Trzeciak's 'thesis'.

Immediately prior to the war, in August 1939, Trzeciak published in the Catholic *Maly Dziennik* an article in which he attempted to prove that Hitler's legislation was based entirely on the ideas of great popes such as Paul IV or Clement VIII. Hitler in his struggle against Jews was inspired by the examples of the fathers of the Church and was therefore accomplishing the will of Providence. Certainly, a large share of responsibility for the anti-Semitic excesses may be attributed to the Catholic clergy. Anti-Jewish animosity was part of an old historical tradition to which the clergy remained faithful in independent Poland.

There were only a few voices among the more enlightened Poles who were critical of Trzeciak. Professor Zaderecki, a respectable scientist, publicly disproved his baseless and false statements. There were also some groups within Polish intellectual circles who opposed the anti-Semitic excesses and who attempted to swim against the current – among them the Polish Socialist Party (PPS), the newly formed Democratic Party (SD), the central leadership of the trade unions, as well as some prominent non-party politicians, scientists and writers. The growing anti-Semitic trend had also been condemned by the

Polish teachers union. The Polish Pen Club almost unanimously rejected a resolution by some anti-Semitic writers calling for the introduction of a so-called 'Aryan paragraph' (which would exclude writers of Jewish origin from the club's membership) into the club's statute.

However, the influence of Polish democratic elements wasn't powerful enough to stem the anti-Jewish trend within the Polish society. They were unable to stop the persecution of Jews organised by growing forces of anti-Jewish extremism who acted with the blessings of the Catholic church and with the approval of the government. The problem was that the majority of Poles were still steeped in religion, uneducated and prone to the influence of people who preached from the pulpits invoking the name of God.

On the eve of the disaster

It would be wrong to assume that the Polish government was totally unaware of the danger and ignored the messages emanating from Germany. A marked change in Polish foreign policy had taken place, especially after the Polish foreign minister, Beck, returned from a meeting with Hitler in January 1939. Beck's statement in the Sejm – 'Peace, yes, but not at any price' – became a popular slogan.

Despite the constant manifestation of anti-Semitism, the Jewish population remained loyal to Poland. It wholeheartedly supported any measures taken by the Polish government to strengthen security. It generously contributed to the Air Defence Loan launched by the government in April. There were long queues in front of the PKO – the state saving bank – in which old and young, man and woman stood for hours to lodge their contributions. The inmates of the Zbąszyń camp on the Polish–German border had resolved to fast one day and to subscribe the savings in food to the Loan. The Jewish press reported gifts made by individuals, elderly Jews sending precious heirlooms, newly married couples their wedding rings, and children collecting money at schools. On 20 August, R. Szereszewski – a well-known Jewish banker – presented several pieces of artillery to the army on behalf of the Warsaw Association of Jewish Merchants. Earlier, the Przeworski family, owners of several sugar mills, offered to the Polish army several airplanes in 1938. The reaction of Poles to this show of patriotism was less than favourable.

Prior to the launching of the Air Defence Loan, a committee was formed to organise its publicity and promotion with the participation of all Polish political parties from left to right, but from which Jews

were excluded. *Gazeta Polska*, the semi-official organ of the government, and *Kurier Poranny*, a popular daily, both criticised the Jewish
population for not contributing enough, despite the official report
which indicated that the Jewish contribution to the Loan was about
33 per cent of the total. The list of contributors to the Polish Defence
Fund contained the names of thousands of Jews, including many
residing in Palestine, who contributed through PKO (the Polish
Savings Bank) in Tel Aviv (*Palestine Post*, 9 July 1939).

On 28 April 1939 Hitler renounced the non-aggression treaty with
Poland. This could only be interpreted as the Nazis embarking upon a
plan of territorial expansion at the expense of Poland, and the possibility of a war with Germany could not be excluded. The question of
national defence acquired first priority. Or, so it seemed. But in reality
the preoccupation with the Jewish problem was still in evidence.
There was a proposal in the parliament to revoke the citizenship of
600,000 Jews who are unable to prove their Polish origin. Another
suggestion, by Dudziński, was the formation of work battalions of
600,000 Jews who would be 'taught' how to work for three years
pending their emigration from Poland.

The culmination of the anti-Jewish parliamentary debate was a
project of a law submitted in the Sejm in the beginning of 1939 by
Benedykt Kieńć and discussed during subsequent sittings. The draft of
the law envisaged stripping Jews of Polish citizenship, depriving them of
electoral rights, military service, work in the state administration and
some state enterprises, the right to public education and to teach in state
schools, banned work in radio, films and press, banned provision of
services by Jewish professionals to non-Jews. The project of the law also
envisaged a ban on banking and the purchase of real estate. Jews were
not to be allowed to open new industrial, commercial and service enterprises. Within one month of the law coming into force, Jews were to be
obliged to declare all their assets. Kieńć clearly attempted to enact in
Poland the same kind of discriminatory laws which, albeit in a much
more drastic form, were already in force in Nazi Germany. It can safely
be assumed that the outbreak of the War in September 1939 had
prevented their adoption (Ros, p. 16).

Outside the Polish parliament the situation was similar. Several
Polish professional associations introduced into their statutes Aryan
principles applicable to membership. The Union of Polish
Combatants (former soldiers) in Poznan adopted a resolution calling
for the expulsion of Jewish members. The union of Polish lawyers
suggested the exclusion of Jews from the profession – even those who

had third-generation Jewish ancestors. In July 1939, only six weeks before Germany invaded Poland, *Technik Polski*, a Polish periodical published by the Union of Polish Engineers, reported with satisfaction that the last conference of the Union adopted some important changes in its statutes: 'It introduced an Aryan paragraph denying membership to the following: Jews, persons of Jewish origin and to those married to a Jewish person' (*Technik Polski*, 10 July, 1939).

On 1 September 1939, the day Germany invaded Poland, the government's statement in the Sejm that Poland would fight to the 'last dying breath', received frenetic acclaim, and the statement by representatives of the Ukraine minority, declaring full support and participation in the defence of the country, was also loudly applauded. But when the Jewish deputy Szymon Seidenman made a similar and much more convincing pledge on behalf of the Jewish citizens, there was icy silence in the House. 'It was an ominous silence – an indication of the Poles' attitude in the coming months of tragedy during which forty generations of continuous Jewish history in Poland virtually ended' (Marcus, 1983), p. 33).

Part III
The Great Catastrophe (1939–44)

5
Onlookers

This wind from burning houses
blew open the girls' skirts,
and the happy throngs laughed
on a beautiful Warsaw Sunday.

Campo di Fiori, Czesław Miłosz (Warsaw, 1943)

Introduction

It is generally assumed that the role of a historian is to record or comment on events as they occur. But a historian cannot describe each and every event unless he considers it to be of some significance. Since he must necessarily be selective in his choice of what he thinks worthy of being recorded, he may not always be entirely objective. This principle is equally applicable to the ordinary person who witnesses events which happen to be of some importance and subsequently conveys them to others. Like a historian he will describe and interpret them in his own way – in a manner in which they are preserved in his memory. Since both suffer from a lack of absolute objectivity, the testimony of a witness to an event is as reliable as an historical account.

The question of historical truth is particularly relevant in regard to the behaviour of the Poles during the German occupation. It is the subject of discussions not only among historians and intellectuals, but also among the general public. Jewish survivors accuse the Poles of anti-Semitism and of betrayal during the German occupation. Poles, in general, take a rather hostile position and accuse the Jews of disloyalty to the Polish state and of anti-Polonism. They also deny, or at least justify, anti-Jewish sentiments within the Polish nation.

85

A significant number of researchers in both camps attempt to find the truth about Polish behaviour during the war. Jewish historians claim that in order to understand the present one must look into the past. They see Polish pre-war anti-Semitism as the source of subsequent attitudes during the war. Poles, on the other hand, reject the existence of anti-Semitism in prewar Poland and deny any connection between this phenomenon and Polish conduct during the Holocaust. Most Poles try to ignore the question and concentrate instead on the suffering of the Polish nation under the occupation. They claim that Poland lost 6 million of its citizens and could do little to help the Jews. (The Poles always quote this number without mentioning that it includes over three million Polish Jews.)

Among all the evidence being offered, there is one undeniable fact: Jews in pre-war Poland numbered about three and a half million or about 10 per cent of the total population. According to the most optimistic estimates, between 40,000 and 80,000 Jews survived the Holocaust; that is, between 1.5 and 2.5 per cent of the pre-war Jewish population. Poland of all European countries had the smallest percentage of survivors. The question that a researcher must ask is why was the number of survivors in Poland so small compared to those in other countries?

An answer to this question presents the greatest challenge to anyone doing research on the subject. In order to be able to draw a correct conclusion, one must look above all at the attitudes toward Jewish citizens adopted by various groups and strata of Polish society, including the average Pole. For, as the present study will indicate, the survival of many victims of the Holocaust depended on this crucial factor.

In this respect, the writings contained in many publications by the Polish underground are a good source of information and indicative of prevailing opinions about the Jewish problem among the Polish population. Some information can be found in documents kept in German archives such as those uncovered relatively recently in Koblenz, Germany, and is an indication of the attitude toward the Jews adopted by a significant part of the Polish resistance, as well as of the relationship that existed between the Polish resistance and the occupying forces. A large amount of material can be found in the testimonies of survivors. This source is disputed by many historians, who question the reliability of witnesses. It is claimed that testimonies taken some time after the events are very often influenced by personal experiences and are far from reality.

These memories cannot be primary materials for history. For oral history is even less reliable than letters and diaries. Belated testimonies seem to be spontaneous but are highly mediated; at such distance from the event memory fades or plays tricks or is contaminated by what the survivor has read or heard. When it comes to Holocaust history, moreover, the requirement to be exact is even more important since slanderers who call themselves revisionists will pick on every discrepancy.

(Hartman, 1996, p. 134)

Aside from the inaccurate names and dates there is also the Rashomon effect. *Rashomon* is the title of a Kurosawa film, made in 1950, in which three witnesses to the same crime give three different accounts.

Nevertheless, even the most ardent denier of oral accounts cannot ignore the sheer number of testimonies coming from thousands of survivors who had similar experiences in hundreds of different locations. In some way they do corroborate each other and cannot be rejected. Of the 25,000 or so testimonies of Holocaust survivors at Yad Vashem, a large proportion are from Poland. Of these, many hundreds of others, if not thousands, confirm their veracity.

The most important evidence of Polish behaviour, however, is the records kept by the Jews themselves at the time of the events. Jewish historians, led by Emmanuel Ringelblum, recorded the history of the ghetto and stored their archives in metal milk containers. During the Warsaw ghetto uprising they managed to hide the material they gathered by burying it. Some of the records were found after the war. Although a great deal of the material was lost, it remains the single most comprehensive contemporary document of the Holocaust and an invaluable source of information. A special section written by Ringelblum was devoted to the question of Polish–Jewish relations and to the problem of Polish behaviour towards the Jews.

What Ringelblum recorded is devoid of any personal moments. He does not write about his life or his family, but tries to present the situation within the context of the life of Jewish society. As for the question of Polish behaviour, Ringelblum clearly tries to find redeeming features in the attitudes of the Poles. In his diary he notes the positive as well as negative sides of their behaviour. He quotes several examples of Poles who behaved in a humane way toward Jews. He desperately tries to be objective.

My own person is a concrete proof that the conclusion drawn in some Jewish circles, that the entire Polish population had been happy to see the destruction of the Polish Jewry, that there were no

cases of goodhearted Poles saving Jews, is far from the truth.
(Ringelblum, 1985, p. 238)

Ringelblum's fate in itself is evidence of this assertion. After the Warsaw ghetto uprising, he was deported to the camp in Trawnik from where he was saved in the summer of 1943 by the Jewish underground assisted by Teodor Majewski – a member of the Polish resistance – and brought back to Warsaw. He, together with his family, was hidden in a bunker at number 81 Grujecka street. In that bunker were also hidden over thirty other Jews. As a result of denunciation, the bunker was discovered by the Gestapo on 7 March 1944. Ringelblum, his wife and son, and all the Jews who were there, together with one of the Poles, Mieczysław Wolski, who helped to create the hiding place, perished at the hands of the Nazis.

However, cases of the general animosity of the Polish population and anti-Jewish excesses, which Ringelblum recorded in every detail, far exceeded the number of humane acts by Poles. When taken in their entirety, the diaries are a document indicting a Polish society which at best looked on indifferently, and in some cases with undisguised satisfaction, at the tragedy of the Warsaw and other ghettos.

Polish apologists more often than not quote Ringelblum out of context, particularly when he tries to be objective and points to the rare good deeds of the Poles. An indication of Polish endeavours to present a positive image of the Polish population during the war, were changes introduced into the first edition of Ringelblum's diaries, published by the Historical Institute in Warsaw. It omitted all negative facts and observations about Polish animosity toward the Jews. That edition introduced many changes in the original vocabulary by leaving out words such as 'anti-Semite' or 'anti-Semitic'. Thus, for example, the quotation 'Nowodworski and other anti-Semitic lawyers', is altered to read 'Nowodworski and other lawyers' (ibid., p. 34). Such an apologetic trend among Polish historians persists to this very day.

The war

The preceding two chapters covering the period between the two wars contain much evidence of anti-Jewish sentiment within Polish society, but in order to understand the development of Polish–Jewish relations during the war, it is necessary to begin with the days immediately preceding the war's outbreak.

The evidence presented in the previous chapters leaves little doubt that the policy of the Polish government had, to a large extent, contributed to the anti-Jewish atmosphere in Poland. The solution to all problems in the country was confined to the solution to the Jewish question. It was only the immediate threat emanating from Nazi Germany that induced the Polish government and indeed the Polish nation to moderate the prevailing anti-Jewish attitudes. The anti-Semitic press, apparently under the instruction of higher authorities, had changed its tone and ceased inciting against the Jews.

The Jewish population actively participated in the preparations against German aggression. The call for volunteers which was issued a few days before the outbreak of the war brought out groups of Jewish men, carrying spades on their shoulders, marching towards the outskirts of the city, parks and other designated places, to dig anti-aircraft trenches to be used as public shelters. Thousands of Jews were busy doing their duty.

> Few Jews lived in this part of Warsaw so that the vast majority of the diggers were Poles, but today, there were no signs of animosity. Many of the Jewish volunteers were bearded religious men wearing the traditional black coats and head cover – something that usually caused the wearer to be insulted or even attacked by the Poles, but on this occasion, in face of a common danger, there reigned a spirit of solidarity ...
>
> (author's recollections)

However, as in the past, the respite in anti-Jewish attitudes was short-lived.

At daybreak on 1 September 1939 the German army crossed the Polish border. Cracow, the second largest city in Poland, fell on 6 September, and that night the Polish government, which only a short time earlier declared that 'we are going to fight to the last breath', fled from Warsaw to Lublin. By 15 September while units of the Polish army were positioned to defend the capital, the Polish government, or what was left of it, including President Ignacy Mościcki and the Polish army Chief Rydz Śmigły, reached a village on the Romanian border from where it fled into Romania. Polish historians do not consider the flight of the Polish government into Romania an act of cowardice, but point to the thousands of Jews who fled the Nazis into the Soviet zone of occupation to save their lives as evidence of Jewish communism. (With regard to Jews in the Soviet zone of occupation, see the Appendix which follows this chapter.)

All eye-witnesses of the September 1939 campaign agree that Jewish soldiers honourably fulfilled their duty on the battlefield. In general, the behaviour of Polish soldiers toward their Jewish comrades in the army was correct, although there were isolated cases of attempts by Polish anti-Semitic elements to create animosity toward the Jews in the Polish army (Ringelblum, 1985, p. 251).

However, after the defeat of the Polish army the old anti-Semitism came back to life. The anti-Semitic atmosphere felt in the last years of the Polish state flared up in prisoner-of-war camps. Many reports indicate that Polish anti-Semites in military uniforms expressed their anti-Jewish feelings in front of the common enemy.

> Our boys behaved in prison in a particularly infamous way leaving a very sullied memory. The [Germans] were enemies of the Poles as well. And here, here only, I got to know the true face of a Pole. From the very moment of becoming prisoner, they all, almost without exception started together, like sheep in a flock, calling aloud 'Heil Hitler' and 'Jude', 'Jude' – pointing their finger at a Jew ... Only here could I discover how the ill-formed character, or rather complete lack of any character, was the essential quality of that fine little nation.
>
> (Kermish, 1986, p. 218)

The anti-Jewish animosity was also evident after the Germans marched into Warsaw. It began when the German NSF (Nazional-Sozialistische Folkswohlfart) organised for propaganda purposes free distribution of bread. During the first days of the distribution Jews were not excluded. But soon after many Poles started pointing out to the Germans who was a Jew to be forced out of the queue (Ringelblum, 1985, p. 255). There were also numerous anti-Jewish incidents among people queuing in front of bakeries, or the few food shops still open.

> I got up before dawn, took an empty bag with me and went hunting. I found the store but there was already a long queue in front of it. The door opened at about 9 in the morning and a few customers went inside. It was orderly until someone said in a loud voice that there were Jews amongst the people in the queue. A commotion broke out with many voices demanding any Jew in the queue to leave immediately. Nobody moved. The man who started the commotion left his place but a few minutes later came back

with a German army patrol. 'Jude! Jude!', he pointed to a woman in the queue. One of the German soldiers grabbed her and threw her to the ground, shouting 'Jude, heraus!' Everybody in the queue burst out laughing.

Poles had a special gift of being able to recognise a Jewish face while the Germans could not distinguish between a Pole and a Jew; they needed Polish assistance which was given enthusiastically. The German soldier assisted by the Pole began to inspect the faces of everyone standing in the queue. Here and there, a man or a woman left the queue without waiting to be apprehended. I did not look particularly Jewish – I have a fair complexion and blue eyes. I wore my school cap – a four cornered typical Polish cap – and nobody standing next to me showed any indication of having recognised me as a Jew. Nevertheless I did not wait for the inspection and left.

(Author's recollection)

From the first day of German occupation it was clear that Jews and Poles were treated differently. According to Nazi racial ideology, the Poles were still a part of the Aryan race, though they constituted a lower stratum. It is for this reason that the outside of the ghetto was defined as the Aryan side.

In spite of the Nazi terror, the great majority of Poles still lived in their pre-war apartments and worked in their pre-war jobs, and urban Poles were quick to improve their lodgings in the course of ghetto formation. An order issued by Himmler called for the moving of all Jews and Poles living on annexed provinces of Poland into the territory of General Government. Subsequently, 1,200,000 Poles and 300,000 Jews were resettled to the east. While the Jews from annexed areas and those living in the eastern provinces were driven into ghettos, Poles found places of abode in the abandoned houses and apartments of the resettled, and later deported, Jews.

As far as the Polish peasantry goes, its economic situation had actually improved. Initially, the policy of the Germans toward the Polish peasantry was not to interfere with their land. The Germans appeared rather benevolent when they cancelled farmers' debts owed to Jewish creditors, eliminated some taxes, and introduced only a few quotas for compulsory food deliveries (Gross, 1979, pp. 103–5).

The Poles never faced total extermination. In fact, the Nazis showed some reluctance to mass-murder Poles lest 'the world hold the Wehrmacht responsible for these deeds', and according to a Nazi official called Halder, 'nothing must occur which would afford foreign countries an opportunity to launch any sort of atrocity propaganda based on such incidents' (Shirer, 1960, p. 794).

Immediate plans for extermination were aimed only at the leading strata of the Polish population, with specific exclusion of unskilled labour, the peasants and workers who, according to a German spokesman, 'basically had shown a willingness to work under energetic German leadership' (Gross, 1979, p. 76). Their fate was to 'be the slaves of the German Reich' (Shirer, 1960, p. 795).

But even in this respect there were some exceptions. On 6 November 1939, the Germans arrested 142 professors and research associates of Cracow Jagiellon University and deported them to the Sachsenhausen concentration camp. This arrest received so much adverse publicity that the administration of the General Government was forced to release the professors from the camps (Wroński, 1974, pp. 401–8).

More revealing of the German plans for Poland is a German document dated 27 April 1942. It clearly indicates that the Nazis never planned the extermination of the Polish nation – an argument put forward by Polish historians who claim that the Poles were destined for the same fate as were the Jews.

> Abschrift NG – 2325
> Geheime Reichsache
> I/214 geh.Rs.
> Berlin 27.4.1942
>
> ... It is quite clear that the Polish problem cannot be solved by way of liquidating the Poles in the same way as the Jews. This kind of solution of the Polish problem would become a burden on the German nation for many years to come, and it would deprive us for ever of any sympathy because other neighbouring nations would have to consider the possibility that in time they will be treated in a similar manner.
>
> (Szafranski, 1960, pp. 29–31)

The assertion that Poles were treated in the same way as Jews is absurd, to say the least. The Jews were condemned to death because they were Jews and they could do nothing to avoid the sentence. The Poles, on the other hand, were persecuted because the Germans wanted to impose obedience and submissiveness. If a Pole accepted this rule he had a good chance to survive. While it is true that many intellectuals, that is, the educated, and those who fought against the occupier were eliminated, this terror was selective – the Germans did not intend to exterminate every Pole.

The ghetto and the Poles

Even prior to the establishment of a ghetto in Warsaw, the activities of anti-Semitic elements were visible everywhere. The trams circulating in Warsaw at first had carriages designated 'for Jews only', but later Jews were forbidden to use them. In many cases Polish hooligans ordered the tram conductor to stop the tram and forcibly removed Jewish passengers. Only on rare occasions did a conductor disobey such an order. There was practically no reaction from the Polish passengers.

Kaplan, an eyewitness to the events, noted in his diary on 2 January 1940: 'For the past few days, incessant attacks occur in public places and in broad daylight' (Kaplan, 1966, p. 161). Ringelblum in his report confirms it: 'Yesterday, 28 January, the Polish gangs roamed the streets. They pulled Jews out of passing horse-driven carriages and beat them with whips' (Gutman, 1993, p. 53). The Polish police closed their eyes and the Polish resistance movement did not react. The hooligans obviously came to the conclusion that the majority of Poles accepted such behaviour.

Anti-Jewish excesses became a daily occurrence, culminating in a pogrom in February 1940. Polish gangs penetrated the area of the Jewish quarter where they attacked anyone in sight. Shouting 'exterminate the Jews!', 'down with the Jews!', 'long live independent Poland without Jews!', they broke into Jewish shops and looted them. The pogrom lasted several days. The Polish police did not interfere and there was no response from the Polish public. There was not a single instance when the Polish onlookers tried actively to prevent what was going on in front of their eyes (Ringelblum, 1985, p. 263).

The ghetto in Warsaw was established in 1940. Jews living outside of the designated area were ordered to move to the ghetto, while Polish inhabitants of the ghetto area were ordered to leave. The Germans sealed all apartments left by Jews, who had moved to the ghetto, and subsequently transferred the apartments together with their contents to Polish dealers and smugglers free of charge (Bartoszewski, 1993, p. 121).

By the late summer of 1940, 400,000 Jews were sealed by a wall from the rest of Warsaw, and on 15 November 1940 the Germans issued an order which forbade Jews to leave the ghetto. Compared to the conditions prevailing on the Polish side, there was indescribable overcrowding and the daily food allocation for Jews was much lower than for the Poles living outside of the ghetto. In terms of nutritional value the daily food ration for Jews in Warsaw in 1941 was 213 calories per person, compared with 760 calories for the Poles (Gutman et al., 1986, p. 45), and on 31 May 1943 Frank informed his associates of his decision to increase rations for the Polish population beginning 1 September (Gross, 1979, p. 163).

To avoid starvation and later deportation, many Jews tried to cross to the Aryan side where they hoped to find someone willing to help. The most common method of crossing was to join a group of Polish workers who were leaving the ghetto after work. At that time there were a few German enterprises employing Polish and Jewish workers (Kurt Rehrich, K. G. Schultz, Brauer and others). This method of escape from the ghetto was used only seldom as quite often the Polish workers would denounce the Jews to the guard when leaving the ghetto. Another method was to leave the ghetto through the gate by paying off the guard, which consisted of Polish police.

After reaching the Aryan side, many Jews were helped or given shelter by their former friends and acquaintances, or paid for false Aryan papers and official registration certificates. It was known as 'life on the surface' – that is, in near legality. However, life 'on the surface' was only available to Jews with 'good' looks. A Jew with Semitic facial features, since he could not show himself in public places, was forced to hide in a bunker or in a concealed room provided either by a friendly Pole or for a reward. In both cases, Jews were constantly under threat of being identified by any Pole who was not well disposed toward them. This could be a landlord, gas employee or electricity meter reader, house janitor, neighbour, or even a passer-by, often on the lookout for a Jew appearing on the street – a practice unknown anywhere in occupied Europe.

Many Jews lost their lives due to denunciation by hostile Polish neighbours. Anti-Semitic neighbours would sometimes on their own initiative conduct searches in order to uncover Jews in hiding. Ringelblum reports of the inhabitants of a building at 39 Pańska street who handed over a number of Jews to the Germans (Ringelblum, 1985, p. 324). In many cases the denunciation came after a Jew registered at a new hiding address. Some employees of the Polish police conducted systematic searches in the books of buildings looking for newly registered persons whom they would thoroughly investigate in order to establish whether they were Jewish (ibid., p. 301).

Adam Czerniakow, who had been appointed by the Germans as the head of the Judenrat, committed suicide in July of 1942 when he was asked to cooperate with the Germans in the deportations of the Jews from Warsaw. In his diaries, which were found after the war (Czerniakow, 1979), he refers to the attitude of the Poles as being sympathetic to the German persecution of Jews. He writes about pogroms on Jewish streets of Warsaw at the end of March, on 31 May and 16 October 1940. An entry dated 9 July 1942 speaks of Polish urchins throwing stones over the wall to Chlodna street [in the ghetto]: 'I have often asked myself the question whether Poland is Mickiewicz and Slowacki [famous Polish poets] or whether it is the [mob].'

One Polish underground publication describes the fruitless endeavours of Jews trying to escape the hell of ghetto life: 'People are hiding in cellars or attempting to get through to the area outside of the walls. But here the escapees are awaited by gangs of blackmailers who, under the direction of two "blue" [Polish] policemen, rob the Jews of everything they carry with them. The problem of blackmail is well known not only to the leaders of the Polish underground but the Polish population at large' (*Dzień Warszawy*, 26 Feb. 1943).

From the moment some Poles began helping the Germans to identify Jews, according to Ringelblum, the street became the link between the Polish anti-Semites and the Nazis. Out of these elements grew the widespread 'profession' of the so called 'szmalcowniks' – blackmailers who terrorised Jews hiding on the Aryan side and together with the Polish police became the allies of the Nazis in their hunt for Jews.

It was enough to mix into the crowd ... and to leave the building on the Leszno street. It seemed simple and relatively without danger, but having left the ghetto, the difficulties and the dangers immediately emerged. Some characters standing there, were watching attentively, vigilantly, trained to recognise the Jew. A Jew having discarded his Star of David armband did not even have time to experience a sense of relief, when one, two, three men wearing raincoats, caps pulled over they eyes, scarves around their necks, hands in pockets tailed him immediately at an accelerated pace. One of them outpacing the victim, the second one squeezing him on the side, sometimes excusing himself politely, while the third one followed behind very close practically stepping on his heels his steps echoing in the victims head, in his temples, in his stomach. By then, even the addresses of friends or of people who were willing to help for money engraved in his mind became useless. What followed depended on circumstances. Some, after being forced into a hallway and given an order, 'pull down your pants!', managed to get out of the situation by paying a ransom. Others were taken to the Polish police where they needed a large amount of money, watches, jewellery to get free.

It was then that my mother decided to send my little brother Olek to the Aryan side. She knew the dangers he was facing. It was a most terrible dilemma for a Jewish mother in the ghetto.

Olek was small, looking less than his eight years. He had a light complexion and blue eyes. His little nose was straight and he did not look at all like a little Jewish boy. But his biggest 'asset' was that he happened not to be circumcised due to my parents secular beliefs ... My mother had given him precise instructions of how he should behave once outside of the ghetto. Night after night she would wake him up and check whether he remembered what she had told him. Once he knew the answers – even half asleep – she decided he was ready to go. And Olek got out of the ghetto. He was a brave little boy. Barely a few steps on the Aryan side, the Polish guys caught him. 'Here, little Jew-boy!' They took him into a hallway. The fact that he wasn't circumcised worked for him.

(Margolis-Edelman, 1997, pp. 54–5)

The activities of blackmailers became so widespread that the *Agencja Informacyjna* (a Polish government-in-exile underground publication) in one of its issues published a communiqué concerning the growing number of denunciations of Jews in hiding outside of the ghetto. The communiqué warned that this kind of act would be punished by the Polish underground authorities and after the war by the Polish courts (*Agencja Informacyjna – Wieś*, 18 March 1943). The communiqué had little effect, as the number of denunciations and incidence of blackmail continued to rise.

For those who succeeded in hiding on the Aryan side, the ordeal did not end there. Very often, the constant fear of being denounced overwhelmed Jews in hiding and they would betray themselves by unusual behaviour such as glancing behind and around them, and by the look of fright in their eyes. It demanded a superhuman effort to put on an appearance of severity and throw harsh stares at Polish passers-by. The Poles soon became experts in recognising a Jew by the expression on his face rather than by his Semitic appearance. Jewish eyes, according to Polish 'experts' , could be recognised by their sadness – due to the years of life under inhuman conditions and loss of their close relatives. In addition to the right looks, a Jew had to possess perfect fluency in the Polish language without a trace of a Yiddish accent. Some Jews with correct looks but poor mastery of Polish pretended to be dumb and deaf (Ringelblum, 1985, p. 291).

There were numerous other ways in which a Pole could recognise a Jew. Michael W., aged 16 in 1943, escaped from the Warsaw ghetto. He had 'good looks' – tall, blond, spoke perfect Polish – but was recognised by a Pole.

> One day, one of the neighbours called me over and said he knew I was Jewish. I denied it, but asked why he thought I was Jewish. He said, he recognised me by the way I did my washing. Apparently I wringed the washing not the way the Poles do it. He assured me I should not worry, he would not report me. I got scared and went back to the ghetto.
>
> (Conversation with the author)

Particularly dangerous was the situation of a Jew on the Aryan side when he became sick. There were numerous cases when a Polish doctor denounced a Jewish patient who was seeking medical help (see Ringelblum, p. 300, quoting the case of a sick Jew who was denounced by a Polish doctor). Polish sources present a sharply contrasting picture: 'A marvellous page in the chronicle of helping Jews was written by the Polish intelligentsia. Of particular importance was the help of Polish doctors who hid sick Jews and wounded Jewish partisans and fighters' (Berenstein and Rutkowski, 1963, p. 38).

Many Jews in hiding on the Aryan side could not bear the tremendous tension of avoiding recognition and returned to the relative 'safety' of the ghetto. They did so not because they were victims of blackmail, but because of psychological stress they could no longer endure. Some felt it was preferable to die with their fellow Jews than undergo the ordeal of living as a Pole.

> I realised that this hiding place would be provided only for as long as there would be money to pay. So I hid the money someplace where the Pole could not lay his hands on, and since he did not know how much I possessed, he helped me for as long as I paid for my 'keep'.
> When I got the signal of the impending danger, I immediately left my hiding place and went back into the ghetto where I felt

more secure, where I could move freely from street to street and feel at home with my people. It was a false sense of security but was in sharp contrast with the conditions on the Polish side where one constantly feared to be denounced.

(From the testimony of Sam G., interviewed by the author)

For a Jew in hiding in the countryside, the situation was particularly difficult. In small towns or villages, where everyone knew everyone else, the appearance of a stranger immediately attracted the attention of the villagers. In most cases a fugitive would be handed over to the German authorities. There were, nevertheless, some exceptions. Some peasants were willing to hide Jews, but this depended on two factors: on the German terror and the surrounding atmosphere. In places with a pre-war anti-Semitic tradition, hiding a Jew was extremely difficult; a brave Pole who was willing to help lived in greater fear of denunciation by anti-Semitic neighbours than of the German terror.

In order to track down the fugitives, the Germans applied a carrot and stick method. Severe penalties, including a death sentence, were imposed for hiding Jews, while a reward in money and kind, including the belongings of a Jew, was promised for catching one. In western Galicia, for example, in Borek Falecki, Wieliczka, Bochnia and Swoszowicz, the reward for catching a Jew was fixed at 500 zlotys and one kilo of sugar. In Wołyń, the reward was three litres of vodka. The latter reward had also been applied in other regions of Poland. This method proved extremely successful and resulted in numerous denunciations. Mass denunciations by the local population took place in the Kielce region, known for its anti-Semitic excesses before the war (and after).

In the town of Częstochowa and its surrounding area there was a small number of Jews who managed to evade deportation. They were caught and handed over to the Germans by the local Polish population. As a result of the combined German–Polish action, Częstochowa, which before the war had a Jewish population of 40,000, was now free of Jews (Ringelblum, 1985, p. 313).

In the town of Lukow a number of Jews were hiding after the deportation in the neighbouring woods. Quite often they were discovered by Polish children who were playing there. Taught from childhood to hate the Jews, they informed their parents about the Jewish presence in the woods. They then informed the local Polish authorities, who in turn alerted the Germans, who took them away to be executed.

The Polish underground and the Polish public at large were aware of these practices, but nothing was done to put an end to them, or at least limit their extent. It did not call for an act of heroism to look away or to try and dissuade a Polish denouncer from doing his sinister work. There was no penalty for not recognising a Jew. It seemed as if all of Polish society was hell bent on assistimg the Germans in their plans. It was sufficient for someone to shout: 'A Jew is escaping!', for a few passers-by to run after the fugitive and to hand him over to the Germans. There were a few cases when the victim proved to be a Pole, a member of the underground, who subsequently perished as a result of mistaken identity. Such incidents must have occurred quite often because the underground press brought this matter to the attention of the Polish public.

> We were both walking down Grzybowska street, just a few yards apart. Suddenly she began to scream. I don't recall exactly how it happened, I mean I don't remember who first noticed the child crawling under the barbed wire. I think she did. But I don't remember the child; all I remember is the woman shouting. She creamed: Jude! Jude! – urging the Germans or Ukrainians or Latvians to perform their duty and shoot a Jewish child.
> ... That was not the only incident of its kind, I swear. No one knows how often it happened. But I was not the only one who heard. It went on and on. That scream: Jude! Jude! ... why was that woman so anxious for the Germans to capture and kill a Jewish child? Did she want to watch a small child die? What was she after?
> (Rymkiewicz, 1994, pp. 42–3)

While all this was taking place the church remained silent, as did the Polish Government-in-exile in London. The only authority who had the means of influencing Polish public opinion under the occupation – the Polish underground – remained indifferent and often hostile to their Jewish fellow citizens. The underground press – there were approximately 1,500 underground papers in Poland – was the government's 'fourth branch' and represented Polish public opinion (Bartoszewski, 1968, p. 56). The volume and diversity of the Polish underground press of this period permit one to state conclusively that the ideas it was expressing were disseminated throughout the entire population. The widely circulated underground press should have made it possible to constantly appeal to the Poles not to cooperate with the Germans in their extermination of the Jews. The reality was that a large part of the press spread anti-Jewish propaganda, while the rest mostly ignored what was happening to Jews.

The resettlements

Terrible as the conditions in the ghetto were, the Jewish population showed exceptional resilience in adapting themselves to the situation. In the beginning there were some cultural activities in the ghetto such as theatre, lectures, even some schooling. And as for the supply of food, smuggling became a widespread activity. Smuggling was not a one-way proposition. Jews sold or traded their property, possessions and clothing for food, and a steady stream of Jewish money, household goods, pianos, and other possessions poured onto the Polish side (Gutman, 1994, p. 92). In this respect, Jews obtained full cooperation from the Poles, who benefited tremendously from this trade. Money and valuables changed hands in payment for staple food and even some luxuries.

However, as the situation worsened, many Jews eagerly accepted the German offer of resettlement for 'work' and presented themselves to the places of transportation. A question that is often asked is why did the Jews in the ghetto passively submit to the deportations? The main reason for Jewish passivity in July 1942 was the German strategy of deception. The promise of resettlement for work was received by exhausted and hungry Jews with relief, and many went voluntarily to be deported to the east.

Ringelblum makes the following comment:

> It is to be regretted that the Polish Government, which was certainly well informed of the fate of the Jews deported from Lublin and Warsaw, did nothing to warn the Jewish community and its leaders. The representatives of the Polish Government in Poland and their agents spread all over the occupied territory, had sufficient information about the methodical murder of the Jewish citizens. Yet it did not make any move. It was only the escape of a few Jews from the Treblinka extermination camp, that opened the eyes of the Jews as to the real purpose of the resettlements.
>
> (Ringelblum, 1985, p. 330)

The evacuations from the Warsaw ghetto lasted 44 days. By that time it was already known that the final destination was an extermination camp. While this drama was being enacted there was utter silence on the Polish side. There was no appeal to render help to Jews fleeing from the ghetto to seek shelter among the Poles. 'A deadly silence reigned on the Aryan side despite the drama that took place in front of hundreds of thousands of Poles. There was no call from the Polish government [in exile] to resist, no expression of sympathy, no promise of help – not even moral support' (ibid., p. 328).

In New York, on 23 June 1943, the Director of the Institute of Jewish Affairs of the World Jewish Congress, Jacob Robinson, had this to say:

> How did it happen that hundreds of thousand of Jews were deported and slaughtered during the course of four months without the slightest reaction on the part of the Polish population, the Polish underground, and the Polish Government-in-Exile? ... This could not happen in any other country. The Nazis were sure that the Poles would not budge, and the Poles in their blind hatred of the Jews were co-responsible for the slaughter.
>
> (Hilberg, 1992, p. 208)

At the beginning of the resettlements, when the Polish population did not know what was happening to the Jews and thought that the transports were really going to the east for resettlement, there was general indifference. The attitudes changed when it was realised that the trains were going to Treblinka, where the Jews were exterminated. But instead of commiserating with the victims, the Poles began accusing them of cowardice and lack of national pride. 'Why didn't you resist? Why did you go like sheep to the slaughter? Why did you not attack the Germans when you knew that your death was unavoidable? We, Poles would not let ourselves to be taken for slaughter, with us they would have had a hard task and would not dare to do what they did to you.' Such were the questions asked by Poles.

Ringelblum admitted that such accusations contained some truth, but he blamed the Poles for not supplying weapons to the ghetto, which the Jews had demanded for months. After many attempts at acquiring weapons, the ghetto received such small quantities and of such poor quality that it was impossible to organise effective resistance against the Nazis.

> We affirm that if the competent Polish authorities would have given moral support and assistance in the form of supply of weapons, the price the Germans would have had to pay for the sea of Jewish blood spilled in July, August and September of 1942 would have been very high. I underline that I have not exhausted the subject of resistance, I have limited myself to interpret the problem within the context of the attitude of the Polish factors.
>
> (Ringelblum, 1985, p. 330)

Armed struggle in other ghettos, did not create much reaction on the Polish side either. No other ghetto had received help from the Polish resistance. Jewish organisations in Vilno and Bialystok managed to establish contact with the local underground and asked for weapons. The Vilno regional command of the AK (Home Army) began negotiations by putting two questions to the Jewish Fareinigte Partizaner Organisation (United Partisan Organisation): 'Is FPO a communist organisation? and whom will FPO support when the Russians are back and a Polish–Soviet conflict arises regarding Vilno?' Replying to these questions, the FPO said that there were some communists in the organisation, but they are a small minority. As to the second question, FPO said that this is a hypothetical question and the position of FPO would be determined when the problem arose. The AK refused to help (Prekerowa, 1992, p. 175).

The attitude of Polish society

Research into this period of Polish–Jewish relations, the documentary evidence and personal testimonies, indicate that the virus of anti-Semitism, which invaded the Polish body and which propagated itself during the pre-Second World War years, had not disappeared after the September 1939 disaster. Polish society entered the Second World War and the Nazi occupation already poisoned by anti-Semitic propaganda. The anti-Jewish policy of the Nazis had encountered fertile ground in Poland. During the Nazi anti-Jewish terror, the dominant contention among the Poles was 'that it is good that the Jewish problem is being solved by the Germans', and that 'at least the Germans are doing something good for us' (Ros, p. 18).

This is why the Poles by and large remained neutral observers of the horrors of life in the Jewish ghettos and of German atrocities perpetrated against the Jewish population. Jan Karski, in his report to the Polish government-in-exile in February 1940, claimed that the elimination of Jews from the economic and social life of Poland, did not give rise to strong condemnation by everyone. 'This lack of condemnation constitutes a narrow bridge, which can lead to a kind of silent agreement between the Germans and the more primitive part of the Polish population' (Prekerowa, 1992, p. 70).

The commander of the AK reported about it in a dispatch sent to London in September 1941: 'Please, accept it as a fact that the overwhelming majority of the country is anti-Semitic ... Underground organisations remaining under the influence of the pre-war activists of the National Democrats and even the Socialist party adopt the postulate of emigration as a solution to the Jewish problem [once the war is finished]' (Gross, 1979, p. 184). Three years later, after the 'final solution' had already been carried out by the Nazis, an emissary of the London government, Andrzej Chciuk (code named Celt), suggested on his return from Poland that various official statements issued by the government-in-exile in London stressing sympathy and solidarity with the Jewish cause should be toned down. 'The Government exaggerates in its love for the Jews, although, understandably, some of the Government statements are determined by foreign policy requirements.' He added: 'the government should restrain its pro-Jewish pronouncements because the country does not like Jews' (ibid., p. 185).

One prominent Polish historian in his attempt to minimise the effects of anti-Semitism has this to say about Polish attitudes toward the Jews during those tragic times: 'Despite German persecution of the Polish people, a small minority of Poles openly approved of German policies toward the Jews, and some actively aided the Nazis in their task. Other Poles showed no outward pleasure at the removal of Jews from Polish offices, professions, and businesses but were not opposed to the economic expropriation involved. These people had anti-Semitic views which were economic, not racial, in character; it reflected an economic anti-Semitic attitude' (Lukas, 1986, p. 126).

Of crucial importance was the attitude of the Catholic Church, the only institution which continued its official activities on the whole territory of the occupied country. The higher church hierarchy did not even once express its views regarding persecution of Jews, nor did it encourage in any way the rendering of assistance to Jews. Part of the clergy continued to accept the meaning of the words of the Jewish crowd mentioned in the Gospel: 'His blood be on us and our children'.

Anti-Semitic sentiments in their most extreme form can be found in a report originating from the Polish Catholic Church. The report covers the period from 1 June to 15 July 1941. It states:

> The need to solve the Jewish question is urgent. Nowhere else in the world has that question reached such a climax, because no fewer than 4 million of these highly noxious and by all standards dangerous elements live in Poland, or to be more precise, off Poland ... the Jewish question ... must be seen as a singular dispensation of Divine Providence in which the Germans have already made a good start ...
>
> (YVA, O-25/89–12, Yad Vashem Archives)

The clandestine press of a number of minor Catholic-nationalist groups continued to issue Jew-baiting statements. Thus, *Prawda Mlodych* for the month of May 1943 wrote: 'The Jews have been parasites living off he bodies of European nations. This is why they have been universally loathed and detested.'

In this the Church was seconded by the Polish resistance underground press. The National-Radical organ *Szaniec* in its issue of 31 January 1942 stated: 'The Jews were, and will be our enemies always and everywhere ... hence the question must be posed, how shall we treat them? ... To this question we have but one answer: as enemies. And certainly no fewer than 90 per cent of the Poles agree with us on that score.' The same *Szaniec* in issue no. 13 of 21 October 1942 said: 'The German-made pogroms of Jews in Poland follow all the rules of modern technology. The job is well done.'

A March 1943 issue of *Pravda*, another underground publication, takes a more conciliatory position, and at the same time reveals the extent of the anti-Jewish feelings within Polish society:

> There is no need for hypocritical talk. No prestige considerations ... shall make us keep quiet about the existence of native Polish canaille who prey upon human grief and misery. The hosts of informers and blackmailers have grown, to reach incredible, terrifying numbers. The blackmailers make life intolerable for the ever growing number of victims of Nazi persecutions.
>
> (Gutman and Karkowski, 1986, p. 114)

Such expressions of outrage were rather the exception – most underground publications displayed undisguised contempt toward Jews.

How to get rid of Jews

As late as 1943–4, that is, after the overwhelming majority of Jews had already been murdered by the Nazis, the preoccupation of many groups of Polish political opinion was the debate about schemes of solving what remained of the Jewish problem. In 1943, 9 out of the 13 listed political groups affiliated with the Delegate's Office (representatives of the government-in-exile) suggested programmes of either forced emigration or extermination of the surviving remnants of the Jewish people. Only four groups adopted the democratic principle of granting the Jews equal rights after the defeat of the Nazis and the liberation of Poland.

The underground press appearing under the auspices of the Delegate's Office or the Chief Command of the Home Army did not even try to conceal its anti-Jewish attitude. The following report of deportations from the Warsaw ghetto was published in London in issue no. 5 of the Reports of the Social Department of the Interior Ministry of 31 August 1943:

> At least some of us, while appalled by the dreadfulness of the methods, and while revolted by the disgrace of murdering women and children, wonder about the meaning of the reported development in terms of the prospects they portend for domestic relations in future Poland. They ask themselves if the prospects are not favourable. For, really, the number of Jews exceeded all proportions! And they were entirely and for ever alien to our culture, our traditions, and our statehood ... There probably is no other human collectivity that would be so repulsive, that would abound with individual characteristics as distinct and as offensive as those which Jews share.
>
> (YVA, M-2/205)

An organ of National-Radical Camp had this to say on that subject: 'Now is the time to resolve that no Jews shall live in Poland any more ... All the Jews who survive the current pogroms will under this law have to leave Poland' (*Placówka*, 21 Oct. 1942). An important Polish underground paper expressed its view on the future place of Jews in Poland in the following terms:

> At present, the majority of Polish society considers that the Germans have entirely liquidated the Jews in Poland. However, this is not so, because a significant number of Jews saved themselves before the liquidation ... Those that survived are physically the most strong – only the old and sick have perished. It can safely be said that, in the country as well as abroad, 25 to 30 per cent of Jews are still alive. In addition, it must be remembered that there are thousands of Jews – 'Polish citizens' – who for a long time did not live in Poland. After the war, all these Jewish elements will attempt to return to Poland in order to again take over the management of our economic life ... as it was before the war ... We must strive that after the war Jews do not return to Poland but remain where they are or go to Palestine.
>
> (*Wielka Polska*, 3 Nov. 1943)

An account of one of the most vicious attacks against Jews by the Polish underground was published on 28 July 1943 in the organ of the Stronnictwo Narodowe – *Walka*. It was thought to be important enough to be reprinted in *Wielka Polska* and *Życie polityczne kraju*. The article analyses the power of the Jews, who despite their reduced numbers present a future danger for Poland:

> There is a danger that the hopes of the 'chosen people' to recover assets robbed by the Germans, will be considered when war reparations are fixed ...
> ... We denounce with all our strength the Nazi bestiality toward the Jews, but we will not give up the economic and political struggle with the Jews, who touched by the crocodile tears of Jewish financiers and politicians, prepare themselves to impose upon us their rule.
>
> (*Walka*, 28 July 1943, reprinted in *Wielka Polska*, 7 Aug. 1943 and
> *Życie polityczne kraju*, 1–15 Aug. 1943)

The government-in-exile

At this stage it would be appropriate to consider the question how much the Poles in London knew about the situation in Poland and what their reaction was. There is much evidence to show that the Polish government-in-exile in London was quite aware of the popular mood within Polish society thanks to the regular reports it received from and through the Polish underground. A report sent to London by the Delegate's Office towards the end of 1940 noted the general attitude of Poles living under German occupation:

> It would be a great mistake to suppose that Polish anti-Semitism belongs to the past. Although Polish public opinion disapproves of anti-Jewish violence, it would most emphatically refuse to tolerate the return of the Jews to their prewar positions and influence ... The Government shows poor comprehension of this attitude: the last radio message of minister Stanczyk which contained commitments to the effect of granting equal rights to the Jews in liberated Poland ... made a very unfavourable impression. It was resented even by working-class elements belonging to the Polish Socialist Party.
>
> (Gutman and Krakowski, 1986, p. 60)

On 25 August 1941, Grot-Rowecki informed the government-in-exile in

London: 'The overwhelming majority of the country is in an anti-Semitic mood. Even socialists are no exception' (Prekerowa, 1992, p. 150).

A member of the Polish underground, Stefan Korbonski, responsible for radio broadcasts from Poland and for the secret radio link with London, wrote in his memoirs (*The Story of the Secret State*) that since the beginning of the deportations in July 1942, he had often been sending messages informing the Polish government about the situation. Polish circles in London did not react to these messages (Korbonski, 1954, pp. 253–4).

The government had also been informed about the deportations and the ultimate fate of the Jewish population. General Tadeusz Komorowski-Bor, one of the leaders of the AK, speaks in his memoirs about the activities of the AK during the deportations: 'Already on 29 July [1942] we received through the railway workers the news that Jews transported to the camp of Treblinka disappear without trace. There could be no doubt that these deportations were the first stage of planned extermination' (Gutman, 1993, p. 349).

When the uprising in the Warsaw ghetto broke out and during the entire duration of the fighting in the ghetto, there was a strange silence abroad, although information was available about the course of the operations from the first day. The news of the Jewish uprising was broadcast on London radio on 30 April – that is, three days after the end of organised resistance and two weeks after the beginning of the fighting. The Polish government responded only on 3 May, when Władysław Sikorski, the then Polish Premier, in his speech mentioned the fighting by Jewish Polish citizens and appealed to render them assistance (*Życie polityczne kraju*, 15–31 May 1943). In his 4 May 1943 message to the Poles in Poland, Sikorski dedicated only part of his message to the destruction of the Warsaw ghetto. The text of the message was placed on the third page of the government organ *Dziennik Polski*.

There was no mention of the current situation in Poland, neither was there anything about what happened in the Warsaw ghetto prior to and after the publication of the message. From the diary kept by Itzhak Schwartzbart – a Jewish member of the Polish parliament – it would appear that Jewish requests for an official condemnation of the persecutions and extermination of Polish Jews and for an alarm to be raised on the world scene remained without reply.

The suicide of the Jewish leader Szmul Zygielbojm, who took his life in London as a protest against the indifference to the Holocaust of the Polish government-in-exile and the world, had been widely commented on, but the Polish underground gave this event a different interpretation. One publication reported that the reason for his suicide was the news from Warsaw that his wife had been murdered in the ghetto. Not a word was mentioned about the suicide note Zygielbojm left in which he explained his real reason:

> ... I must also assert that although the Polish government has to a large extent contributed to the arousal of world opinion, it did so inadequately, and did not dare to do something extraordinary that would correspond to the magnitude of the drama that takes place in the country.
> ... I cannot remain silent and I cannot live when the remnants of the Jewish population, which I represent, are perishing.
> ... With my death, I wish to express my deepest protest against the inaction with which the world looks on and allows the extermination of the Jewish people.
>
> S. Zygielbojm

> (This version of Zygielbojm's letter corresponds to the text of the photocopy published in *Documents on the Holocaust*, by Y. Arad, I. Gutman and A. Mavgaliot (eds), Jerusalem, 1988)

Subsequently, the underground papers sharply criticised the Polish government-in-exile for the glorification of the death of Zygielbojm and the Warsaw ghetto uprising:

> The glorification of this Jewish 'attempt', which in other circumstances would have been directed against the Poles, should have been left for the Jews.
> ... The presence at the funeral of the tragically deceased chairman of Bund of as many as three Polish ministers and the chairman of the National Council, is out of proportion with the role of this organisation in Poland ... It is a continual mistake of our emigration [government], which does not realise the changed character of the Jewish question in Poland, and of the fact that world Jewry is waging decisive actions against the restoration of a strong and independent Poland.
>
> (*Wiadomości bierzące* NSZ-1A 6 June 1943)

Polish government in London attempts at reconciliation between Pole and the Jew were met with fierce opposition from the Poles in occupied Poland. The celebration of the day of the Jewish–Polish soldier in London on 3 November 1943 provoked a hostile reaction in the Polish underground press:

> The London celebration is not an isolated event, but a planned and large scale action to whitewash the Jews in the eyes of the Polish society, which remembers well all their treacheries and machinations with the enemies of Poland.
>
> ... Despite the terrible German atrocities, the Jews hate the Poles more than they hate the Germans, and have often threatened that they will repay us with interest for the German persecutions, because, they claim, it was our duty to defend them from the Germans.
>
> (*Wielka Polska*, 3 Nov. 1943)

The ambivalence of the Polish government-in-exile on Jewish issues could be accounted for by two conflicting considerations. On the one hand, the government feared that public opinion in Poland, anti-Semitic as it basically was, might blame it for being too good to Jews. On the other hand, it badly wanted to appear committed to democracy and to equal rights for national minorities in the eyes of Western public opinion.

The Warsaw Ghetto uprising and the Poles

The dramatic news, unbelieved at first, that resettlement meant death in the gas chambers, deprived the Jewish population of hope of surviving the war. It dawned on many Jews that there was no sense in passively submitting to German orders. It was the beginning of resistance to the Nazis. However, for the resistance to be effective there was desperate need for arms. These could only be obtained from the Aryan side with the help of the Polish resistance, but the request for weapons was met by complete silence from the Polish underground.

Nevertheless, a shipment of weapons from the Polish side reached the ghetto in the first week of August 1942. It consisted of five pistols and six hand grenades (Gutman, 1994, p. 155). According to Wolinski (codename Wacław), who headed the department for Jewish affairs within the Polish underground, as a result of the urgent requests from the Jewish Fighting Organisation (ZOB), ten pistols and a small quantity of ammunition were supplied to them by the high command of the AK in December 1942. Wolinski claims that 'these weapons were in a very poor condition and were only partially useable'. The ZOB viewed this gesture as far from satisfying their most basic needs and continued to demand an increased supply of arms. Their request led to the supply of ten additional pistols and a small quantity of explosives (ibid., p. 173).

Furthermore, the Jewish leaders of the Warsaw uprising had no military experience and did not realise the ineffectiveness of hand pistols in street battles. By contrast, the AK command, mostly professional officers, knew how to conduct military operations and what kind of weapon was needed. In his last letter to Cukierman – the Jewish contact on the Aryan side – the leader of the uprising, Anielewicz, expressed his disappointment: 'Remember that pistols are of no use to us. What we urgently need are grenades, rifles, explosives' (Mark, 1963, p. 262).

Despite the claims by the AK that its stock of weapons did not allow for larger supplies, the quantities that the AK agreed to supply the Jewish ghetto fighters were minuscule compared to the reserves of arms at its disposal. According to information supplied by the representative of Polish government in the US, the AK had at its disposal in the spring of 1943 25,000 guns, 6,000 pistols, 30,000 grenades, as well as heavy weapons (Mitkiewicz, 1972, pp. 95–156).

Another reason for the reluctance to supply weapons to the Jews put forward by the AK, was that Jews were not capable of armed resistance. A message sent by Rowecki on 1 January 1943 clearly characterises the attitude of the chief of the AK regarding help for the Jews: 'Jews of diverse groups, including communists, are approaching us with requests for weapons, as if we had full stores. As a trial, I gave them a few pistols. I am not sure if they will use them at all' (Gutman, 1993, p. 352). There was also the suspicion that Jews were communists.

There is no evidence to suggest that the Poles discussed the defence of the ghetto and that they tried to render effective help. A letter from Anielewicz to the representatives of the Coordinating Commission, operating on the Aryan side, dated 13 March 1943 indicates the attitude of the Poles to the Warsaw ghetto fighters:

> Please, convey to the [Polish] authorities that if no significant help is forthcoming immediately, we will consider it as a sign of indifference of the authorities toward the fate of the Warsaw Jewry. The supply of armament without ammunition appears to us as a cynical mockery to our fate and as a confirmation of the fact that the venom of anti-Semitism continues to poison the government

circles in Poland despite the cruel and tragic experiences of the past three years. We do not have to convince anyone about our willingness to fight. Beginning with 18 January the Jewish community is in a state of permanent struggle with the occupier and his servants. Whoever is denying it or has any doubts, is a malicious anti-Semite. Commander of ZOB.

(Gutman, 1993, pp. 475–6)

The extent of Polish assistance to the Jewish ghetto fighters can be seen from a report by a German army commander named Stroops, who on 24 May 1943 in answer to a series of questions about the destruction of the Warsaw ghetto, had this to say about the state of Jewish weapons: 'as for the spoils, these consisted of 7 Polish rifles, 1 Russian rifle, 1 German rifle, 59 revolvers of various calibres. A few hundred hand grenades, which included Polish home-made grenades, a few hundred Molotov cocktails, home-made bombs and detonators, and quantities of explosives, and munitions'.

The uprising

The reaction of the Polish underground to the Warsaw ghetto uprising was, with very few exceptions, negative and often hostile. The uprising was seen as communist inspired and assisted by the Soviet army. It was also considered a threat to Poland because it was thought that the Jews would use their weapons against the Poles when the war came to an end. Many underground publications saw the uprising as a final solution to the Jewish question in Poland:

> For us all this [the ghetto uprising] is a matter of indifference. We rejoice with the death of every German, but we also reflect on ... the immaturity of the Jews as a nation (some surrendered, some did not even attempt to fight); they only think of preserving their life, while we – Poles – rally around one idea.
>
> (*Polska Żyje*, 24 April 1943)

On Good Friday, 23 April 1943, the Jewish Fighting Organisation issued an appeal to the Polish population, declaring that the struggle in the ghetto upheld the time-honoured motto 'For your freedom and ours', and stressing that the Jews and the Poles had become brothers in arms (Korbonski, 1978, p. 132). The response by the Polish population at large to the appeal is unknown. But the following excerpt clearly indicates the attitude of many Poles to the ghetto uprising. It shows deep-seated prejudice that was not affected by the tragedy unfolding in front of their eyes.

> Here is one interesting detail of the fighting. During the first days of the operations, the Jews hoisted Polish and Zionist flags on the Muranowski Square. This expression of Polish patriotism is laughable, to say the least, if not cynical. Of course, we do not condone the Nazi mass murders perpetrated on the Jewish or other nationalities, but we consider that the 'chosen people' have linked their ideologies, sympathies, hopes and interests with the red flag from the Volga rather than with the Polish White Eagle ... We know about the uncountable losses that the Polish nation has suffered precisely because of these Jews, and it is for this reason that their fate, terrible as it is from the purely humane point of view, appears to be just. The historical Nemesis always pays back crimes and faults – it punishes even entire nations.
>
> (*Nurt Młodych*, 30 April 1943, also in *Przegląd prasowy*, 12 May 1943)

Numerous Polish publications, in an attempt to diminish the importance of the Jewish ghetto uprising, resorted to distortions and more often than not to plain lies. The most recurrent argument was that the uprising was communist inspired and that the Jews were armed to the teeth and were directed and instructed by Soviet advisers. A popular notion was that members of the Soviet army were directing the rebellion. Such falsehoods evidently found willing ears, for in June 1943 the minister of security of the Polish government-in-exile, General Marjan Kukiel, in a message from London to Warsaw, asked 'whether there is any truth in the claim that the opposition of the Jews in Warsaw during the destruction of the Jewish ghetto was led and organised by Soviet officers and other ranks, who were parachuted from the air, and whether arms, munition and antitank guns were supplied in the same way' (Gutman, 1994, p. 230).

A special report by 'S' (code-name Strzelec) of 2 May 1943 provided the following 'data' about the armed forces of the Warsaw ghetto:

> The ghetto armed forces consist of the following units:
>
> Members of Bund and Jews-communists, who until now have concealed their activities and worked in the German war industry while preparing themselves for sabotage and armed resistance;
>
> German Aryan communists, who were pardoned after the signing

of the German–Soviet Pact, but who were again persecuted after the collapse of the agreement. They ... found secure asylum among their Jewish 'comrades' in the ghetto;

German Aryan deserters who fled from the eastern front, and who were unable to find shelter among the Polish population ... found a friendly reception and understanding in the ghetto;

Soviet emissaries, Jewish and Aryan, who infiltrated the ghetto by way of air-parachute drops and supplied in this way weapons and ammunition, and who are expert instructors in revolutionary struggles and sabotage;

Polish soldiers and officers of Jewish origins – many of them converts and assimilated within Polish society – who because they were not Aryan or were of mixed origin, were forced to enter the ghetto and are above all seeking their own liberation.

The armed operations of these organisations are financed or helped by:

Rich local Jews and Jews abroad, who were displaced into the ghetto, and who thanks to money and connections were able to save themselves from deportation; communist organisations active abroad;

German speculators, who act as middlemen in the supply of weapons, Volksdeutche who operate within local institutions and who under the pretence of smuggling food to the Jews in service tramways, even in military vehicles, supplied the Jews with weapons and ammunition.

(*Agencja A.*, nr. 2, 5 June 1943)

Similar views were expressed by most underground publications – the Jews with the help of the Soviets are fighting the Germans with the ultimate objective to attack the Poles.

The resistance and the supply of weapons for the Jewish community still numbering in the thousands, has been organised by the Bund and the Communists. These are actually the elements who during the entire period of occupation, were the most hostile to the Poles and have been able, within the communist organisations, to perpetrate bloody revenge on the Poles ... Stocks of weapons and communist headquarters, from which Soviet officers controlled sabotage, were located in the ghetto.

(*Polska Informacja Prasowa*, 7 May 1943, reprinted in *Agencja A.*, 15 May and in *Wielka Polska*, 18 May 1943)

Even those who acknowledged the bravery and greatness of spirit of the ghetto fighters did not call on the Poles to help the Jews. Some Polish accounts of the Warsaw ghetto uprising attempted to paint a positive picture of the Polish attitude toward the Jewish fighters, but such depictions were rather deceptive. According to one Polish source: 'the leaders of the Jewish ghetto resistance had no doubts about the attitude of the Polish underground; they were conscious of the mood and feelings of the Warsaw population. They perceived the sympathy and the moral support of the Polish side' (Arczynski and Balcerak, 1983, p. 150). Another underground source reported that: 'ZOB was able to prepare itself for the first act of resistance against the Germans thanks to the help by the Polish underground' (ibid., p. 140).

Many publications by the Polish underground, especially by the nationalists, concerning the Warsaw ghetto uprising were rabidly anti-Semitic and their contents not very different from what was appearing in the Nazi press. One of their organs, *Młoda Polska*, asserted: 'today, despite the tear in the eye over the burnt out ghetto, all Polish groups are in agreement on the elimination of Jewish influence. Victory has been achieved!' (*Młoda Polska*, 13 Oct. 1943, reprinted in *Przegląd Prasy Polskiej*, nr. 23)

Jewish cowardice

A recurring theme in the Polish underground press was that the extermination of the Jews by the Germans was made easier because of the absence of Jewish active resistance against the deportations. It was also allegedly facilitated by the collaboration of many Jews who wanted to save their own skin. The AK press expressed its position in the following terms:

> We, therefore, who looked at the life in the ghetto and its subsequent liquidation – saw above all a tragedy of a people too coward to wage a war and perhaps because of its cowardice experiencing terrible sufferings.
>
> ... Until it came to the actual fighting in the ghetto, Jews were selling each other – the rich selling the poor to the Germans – and when at the end there was only a handful of the 'most enduring' – simply the richest – and it became clear that the Germans will take even them, and there will be no one to pay for them – then those who were still left threw themselves into a hopeless battle ... One can only speak of a Jewish tragedy not of Jewish heroism.
>
> (*Walka*, 25 May 1943)

Another underground paper openly showed its contempt for the fighting Jews:

> In those tragic days, the Jewish community displayed an unheard of attitude of resignation and complete lack of national solidarity. Every Jew pushed another one to his death hoping that perhaps he will survive, that something will happen. In the meantime others should go to the slaughter.
>
> (*Wielka Polska*, no. 19, 5 May 1943)

Expressions of genuine sympathy were very rare and came mainly from little-known underground circles with only weak influence on Polish public opinion:

> The until recently Jewish position, so extraordinarily passive, has been met with a completely negative reaction from Polish society. However, the present fighting on the streets of the ghetto lasting already 10 days, deserves the highest sympathy of Polish society, which cannot actively help the Jews in their struggle, but gives them its full moral support.
>
> (*Tydzień*, nr. 6, 29 April 1943)

It is worthwhile noting that Polish documentation of the period does not contain one example of an open armed revolt of the Poles (the Warsaw 1944 uprising came much later and had political motives). There is no known case of armed resistance of Polish inmates of German concentration camps. The April 1943 Warsaw armed uprising by the Jews was the first open act of resistance in occupied Europe (except Yugoslavia). Revolts and escapes from the extermination camps in Treblinka and Sobibor, as well as the revolt of the Sonderkommando in Auschwitz, Chelmno and Nerem, are another pointer to Jewish resistance compared to the absence of resistance on the part of the Polish population and the underground.

A close scrutiny of the behaviour of the Polish population under the occupation indicates a large degree of submissiveness. Hundred of thousands of Poles were transferred to Germany for forced labour without any signs of active resistance; 'even in Warsaw the centre of the Polish underground, the overwhelming majority of Polish society was only concerned with surviving the war. They obediently went to work every morning and tried to make their life under occupation as bearable as possible. In a large number of smaller towns and in hundreds of villages, the peasants obediently supplied the required quotas of food to the Germans' (Pekerowa, 1987). Apart from some outstanding exceptions, the Poles offered no resistance. (See Chapter 7.)

Onlookers

While the ghetto was in flames, and hundred of Jews attempted to flee to the Aryan side, gangs of 'szmalcowniks', police agents and uniformed Polish policemen threw themselves upon the victims 'like hyenas on a dead corpse' (Ringelblum, 1985, p. 340). Ringelblum reports an attempt to flee the burning ghetto by a group of about ten Jews who were forced back by a gang of 'szmalcowniks'.

Ringelblum also notes that even the Polish working class was not free of the anti-Semitic virus. Working-class mothers still threatened their children with 'the Jew who will take you away in a bag if you misbehave'. Nevertheless, many Jews found shelter in working-class apartments. In many cases some Polish railway workers helped Jews to escape from trains going to Treblinka. However, as Ringelblum reports, anti-Semitic railway employees caught many escapees from the death trains, robbed them and then handed them over to the Germans. 'The railway workers on the bloody trail leading to Treblinka, and the inhabitants of the neighbouring villages, have many Jewish lives on their conscience.' Ringelblum concludes: 'even in the best of times there never was an active action against anti-Semitism. There was a general fear of expressing opinion favourable to Jews because no one wanted to go against the trend' (Ringelblum, 1985, p. 289).

Rebutting the reports of Poles attacking fugitives from train transports, one Polish source speaks of: 'peasants from the village of Bar [Lvov region] who helped Jews who jumped from the "death trains". Peasants from the same village supplied food to a group of 18 Jews hiding in a nearby forest. Thanks to the help by the Warsaw railway workers, some of the Jewish forced labourers managed to escape before the deportation' (Berenstein and Rutkowski, 1963, p. 37).

While the desperate fighting in the ghetto was going on, life on the Polish side of the wall continued normally. In an internal report of events in the Warsaw district in April and May 1943, the governor of the Warsaw district, Dr Ludwig Fischer, wrote: 'Despite the battles in the ghetto which continued for many weeks, economic life in [Aryan] Warsaw has gone on undisturbed. There was no sabotage at workplaces because the Polish workers and employees displayed admirable discipline' (Gutman, 1994, p. 253).

During the first days of the fighting, the population was overwhelmed with a sense of curiosity. A few expressed sympathy for those who bravely withstood the Nazis, but the majority of the onlookers represented bystanders for whom the sight of the burning ghetto did not arise any emotions. A Polish reporter describes a group of a few dozen people standing, side by side, on the ruins of a destroyed house and staring at the fight that was going on only two hundred paces from a house destroyed by the artillery (Szapiro, 1992, p. 215). After a few days of uprising in the ghetto, the onlookers displayed total indifference.

> It was a sunny day and the square was packed with people. The small cafes were bursting with young men eating and drinking. Well-dressed Poles moved along at a leisurely pace while children were enjoying the merry-go-round. They were quite oblivious of the heavy smoke of the burning ghetto rising from the other side of the wall. The music kept playing, the Poles with their children were having fun, completely indifferent to the great tragedy taking place in front of their eyes.
>
> (Gutman, 1994, p. 233)

Ringelblum reports a 'hint' of anti-Semitism in the conversations of the onlookers, as well as gratification at the happenings in the ghetto. Sympathy was expressed by saying 'that although the victims were Jews, they are after all human beings'. Some Poles regretted the burning of the buildings more than that of the human beings inside of them.

> While the ghetto was burning, many Poles climbed to the top of the roofs to observe the sorry spectacle. Although my heart was bleeding when I watched the destruction of the remnants of Jewish Warsaw, I had to listen to the comments made by the bystanders and also to pretend to be a spectator. These were the remarks I heard – not one expression of any kind of sympathy.
>
> (From the testimony of Michael W., interviewed by the author)

Ringelblum records similar reports by witnesses:

> One, obviously a God-fearing woman, said: 'During Easter week Christ was tortured by the Jews [the uprising began on the eve of the Passover], so it is only right that the Jews should be tortured by the Germans.'
>
> Another middle-aged woman made the following comment: 'It's

frightening to see what is going on in the ghetto. It's terrible. But perhaps just as well. The Jews used to suck our blood. They used to say: The streets are yours but the buildings are ours. Now let their buildings burn.'

One old man said: 'It's a good thing the Germans are doing. Can't you see? The Jews have a large military force in the ghetto. If they hadn't turned it on the Germans, they would have turned it on us.'

Another commented: 'Even if the Jews burn, that's still only a drop of what they deserve.'

(Ringelblum, 1985, p. 341)

Some Polish historians attempt to offer a justification for the behaviour of the Poles while the ghetto was burning. One of them, Richard C. Lukas, asserts that 'the destruction of the Warsaw ghetto in 1943 was justified to the Varsovian at least partially because of the mass graves found in Katyn, implying Jewish–Bolshevik guilt' (Lukas, 1986, p. 129). He omits to mention that among the Polish officers executed in Katyn were over 300 Jews. Furthermore, at the time of the uprising it was not yet established that the Soviets were responsible for the death of the Polish officers. Poles at large accepted the German version because according to German propaganda it was the Jews and communists who perpetrated the crime. It suited the Polish general attitude.

Another argument offered by the same Polish historian to justify the lack of Polish assistance to the Jews was that 'since the Poles had experienced progressive pauperisation during the German occupation and lived in conditions of bare subsistence, most Poles could not offer assistance to Jewish refugees even if they wanted to. When Jews gave money to the Poles to keep them, it was accepted not out of greed but out of poverty' (ibid., p. 144).

The Polish underground offered a different justification for Polish attitudes towards the Jews; it was the behaviour of the Jews in 1939 under the Soviet occupation.

Jews disarmed our soldiers everywhere, they murdered and denounced our community activists to the Bolsheviks and openly went over to the side of the usurper. In Siedlce ... Jews constructed a triumphal arch for the Soviet armed forces and all put on red bands and ties ... Everyone in Poland remembers that.

(Wielka Polska, no. 19, 5 May 1943; see also the appendix
following this chapter)

While the fighting was going on, the Jewish resistance and indeed the remaining survivors of the ghetto still hoped for some help from the Poles. None was forthcoming. One could only guess the feelings of the Jews who were under constant attack by the German troops and experiencing a barrage of bombardment from the ground and the air. The following excerpt from Ringelblum's archives dramatically expresses the desperate situation of the Jews and their perception of the indifference or hostility of the Poles:

What did our neighbours do when the German occupant, armed to the teeth, attacked the defenceless Jews? Did they, despite the reigning German terror, offer shelter to the victims of Nazism who escaped from the ghettos to the so-called 'Aryan' side? Did the shelters only function when they were paid for, and ended when the funds run out? Why, when the death trains were moving from all direction toward Treblinka or other places of extermination, did the last look of the victims fall on the indifferent and even happy faces of their neighbours? Or when last summer [1942] trucks loaded with Jewish men, women and children passed through the streets of the ghetto, it aroused laughter from the Polish mob? ... Why, may we ask, when it was possible to lessen the gangrene of spying and collaboration of many Poles with the Germans, nothing was done to reduce the large wave of blackmail and denunciations aimed at the remnants of the Polish Jews ... ? This is a question that the quarter of a million surviving Jews, who expect only a miracle to save them, are asking ... Why did the anti-Semitic press continue to incite the Poles against the Jews, while the government press only on rare occasions came out in their defence?

(Ringelblum, 1985, pp. 239–40)

For the ghetto's inhabitants, the entire world was reduced to the Nazis and their helpers. The outside world neither reacted nor helped. No encouragement or assistance in any form was forthcoming from the Polish side (Gutman, 1994, p. 147).

APPENDIX: Jewish Refugees in the USSR

On the night of 16 to 17 September, we heard a communiqué from Moscow in the Polish language announcing that since the Polish state has ceased to exist, the Red Army is marching into Poland to take under its protection the Ukrainian and Belorussian brothers. 'This is the fourth partition of Poland. The bloody Bolsheviks got together with our worst enemies!', somebody angrily said.

Rumours began to circulate that the Red Army was approaching Warsaw and some swore having seen a red flag on the roof of the Warsaw town hall. Someone commented that since Warsaw was under Russian rule prior to WWI, it would certainly become once more their domain and we might be safer under the Bolsheviks than under the Nazis.

(Author's recollection)

This is what Jews sheltering in cellars during the German air raids of Warsaw in September 1939 hoped for. However, according to the secret agreement between Germany and the Soviet Union, Poland was to be divided between the two countries. The final borders were drawn on 28 September, after the fall of Warsaw.

Fearing the worst under Nazi rule, Jewish refugees from the German occupied zone began arriving in the Soviet zone well before 17 September 1939. The flight of Jews from Warsaw was particularly heavy after 7 September when an official order was issued calling all men of military age to move to the eastern province where a new line of defence was to be established. It never eventuated and many Jews returned to Warsaw. However, after the collapse of the Polish state, and as a result of German atrocities committed against the Jewish population under German rule, the flight of Jews toward the relative safety o the Soviet zone took massive proportions. It lasted until 30 October when the borders between the two zones were officially closed.

Before the final demarcation, the refugees did not encounter any difficulties in crossing the border, but even later, the flight of Jewish refugees did not stop and lasted almost until the German invasion in June 1941. Available evidence indicates that Soviet policy regarding the refugees was determined by the more general considerations rather than by a desire to provide an asylum for the Jews. Moscow maintained the fiction that it came to 'rescue and liberate the oppressed Belorussian and Ukrainian population'. In fact, after the conclusion on 16 November of the German–Soviet agreement on population exchange, the Soviet authorities allowed only those who qualified under the agreement to enter their territory. Since the agreement covered an exchange of Belorussians and Ukrainians living in German territory for Germans living in the Soviet zone, Soviet border guards refused to admit victims of persecution and in many cases forced back Jewish refugees (*Jewish Social Studies*, March 1987, p. 144).

Generally, the Soviet authorities treated the Jewish population in eastern Poland in the same way as they treated Jews in the Soviet Union. They had the same civil rights without, however, any autonomy. All Jewish institutions and organisations were closed down and some of their functions were taken over by state administration. The generations-old Jewish community structure ceased to exist (Prekerowa, 1992, p. 61).

Nevertheless, the stream of refugees continued throughout the winter of 1939–40. Thousands escaped from towns and villages close to the border; entire families attempted to reach the Soviet zone. The attitude of the Soviet guard differed from place to place. Occasionally hundreds were allowed to cross, but many who were caught crossing the border were tried for espionage. As for those who succeeded in gaining residence in the Soviet zone, they came face to face with a system which did not allow for any other but communist ideology. People suspected of having past connections with either the Bund or the Zionist movement ran the danger of being deported to a Soviet labour camp. Even members of the Polish Communist Party were not spared and ended up in Soviet prisons. The Soviets considered the refugees to be a security risk as they had family connections across the border and were thought to be likely candidates for espionage.

In addition, the general Jewish refugee community also faced an economic problem. Only a small fraction of the refugees could find employment in the Soviet zone. It is not surprising that when the

Soviet authorities offered jobs in the USSR, many accepted the proposal and registered for work. Those who agreed to work in the USSR were given free transportation, advance payment and were promised tempting conditions. 'Many wanted to leave Bialystok, where they found it increasingly difficult to get housing, food ... They were ready to go to the Caucasus, the Urals, to sunny Tashkent.' All 'volunteers', with rare exceptions, went to work in the Soviet Union for non-ideological reasons – simply in order to survive (Sword, 1994, p. 12). But once inside the Soviet Union, they were subjected to the same harsh regime as the ordinary Soviet citizen.

The majority of the refugees, however, refused the offer of resettlement, which presented the Soviet authorities with a problem regarding the status of the refugees. On 29 November 1939 the Soviet Citizenship Law was extended to eastern Poland, according to which all former Polish citizens who were living in the territory incorporated into the Soviet Union automatically became Soviet citizens.

From the onset the refugees had adopted a negative attitude towards the Soviet Citizenship Law because they thought that their stay under Soviet rule would be temporary, and feared that by acquiring Soviet citizenship they would sever the links with their families left behind in Nazi-occupied Poland. Many simply refused to become citizens of a regime they hated. The number of refugees arriving into the Soviet zone decreased in the spring of 1940 and ceased almost completely during the summer. At the time when increasing numbers of Polish Jews under German rule were pushed into the ghettos in the summer of 1940, the Soviet border became more difficult to cross.

In April 1940 the Soviets established a special commission to register the refugees. It offered two alternatives – either to become a Soviet citizen or to declare the wish to return to the German zone of occupation. The vast majority decided to register their intention to return. There is evidence available to show that during that time a number of refugees succeeded in returning to their former homes in Nazi Poland (Jewish Social Studies, March 1987, pp. 152–3).

It was during those sleepless nights in the small Russian town of Propoisk that I experienced the feeling of being homesick. I began to regret my escape from Warsaw ... I had fits of crying, I wanted to go back. The urge to return home became an obsession when I received a letter from my father, which was posted in Lvov. Obviously, life under the Germans had become unbearable and father also fled to the Russian zone. I was overjoyed – I was no alone in Russia. My joy was short-lived. In the second letter, that followed a few days later, father told me that he could not bear the thought of having left mother, my sister and grandfather in Warsaw and decided to return. He went back.

(Author's recollections)

The attempt by some Jewish refugees to return to a regime that publicly announced its hatred toward Jews was considered by the Soviets as proof of opposition to the Soviet regime. Rumours were circulating about anti-Soviet demonstrations by refugees. The refusal of most to accept Soviet citizenship induced the Soviet authorities to a radical solution – massive deportation of the refugees.

Sometime during the spring of 1940 the Soviet authorities opened offices to register all those unwilling to become Soviet subjects. Many registered, which only increased Soviet distrust. It is interesting to note that while hundreds of Jews were openly demonstrating their opposition to Soviet rule, there is no evidence of Poles showing any signs of resistance to communist rule.

The deportations were over within a few weeks. In some towns it lasted only a few days and nights. The secret police with the assistance of the Soviet government apparatus rounded up all those on the list, put them on trucks, then transferred them on to trains that took them into labour camps located in remote areas of Russia. During the second half of 1940, most Jewish refugees were removed from eastern Poland. While it is impossible to ascertain the exact number of deported Jews, there is little doubt that the vast majority of refugees were deported. The number of Jews deported from the occupied zone is estimated at about 250,000.

The Soviet deportation machine was well prepared for its task. Years of experience in uprooting and hunting down thousands of victims during the collectivisation and the great purges showed their results in June 1940, when most of these deportations took place.

On arrival at the labour camp the deportees were treated like criminals. Every morning they would be taken outside the camp perimeter into the forest where they were to cut down trees. This came with a warning that: 'one step to the right or to the left will be considered as an attempt to escape in which case firearms will be used' (testimony of a former Jewish inmate of a Soviet labour camp). Conditions were very harsh. Little food was supplied, and with no proper clothing many succumbed to the cold of the Siberian winter and died.

Conclusion

Polish apologists in their attempt to put the blame for anti-Semitic sentiments within Polish society during the War on the Jews themselves, use the situation of the Jews under the Soviet occupation as a justification of Polish behaviour. Polish historians point out the reception of the Soviet troops with ovations and flowers by the Jewish population, which the Poles saw as a demonstration of lack of loyalty to the Polish state. However, it is recognised that not all Jews rejoiced – most did not. There was certainly little joy among the religious Jews, those engaged in commerce and industry, and members of Jewish political parties and organisations (Bund, Zionists), who had much to fear from the Soviet authorities (Prekerowa, 1992, p. 15). Accepting Soviet occupation did not mean an anti-Polish attitude. For the Jews who found themselves under Soviet rule, the occupation by the Red Army meant safety form the Nazis.

Some Polish historians claim that the NKWD created a net of informers in the occupied zone in which Jews, particularly former members of the Polish Communist Party, as well as newly converted Jewish communists, played a major role. The reality, however, was that the Polish Communist Party was dissolved by the Comintern in 1938 under suspicion of being infiltrated by Trotskyites, and any one declaring his or her membership of the former Polish Communist Party was promptly arrested by the Soviets.

It is a well-known fact that an NKWD net of informers existed in the whole of the Soviet Union and was not confined to eastern Poland alone. The recruitment of a collaborator was never voluntary but resulted from an approach by an NKWD officer who usually enlisted one under threat. Furthermore, the victims of denunciations were Jews and non-Jews alike. It created an atmosphere of suspicion and fear among the Jewish population, but among the Poles it became a source of animosity toward the entire Jewish minority. Such false rumours infiltrated the German occupied zone, and being relayed from mouth to mouth, reinforced accusations against the entire Jewish population (Prekerowa, 1992, p. 65).

6
Looters

And you shall say to him, 'Thus says the Lord, "Have you killed, and also taken possession?"'

(1 Kings 19)

Many Polish historians (such as Orlicki, Michowicz, Arczynski and Balcerak) justify the behaviour of some Poles during the war as economically motivated; that is, they disregard ethical imperatives in favour of material benefits. Indeed, a cursory examination of available evidence indicates the economic benefit Poles derived from the Jewish tragedy.

The elimination of Jews from Poland's economic life under the occupation, and the confiscation of Jewish enterprises by the Germans, provided from some Poles significant windfalls. For example, the proportion of Jews engaged in liberal professions was close to 50 per cent, with 55 per cent of medical practitioners being Jewish (Michowicz, 1982, p. 318). Given the fact that under the German occupation Jews were totally removed from professions servicing Polish clients, and generally from all commercial activities, it can clearly be seen that by taking over the place of Jews in the economy and by replacing Jews in the liberal professions, many Poles benefited from the war.

Then there is the question of Jewish assets. Since the number of Jewish survivors was negligible, we can only assume that the bulk of their assets were either destroyed, expropriated by the Germans, or appropriated by the Polish government or population. Some of these assets remained in the former Polish territory annexed by the Soviet Union. It is very difficult if not impossible to quantify the value of the assets that were transferred from Jewish owners into Polish hands. A rough assessment of value can be derived from the estimation by

Polish historians of the Jewish share of Polish national wealth, and especially their share of commerce and industry in pre-war Poland.

Before the war, Jews represented about 10 per cent of Poland's total population. Assuming that national wealth was evenly distributed, Jews owned about 10 per cent of Poland's private assets. One Polish source reports that in the entire Polish state as much as 61.9 per cent of people engaged in commerce belonged to the Jewish minority. Generally, Jews were in control of 42.2 per cent of industry and 36.6 per cent of commerce (*Mały rocznik statystyczny*, 1939, p. 32). If we take that into account along with claims of Polish historians about Jewish dominance of the Polish economy, then the value of Jewish assets appropriated by the Poles would be very considerable.

From the early days of occupation, the German authorities offered rewards to encourage Poles to inform about the places in which Jews hid their valuables. Later the reward also comprised half of the confiscated assets of those caught (Berenstein and Rutkowski, 1963, pp. 18–19). It was one of the reasons why many of the Polish beneficiaries were in favour of the anti-Jewish policy of the Germans. These included many Poles who were appointed by the Germans as 'commissars' (managers) of Jewish enterprises.

In order to save their assets many Jews handed over their property for safe-keeping to Polish acquaintances. In some cases these items were indeed held for the Jews who deposited them, and there were cases after the war where properties were returned. But most of the Polish families appropriated them, especially as very few Jews survived to reclaim their assets (Bauer, 1978, p. 54).

Occasionally Jews had their business registered in the names of Poles, resulting in a considerable volume of such assets being transferred into Polish hands. Polish sources try to interpret this practice in a much more favourable light. The safe-keeping of Jewish assets, they claim, is evidence of goodwill rather than an act robbery. It was a sign of 'simple human honesty' (Berenstein and Rutkowski, 1963, p. 20).

It is beyond doubt that the confinement of Jews in the ghettos brought great benefits to Polish merchants and artisans, to a segment of the intelligentsia, and to those workers who turned to trade and handicraft in a move aimed at taking over the places previously filled by the Jews. When Jewish enterprises were liquidated, the non-Jewish manufacturers and distributors automatically gained market shares.

Poles who had economically benefited from the move of Jews to the ghettos by acquiring Jewish homes and businesses, opposed the Polish government-in-exile's decree that all such actions under German occupation were illegal. 'We will not return the shops and factories [to the Jews]', was an all-familiar Polish cry (Iranek-Osmecki, 1971, p. 24). In addition, thanks to the German occupation, many Poles who were indebted to Jewish financiers and businessmen were suddenly freed from their obligations to repay the debts.

There can be little doubt that a great number of Polish people bene-fited from the theft by the Nazis of Jewish property, though a large proportion of the loot remained in Nazi hands (Bauer, 1978, p. 54). The greater the benefit the Poles received from occupying Jewish apartments, taking over Jewish businesses and livelihoods, and taking away Jewish-owned furniture and clothing, the greater was their inter-est in not seeing the Jews return to claim their property.

Of the 25,000 or so testimonies of Holocaust survivors at Yad Vashem, a large proportion are from Poland. Of these, many hundreds, if not thousands, testify to the accuracy of the generalisa-tions just made. As time went on, Poles could be heard to say that with all the disaster Hitler had brought to Poland, he had at least dealt with the Jewish question and solved it (ibid., p. 57).

The attacks by the Nazis on Jewish personal property were followed by the confiscation of savings and cash. All money kept in bank accounts was forfeited to the Nazis. Jews were forbidden to possess more than was needed for daily expenses, making it impossible for them to continue to operate their businesses. As a result, the old pre-war Polish policy of *numerus nullus* in industry, commerce and generally in the economy, became a reality. It was due to the elimination of Jews that Christians became the owners of many Jewish commercial and indus-trial enterprises. Some Poles got rid of their Jewish partner at no cost. The Poles also succeeded in the appropriation of Jewish market stalls and in taking over the small trade without much difficulty. The Nazi plan of exterminating Jews enabled the Poles to acquire billions worth of Jewish assets accumulated over the centuries.

Methods of the transfer of Jewish assets

While it is difficult to estimate the total gain for the Polish population as a result of the elimination of Jews from economic life, it is relatively easier to determine the way in which assets and other economic bene-fits were transferred to Poles.

In the winter of 1940, many Poles seized any opportunity to take advantage of the terrible situation of the Jews, when the Germans issued an order to stamp all Polish banknotes at the bank. This order hit the Jews more than it did the Poles. An earlier order forced Jews to surrender amounts over 2,000 zlotys to the German authorities, which meant that Jews could not change more than 2,000 zlotys, and even this was very difficult because Jews were often forcibly removed from the queues in front of the bank. As a last resort, Jews were forced to seek help from Poles, who usually charged a hefty commission of up to 20 per cent for changing the money at the bank. At a later stage, the level of commission charged by a Pole reached 75 per cent. Thousands of Jews lost their entire fortune because they did not have a Polish intermediary who would change the banknotes (Ringelblum, 1985, p. 274).

An important feature of Polish–Jewish economic relations during the war was the problem of Jewish possessions that were given to Poles by Jews for safe-keeping – a practice which began prior to the establishment of the ghetto. When the Germans ordered Jews to surrender all fur coats, a Jew who had a Polish friend would give it to him for safe-keeping. If the Jew had a business, he would enter into a partnership with a Pole, thereby making him a co-owner. Ringelblum asserts that the outcome of such an arrangement was in most cases rather negative. 'It was perhaps due to the general demoralising influence of the war that people who were otherwise honest, became devoid of any morality and appropriated for themselves the goods placed in their trust.' The Jews who were still alive were considered as 'corpses on holidays' who were destined to be eliminated sooner or later (ibid., p. 273).

Jewish assets were quite often the reason for blackmail and denunciation. Both were used as a means of getting rid of the owner of the assets. There were, nevertheless, known instances of Poles who hid Jewish belongings. In this way they contributed to the saving of a number of Jews for whom hidden assets were the only resource enabling them to survive. Ringelblum comments that 'the number of such noble individuals who resisted the temptation of appropriating Jewish assets was very small'.

Ringelblum also mentions hundreds of instances of real estate sales by Jews to Poles in Warsaw. Earnings from real estate were a significant source of income for many Jewish families in Warsaw. This source dried up immediately after the Germans issued an order placing all Jewish-owned real estate under a nominated administrator. Jewish owners were forced to sell properties in their entirety or in part to a Pole, predating the contract of sale prior to September 1939. Such contracts were based on mutual trust, that is, the Pole pretended to have lent money to the Jewish owner under the guarantee of the property, which would return to its owner after the war on the repayment of the 'loan'.

A default in payment meant that the property remained in the hands of the Pole. It is impossible to estimate the value of the real estate that remained in Polish hands, as most Jews did not survive the war.

A significant amount of money and valuables changed hands as payment for hiding or providing false documents. Among the Poles who participated in saving Jews were people who were motivated by religious, ideological or humane considerations, but probably the majority of survivors managed to find a hiding place by paying large amounts of money. There were cases when a Pole, who provided a hiding place, tried to appropriate the liquid assets of the Jew as quickly as possible, and when the Jew ran out of funds, he was thrown out or simply handed over to the Germans (Gutman, 1993, p. 363).

Jewish assets had also been acquired by the Polish 'szmalcowniks' and blackmailers. The former operated in the street, the latter in apartments. A szmalcownik would first observe people in the street or in a cafe, and when he spotted a Jew would follow him to find his place of abode. From then on the blackmailer would take over, and with the cooperation of the agents of the Polish police would try to squeeze out as much money or valuables as were in the possession of the victim. In most cases, when a Jew was discovered hiding in an apartment, he would simply flee, leaving all his possessions to the blackmailer. These activities became the livelihood and a sport for participants who wanted to inherit Jewish assets. 'In this orchestra, money-grabbing Polish police played first violin' (Ber, 1975, p. 64).

The blackmailers were encouraged by the fact that they went unpunished and there was no visible reaction from Polish society. Jewish political and social organisations consistently demanded from the Polish underground some action against the blackmailers. However, the main Polish resistance movement – the AK – and the government delegate within it, did nothing to protect Jews hiding on the Aryan side. The only – albeit belated – step against blackmail was a warning issued by the representative of the Polish government-in-exile that blackmailing Jews was a crime which would be punished after the war. The warning did not have any effect; the practice of blackmail continued unabated.

In fact it had the opposite effect. In a document emanating from the Delegatura – the official representative council in Poland of the Polish government-in-exile – which was forwarded to London, the Delegatura informed the government that the Polish people would forcibly prevent any surviving Jews from repossessing their homes and businesses. The Polish government did not respond officially to the Delegatura's threats, but it was a clear warning that any attempt at

restitution of lost assets and posts to Jews would be met with determined resistance by Polish society.

Roman Knoll, who held the post of the Foreign Department director of the Delegate's Office on the Jewish Question, took a long-term
view on the question of restitution of Jewish assets. In a memo written
in the summer of 1943 he made the following comment:

> The German mass murder of Polish Jews will reduce the scale of the
> problem, but they cannot eliminate it entirely. In all certainty, a
> considerable number of Jews will survive. Others, who are now
> abroad, will re-enter Poland. If the mass of the Jews ever returns, our
> population will not recognise their restitution claims, but will treat
> them instead as invaders, resisting them by violent means if need be.
>
> (YVA, M-2/334)

The Polish underground press had also incessantly warned the Polish
government not to allow the surviving Jews to remain in Poland,
while warning the Jews not to attempt to recover their assets from
Poles. Such a warning had the effect of diminishing the criminality of
blackmail in the eyes of Polish society.

Smuggling was another way of benefiting from Jewish misery. Jews
sold or traded their property, possessions and clothing for food; and a
steady stream of Jewish money, household goods, pianos and other
possessions poured onto the Polish side. This is how a Pole described
the situation at the time:

> When the Jews were forced into the ghetto, they took with them
> some of their money, gold and jewellery. After a while the Jews
> began to part with the money. This happened because they were
> short of food and other things they needed. So they resorted to
> smuggling. What they did was to bring valuables out of the ghetto
> and exchange them for food. Some Jewish smugglers were also
> making money, but as the Germans closed off most of the exits
> from the ghetto, it became much harder to smuggle, resulting in a
> rise in the price of food. Those were the days when one brought a
> bag with bread into the ghetto, and one would take out a bag full
> of gold. That shows you how rich the Jews were.
>
> (Author's conversation with a Pole after the war)

A special case of benefiting from the situation was the behaviour of
Polish employees of the taxation authorities. The conduct of Polish

tax collectors employed in the Warsaw ghetto is described thus by
Emmanuel Ringelblum:

> For the ghetto, the tax collectors were a sheer nightmare. They
> demanded the payment of taxes of burnt down or bombed
> commercial or industrial enterprises. They demanded payment of
> tax for previous years knowing that the majority of Jews would
> have lost the receipts during the bombardments of Warsaw.
> Whenever there was resistance against such brutal measures, they
> would come with German trucks and appropriate anything they
> liked. Whoever did not want or could not pay instantly, had his
> belongings confiscated on the spot. Property seizure amounted to
> sheer robbery. Especially cruel were the employees of the 15th,
> 16th, and 17th local tax offices.
>
> (Ringelblum, 1985, p. 47)

Another way of depriving Jews of their money was the fabrication
of fake letters supposedly sent by Jews deported to the camps. The
extent of the extermination was so staggering for the remnants of the
Jewish community still alive at the end of 1942, that they simply
could not explain to themselves what could have happened to those
who were deported. Where have 3 million Jews disappeared to? In
their eagerness to find out about the fate of their relatives and friends,
Jews were ready to pay for any information or letters supplied to them
by unscrupulous Poles. Some Poles offered to help in finding the
whereabouts of a deported person for a hefty reward of hundreds and
even thousands of zlotys. There were many Jews who paid large
amounts of money to find out about their close ones. In the end they
realised that they were already all dead.

> No matter how many times such cheating about the whereabouts
> of relatives was uncovered, there still are those who cannot forget
> those who were taken away, and are ready to spend a lot of money
> in order to obtain any information about them.

Ringelblum concludes:

> If the frauds involving letters from individual Jews or from camps
> are becoming more frequent, this is due to the great number of
> swindlers who exploit the situation for their personal interests, and
> to their ability to play on people's fantasies and on their dreams

that the millions of deportees are working and still alive. How unfortunate must be a people to believe in such impossibilities!

(ibid., p. 43)

Much can also be said about the role in the looting of Jewish assets played by the so-called Polish 'Blue' Police.

The Polish Police (Polnische Polizei) was established according to an order issued by the occupying powers in autumn of 1939. They were so named because of the colour of their uniforms. The Blue Police were mainly members of the pre-war state police as well as volunteers. Although they had their own command post (Kommando der Polnischen Polizei), in fact they were partly subordinated to the German law and order Police (Ordnungspolizei). The police was mainly used as an auxiliary force supporting the German gendarmerie. They were assigned to the Aryan quarters and had the task of catching Jews, which many of them accomplished with great zeal (Prekerowa, 1992, p. 156). They performed acts of a clearly exterminationist character (round-ups and executions) aimed against the Jewish population.

The German authorities instructed the agents of the Polish criminal police, agents of the Gestapo and members of the Polish Blue Police to search for Jews hiding on the Aryan side. The uniformed members of the Polish police who lost their positions in the Jewish quarter after the destruction of the Warsaw ghetto, began concentrating their efforts on tracking Jews living on the Aryan side. For them it was not only a question of denouncing Jews but also a source of income. They spared Jews who were able to pay them off, but a poor Jew had no chance when caught by a Polish policeman. Documentary evidence of the material benefits that the Polish Police derived from the situation can be found in the reported interrogation of Jürgen Stroop, comman-der of German forces which suppressed the Warsaw ghetto uprising. In his report, Stroop underlines the zest with which the Polish Police executed German orders; especially, Stroop asserted, after he issued instructions to distribute to them one-third of the property found with the Jews (*Materiały* i Dokumenty, 1946, p. 133).

A significant volume of Jewish assets came into Polish hands after the deportation of Jews or the destruction of a ghetto. When Jews had already been deported, the looters became busy. In the Radom District they rummaged in emptied ghettos tearing out everything they could. On the site of Belzec, where Germans had shut down a death camp, they searched for gold in the ashes (Hilberg, 1992, p. 214).

On 19 August was the turn of the ghetto at Rembertow. Rembertow was now 'free of Jews'. On the following day, Poles from the town entered the ghetto looking for gold. They left the ghetto loaded with whatever they could carry – furniture, bedding, pots and pans – returning the following day for a final session of looting.

(Gilbert, 1985, p. 429)

Calel Perechodnik noted in his diary what he saw after the liquidation of the ghetto in the town of Otwock near Warsaw:

I returned an hour later. The whole apartment has been smashed up. The Poles have ransacked it from top to bottom. The entire ghetto [in Otwock] is still surrounded by Polish scum. They keep jumping over the fence, axing doors open, and plundering every-thing. Sometimes they stumble upon corpses that are still warm, but that doesn't deter them. People tussle over corpses to wrest away a pillow or a suit.

(Rymkiewicz, 1994, p. 229)

In their search for Jewish assets, some Poles resorted to desecration of graves in Jewish cemeteries. This practice became more prevalent when it was realised that any acts directed against the Jews were not subject to law – that is, they remained unpunished. An additional factor was the absence of any adverse reaction from Polish society. One eyewitness account contains a vivid description of the scene at the Jewish cemetery on Gęsia street in Warsaw:

Wherever I turned, there was nothing but overturned tombstones, desecrated graves and scattered skulls – their dark sockets burning deep into me, their shattered jaws demanding, 'Why? Why has this befallen us?'

Although I knew that these atrocities were the handiwork of the so-called 'dentists' – Polish ghouls who searched the mouths of the Jewish corpses to extract their gold-capped teeth – I nevertheless felt strangely guilty and ashamed. Yes, Jews were persecuted even in their graves.

(Meed, 1973, p. 335)

An article published in *Prawda* – an underground publication – most probably written by its leader, the well-known writer Zofia Kossak-Szczucka, draws particular attention to the indifference of the population who lived in direct proximity to the extermination camps. There were numerous reports about criminal elements who managed to enter the camps and left with the money of those who were gassed. They also attacked those who succeeded in escaping from the camps, or those who jumped from the trains, robbing them of whatever valuables they had on them. 'The surroundings of Treblinka or Sobibor became a gold producing region which attracted people from far away places in Poland' (Prekerowa, 1992, p. 155).

The economic situation of the Polish population was certainly poor, but there were no reports of starvation or excessive poverty. It was rather the personal greed of some Christian Poles combined with anti-Jewish sentiments that played an important role in their behaviour toward the Jews. Anti-Semitism was clearly prevalent among various social groups. The Directorate of Civil Struggle issued in March 1941 a communiqué stating that 'there are individuals without any conscience, who created for themselves a new source of income through blackmail of Poles who are hiding Jews and through blackmailing Jews' (ibid., p. 153).

The gold rush after the liberation

The hunt for Jewish 'treasures' did not end after the liberation of Poland. Thousands of Christian Poles became 'gold diggers' on the grounds of Treblinka and other camps. Using a sieve they would sift the ashes of the dead to find the gold in teeth or hidden jewellery. By detonating small explosives charges they raised the dust of the ashes so that heavier metal particles would fall first to be picked up. 'Month after month one could see small hand carts doing the rounds between Treblinka and the surrounding villages. A new commodity appeared on the market: the bones of the victims. There was some trade in this commodity because it was thought that they contain some precious metals' (Auerbach, 1952).

Dr Tenenbaum, in his book *In Search of a Lost People*, reports that in Birkenau after the liberation, the latrines of the camp were emptied by the inhabitants of the surrounding villages. They removed the excrement from the latrines to search for the gold and diamonds of former inmates. Apparently they found real treasures – pearl necklaces, golden chains and rings that were thrown in so as not to hand them over to the Germans.

The hunt for Jewish treasure went on as late as 1946. By then the location of the hunt shifted to the area of the former Warsaw ghetto. It was thought that underground bunkers built by the Jews during the war could still be found under the ruins and would probably contain some valuables.

> Looking behind me I saw from a distance the silhouette of people busy digging the ground. I noticed them earlier, but had not paid much attention to their activities; I thought they were cleaning the ruins. It was my companion who broke the silence and pointing in the direction of the diggers said: 'What do you think the people over there are doing? They are searching for Jewish gold and jewellery which they believe are still buried in the ground. They hope to uncover some of the bunkers built by the Jews in the ghetto, where, they think, the Jews had hidden their valuables. They usually come here at dusk and work through the night. You see, this is not strictly legal but there is nobody to prevent them from going about their sinister work.'
>
> (Author's recollections)

Among Poles who were engaged in the hunt for Jewish treasures, the memories of the 'good old days', when money could be made of Jewish misery, were still alive.

> I could not avoid overhearing the conversations of those sitting next to me in the train. What horrified me most were the constant references made to the 'good old days' under Nazi rule. Almost every Pole in the compartment had a story to tell how he managed to live well by taking advantage of the position of the Jews created by the Germans.
> One said: 'we all knew how rich the Jews were, but we could do nothing about it until the Germans came. It was easy to get hold of their wealth. When they were deported from my town, I became the owner of a shop that belonged to a Jew. Before the war I could not even dream of having my own business; everything was in Jewish hands. Whatever you say against the Germans, you must admit that they did a good job – one that even our own government could not do.'
>
> (Author's recollections)

Another chapter of the saga of Jewish assets was written in 1946, when the then Polish government tried to recover unclaimed Jewish assets from Swiss banks. On 2 February 1946, Max Troendle, the then Swiss Trade Minister, began negotiations in Poland regarding supplies of fuel to Switzerland. During those early discussions, Polish officials mentioned that many rich Jews who perished during the Holocaust must have deposited money in Switzerland or have invested in life assurance policies. That money, the Poles asserted, belonged to the country of origin of the depositors. According to Troendle, the Poles requested the transfer of assets of missing Poles deposited in Swiss banks and insurance companies. The money was to be handed over to the Polish government in the form of bilateral compensation for Swiss assets in Poland appropriated by the government (Bower, 1997, p. 232).

On 24 January 1947, the Polish ambassador's request for the heirless assets was rejected. Two years later, in April 1949, the issue resurfaced during negotiations of a new trade agreement between Switzerland and Poland. Again, the Poles claimed that many Poles who died deposited funds in Switzerland. During the negotiations, Rudolph Speich, the chairman of the Swiss Bank Corporation, told the Poles that the bank held 'at least 2 million SF' in Polish heirless assets (ibid., p. 233).

On formally signing the agreement on 25 June 1949, the Swiss government undertook in a secret clause that after 1 July 1954 Switzerland's banks and insurance companies would release the assets of Polish nationals whose accounts remained unclaimed and dormant for five years since the end of the war. The secret leaked out eventually. Max Isenbergh, a representative of the American Jewish Committee, made the following comment: 'It's a cruel irony that the Poles who persecuted the Jews should receive the Jewish money' (ibid., p. 241).

The question of former Jewish assets in Poland is slowly emerging into the open. Some Jewish community assets such as synagogues, and in some cases real estate, have been returned to their owners or their descendants. In November 1998, as part of its commitment to return communal property to the small Jewish community which continues to live in Poland, three new synagogues were established in Watslav, Opol and Osviencim, the town which replaced Auschwitz. But the fear of massive claims still persists, especially among Poles who now live in former Jewish houses and apartments.

The fear of Jewish claims has stirred up severe anti-Semitic manifestations in Poland. According to sources in Poland, claims made by Jewish organisations against Swiss banks, as well as several large German and Austrian companies who used Jewish labour, demonstrate the approaching Jewish threat. According to one Polish source: 'now, with all the lawyers coming from America to Europe chasing after compensation money for Jews, and the fear that the Jews will return to Poland asking for the return of their stolen property, I feel a lot of tension in the air. The issue of the property is explosive' (Tal, 1999).

7
Polish Resistance and Collaboration

> We, with rifles on the barricades, amongst the ruins of our bombed from the air family homes; we – soldiers of freedom and honour ...
> ('My Żydzi Polscy' ('We Polish Jews'), Juljan Tuwim, 1942)

Poland stands out amongst the Nazi occupied countries of Europe in its apparent reluctance to collaborate with the Germans. Polish historians are very proud of the fact that the Poles did not supply the Germans with a Quisling government during the war. While this may be true in a general sense, it is a fact that a section of the Polish population did cooperate with the Germans in their plan to exterminate the Jews. The evidence presented in this study allows one to conclude that the degree of collaboration was not so much a result of Polish unwillingness to cooperate with the invader as of the German perception that they had no need of a Polish collaborationist government for their plans of exterminating the Jews: the Germans felt they had the tacit approval of the Polish population.

The reception given the invading German army in the Polish countryside has not been a very fashionable theme in Polish historiography, which tends to picture the war period as one of heroic struggle by a united society against the invader. None the less, several sources specifically state that the German victory was received with joy by the peasants in certain areas and that the entering German army received a friendly reception from the population in many ethnically Polish hamlets and villages (Kersten and Szarota, 1968, II, p. 24; also Kisielewski and Nowak, 1968, pp. 387–8).

Collaboration

There is some evidence of German attempts at recruiting Polish collaborators. In the early days of occupation, the Germans envisaged the creation of a 'token Polish state' – a *Reststaat*. Two groups within Polish society were sounded out about their willingness to cooperate in such a project. In March 1940 the Germans approached the peasant leader Wincenty Witos, who at the time was in detention in Czechoslovakia. In spite of his refusal to cooperate, the conditions of his confinement remained very generous. After five months in Rzeszow, Witos was taken to a jail in Berlin for another five weeks and, upon release, committed to a sanatorium in Potsdam (Madajczyk, 1970, I, p. 105).

Another group approached by the Germans were prominent aristocrats holding conservative views and with traditions of loyalty to and collaboration with the Austro-Hungarian monarchy before the First World War. One of them was professor Stanisław Estreicher; the names of Princes Zdzisław Lubomirski and Janusz Radziwill and that of Adam Ronikier were mentioned as other candidates (Landau, 1962, I, p. 91). The reaction of these men is unknown.

The Germans were much more successful in their attempt to find willing collaborators among the Polish population. In this respect, they encountered few problems within the local Polish administration, and the Gestapo in particular frequently found confidants among the local population (Kisielewski and Nowak, 1968, p. 151). As a rule the Germans would leave the old *sołtys* (village head) in their posts, thereby making sure that they would follow German orders. In fact, 73 per cent of the *wójts* (chief administrative officers) at the *gmina* (township) level and mayors in the General Government were Polish (Madajczyk, 1970, I, p. 222).

When the Germans began to round up Poles for work in Germany, and imposed 'human quotas' on rural communities, it was the local Polish officials who were personally charged with selecting the people who were to go to work in Germany. It was not uncommon for a soltys and his cronies to form a closely knit clique that exploited the situation for their own advantage and to use their position to extract favours and bribes (Gross, 1979, p. 143). A comparison can be made between Polish local officials and the Judenrat – a German-appointed Jewish authority.

The German invasion of Russia elicited mixed feelings from the Poles. There were Poles in exile in England and Italy who regarded the Germans as the lesser of two evils facing Poland. As the Germans kept advancing into Soviet territory in 1941, they believed that in the face of imminent Soviet defeat the Poles should try to establish a compromise with Germany (Lukas, 1986, p. 111). In October 1941 the German embassy in Geneva reported to Berlin that a Polish exile circle in Switzerland, hostile to Sikorski's Polish government-in-exile, wanted to reach an understanding with the Germans aimed at creating a new Polish state. However, Joachim von Ribbentrop, the German foreign minister, ordered the contact between Poles and Germans to be broken off.

The Germans found a more responsive ear in Leon Kozłowski, a former Polish premier. Kozłowski, who had been released from a Soviet prison, deserted from the Polish army in the Soviet Union, and made contact with the Germans. Kozłowski appeared to have been offered an opportunity to head a puppet Polish government but imposed conditions the Germans would not accept – namely, the release of Poles from concentration camps. Compromised in the eyes of fellow Poles, Kozłowski remained in Berlin, where he subsequently disappeared. A former Polish finance minister, Wincenty Jastrebski, together with a Warsaw academician, Tarlo Mazynski, approached the German embassy in Paris in May 1943 with an offer to establish a Polish National Committee to collaborate with Germany (Irving, 1967, p. 39).

At the same time, the German governor of Poland, Frank, made a few endeavours to alter the image of the Nazis and to persuade the Poles to support Germany. In October 1943 he allowed the opening of a Chopin museum, and by early 1944 the opening of a Polish theatre in Cracow. He opened some seminaries that had been closed in 1939, and even contemplated opening secondary schools and a school of medicine in Cracow staffed by Polish professors. He also ended the requirement of passes for Poles using trains, and increased the food rations for the Polish population. All this was part of a German campaign that described German rule in Poland as 'hard, but just' and the majority of Poles as loyal collaborators.

Another indication of acceptance of German rule, was the willingness in 1943 of many farmers to claim German origin to join the DVL (German National List). It is estimated that about 100,000 people living in the General Government signed the DVL, thereby becoming the so-called *Volksdeutsche*, although the majority of them probably had little German blood (Pospieszalski, 1958, VI, p. 22). The Polish Bishop in Silesia, Stanislaw Adamski, ordered the clergy and people to assume the status of *Volksdeutsche* (Lukas, 1986, p. 14). By early summer of 1944, the number of such Poles rose to between about 850,000 and 1,000,000 (Gross, 1979, p. 166). The Polish underground did not think of these people as being traitors, because it considered that they became *Volksdeutsche* out of self-preservation (Lukas, 1986, p. 25).

The Blue Police

Despite the Germans' unsuccessful attempts at enlisting Polish collaboration on the official level, there was no shortage of Poles eager to assist the Germans in exterminating Jews. A major role in such cooperation was played by the Blue Police. They executed German orders against Jews and assisted the Germans in their Final Solution plans. Their duties included: guarding the exits from the ghettos, and the walls and fences surrounding the ghetto and the Jewish quarters; participating in the deportation operations by capturing Jews and escorting convoys of Jews destined for deportation to extermination camps; participating in capturing Jews who went into hiding after the deportation operation; and executing Jews condemned to death by the Germans (Ringelblum, 1985, pp. 309–10).

According to Ringelblum, 'the Polish police played a lamentable role during the deportation operations. The Polish police is responsible for the death of thousands of Polish Jews caught with their assistance and pushed into the death trains.' Ringelblum quotes as an example the town of Biała Podlaska, where the Polish police took part in the deportations of October 1942. One eye witness reported that in the house where he was hiding it was the Polish police together with the local fire brigade who discovered 60 Jews. In most such cases the Jews were robbed of everything they had on them. They would then be handed over to the Germans.

In the city of Chęstochowa, the Polish police kept watch over all exits during the deportations, escorted the deportees to the railway station, tracked dawn those who evaded the deportations and handed them over to the Germans. During the deportation of Jews from the town of Lukow, the Blues went through the apartments after the end of the operation in search for any Jews who had avoided deportation or were attempting to escape. Without the assistance of the local police, it would have been hard for the Germans to find the Jews, because the Germans were generally unfamiliar with the layout of a house and ignorant of the existence of cellars or attics. 'It is difficult to estimate the number of the victims due to the collaboration of the Polish police – they certainly run into tens of thousands' (ibid., p. 311).

References to the participation of the Blues in the massacres of Jews can be found in the Ringelblum archives. He recalls: 'The largest grave contained a thousand bodies, and the two smaller graves contained five hundred bodies each. We learned of this massacre from the Polish police themselves. They told Moshe Hersh about it in minute details, because they themselves had taken part in that slaughter ... we have concrete evidence what happened in the winter of 1941–2. In another instance, some twenty Jews, mostly women and a 10-year-old child, accused of leaving the Jewish ghetto illegally, had been shot by the Polish police within the compound of the Warsaw central ghetto custody house on Gęsia street.' At the same time, according to Ringelblum, the Blue Police accepted hefty bribes and actively participated in the smuggling operation at the gates of the ghetto or surrounding walls. They appropriated the lion's share (close to 60 per cent) of the proceeds of smuggling.

Equally submissive to German orders was the Polish fire brigade, who in the course of the deportations blocked all exits from houses and searched for those hiding in attics and cellars. 'We have concrete evidence of such collaboration by the Polish firemen in Kałuszyn and Biała Podlaska' (ibid., pp. 311–12).

In such a situation, a Jewish escapee from the ghetto had to face many difficulties, the most immediate being caught by the Polish police. After a Jew succeeded in evading the Blues and reached a village in which he found favourably disposed or neutral villagers, he had to rely on good luck. For if he found himself in the region of activities of the NSZ or of a unit of the AK hostile toward Jews, he perished as a 'bandit' or 'communist agent'.

After the Jewish uprisings in several Nazi camps, a number of fugitives lost their lives at the hands of members of the underground and the surrounding Polish population. Instances of participation by Poles in raids on Jewish fugitives have been authenticated as having occurred in 172 localities, and murders committed by Polish underground formations (NSZ as part of the AK) as having occurred in 120 localities. Beyond any doubt these figures are incomplete.

Throughout the winter of 1942, Polish peasants took part in raids organised by the Germans to track down Jews in hiding. 'The peasants,' notes Zygmunt Klukowski in his diary on 26 November, ' ... are hunting down the Jews in the countryside; ... they bring them to the towns or sometimes they kill them on the spot. Generally speaking, Jews are treated as if they were wild animals' (Wasserstein, 1979, p. 138; an extract dated 26 Nov. 1942 from the diary of Dr Zygmunt

Klukowski). Klukowski adds: 'Generally, a strange brutalisation has taken place regarding Jews. People have fallen into a kind of psychosis: following the German example, they often do not see in the Jew a human being but instead consider him as a kind of obnoxious animal that must be annihilated with every possible means, like rabid dogs, rats, etc.' (Klukowski, 1959). In many cases residents of nearby villages and small towns participated with Germans in the hunting of Jews. In the village of Kreznica, Lublin county, a local priest named Pankowski in his Sunday Mass sermons called upon the parishioners to murder Jews (Gutman and Krakowski, 1986, p. 244). One German account noted that 'Polish peasants ... had beaten thirteen of them [Jews] to death' (Hilberg, 1992, p. 208).

A sad chapter in the story of Polish collaboration with the Germans was the situation of the Jews who managed to escape from the ghetto and other places and tried to join the Polish partisans in the forests. Some, particularly in the eastern provinces of Poland, formed their own, Jewish, partisan units. They expected that the Polish resistance movement would join forces with them in the struggle against the Germans. The opposite happened. Instead of incorporating them into the body of the Polish resistance to fight against the common enemy, the Polish underground waged a war against the Jews. Groups of Jewish partisans were eliminated by the forces of the Polish underground and by local villagers who tracked them down and handed them over to the Germans (Ringelblum, 1985, p. 359).

Based on Polish sources, it can be shown that anti-Semitic attitudes dominated Polish society not only in areas under German control, but also in the Polish resistance units. It was this stance that severely limited the possibility of Jews joining the Polish underground movement. The belief that Jews were essentially an alien presence in Poland determined the attitude of the resistance.

The Home Army (AK)

Of the two major resistance groups in Poland, the AK (Armja Krajowa – Home Army) was the most important one, and in constant communication with the Polish government in London. As a general rule, Jews were not accepted into the ranks of the AK, except when a Jew knew a commander of a resistance unit personally. A few hundred Jews managed to join it – mostly under an assumed name as an 'Aryan' (Prekerowa, 1992, p. 187).

I begged them to use their influence to help me join [the AK]. After two weeks without a reply, I asked my friends to tell me the whole truth ... After a lengthy silence, they told me: 'the AK did not want Jews.'

(Verstandig, 1995, p. 168)

Another witness to the events of the time reports:

I knew Tadeusz very well from before the war ... Now he was an AK soldier, already an experienced fighter. I thought my great chance had come at last and passionately begged Tadeusz to help me join the Home Army at once. He said it was a splendid idea and told me to get ready and wait for him; he first had to notify his commander. He disappeared for half an hour, then came back upset and confused. His commander refused to take me because I was Jewish.

(Bauman, 1986, p. 157)

There were many cases when the leadership of an AK partisan unit issued an order to check the 'purity' of a prospective member and to find out whether he was of Jewish origin. Instances are known of individual Jews joining the Home Army as Poles, to be murdered by their comrades-in-arms when their real ethnicity was revealed (Gutman and Krakowski, 1986, p. 132).

Polish sources agree that the number of Jews within the AK units was relatively small, but most deny that anti-Semitism was a major factor in the low number of Jews in the AK. They do, however, agree that anti-Semitism did exist in its ranks. The main reason there were few Jews in the AK, they say, had less to do with anti-Semitism than with the fact that most Jews were unassimilated – that is, they did not know Polish well or at all – and their facial features gave them away (Lukas, 1986, p. 79). Polish sources do not reveal by whom they would be given away.

Another reason for Polish hostility toward Jews put forward by Polish historians was the alleged close association of Jews with the Polish or Soviet communists, who were regarded as enemies of Poland. Long-standing Polish charges of Judaeo-communism were confirmed in the eyes of Poles who saw Jews collaborating with Poland's 'other enemy' – the Soviets – and this revived anti-Semitic feelings in some Poles (ibid., p. 80). One Polish historian, while agreeing that there were incidents of AK units attacking Jewish partisans, asserts that most of these seem to have been motivated primarily by political rather than anti-Semitic reasons, meaning that all Jewish partisans were indeed communists (Iranek-Osmecki, 1971, p. 262).

Another argument used to justify attacks against Jews by the AK was 'that ... everyone, including the Jews who lived and operated in this bitter world, was affected by it. Jews were also involved in robbery, rape, and pillage. Often Poles were victims. Frequently Jews joined groups of bandits or formed groups of their own' (Lukas, 1986, p. 82).

Despite general knowledge of the systematic murder of Jews, the AK did not issue an order nor a recommendation to its forces to undertake action against the Germans. The Central Command of the AK took a neutral position, justifying it by the fear that after the extermination of the Jews, the Germans might begin exterminating the Poles – a view largely disproved. An order by General Rowecki (no. 71, dated 10 Nov. 1942) expresses this position:

> The Polish community fears that after the end of these operations the Germans will start to exterminate the Poles ... If the Germans really undertake such attempts, they will meet with our active resistance. Regardless of the fact that the time for an uprising has not yet arrived, my units will undertake an armed struggle in the defence of the life of the nation.
> (Caban and Mankowski, 1953, II, p. 60)

This order is an unambiguous indication that the question of defending the Jews wasn't considered important enough to require any action. Intensification of the activities of the AK was only anticipated in case of a danger to Poles. Polish citizens of Jewish origin were excluded.

The AK and armed resistance

Research into the activities of the Polish underground, does not show acts of sabotage significant enough to be considered as armed resistance. In contrast to the Jews, Poles possessed a substantial arsenal of weapons of all kinds, but did not use them until the Warsaw uprising of August 1944. It should also be noted that the Poles were rather late in establishing a partisan movement. They started to organise such units at the end of 1942, began serious military operations only in 1943, and went into full swing as late as 1944, while Jewish partisan units began operating in the east as early as the end of 1941.

The escalation of the activities of the AK was not prompted as much by the desire to harm the Germans as by the advance of the Soviet army into Poland. The AK issued a call to prepare for the decisive moment, after the victory of the Soviet Union over Germany, so as to be able to fight the Soviets. Until then they preferred to remain idle, their weapons at their feet (*Sefer ha-partizanim ha-Yehudim* ('The Book of Jewish Partisans'), 1959, I, 26). Generally, the scale of Polish fighting against the Germans was insignificant, and the idea of actually engaging the enemy in battle came rather late – during the 1944 Warsaw uprising.

Stefan Korbonski, a member of the Political Coordinating Committee which directed the entire Polish underground fight against the Germans, provides some information about the extent of Polish active resistance. 'No compilation exists of combined total results of joint sabotage activities conducted by various organisations', Korbonski asserts. He nevertheless supplies some statistics of acts of sabotage between 1 January 1941 and 30 June 1944. A close examination of the statistics shows that they include items such as the number of 'defective parts for aircraft produced – 4,710, defective artillery shells produced – 92,000', and so on. He also mentions 732 transports being derailed and 'in April 1943, thirty-seven railroad transports attacked and six carloads of arms captured' (Korbonski, 1978, p. 87).

The Polish underground was completely inactive regarding sabotaging railway lines and trains transporting Jews to the extermination camps. The existence of such camps was well known to the Polish underground and, in contrast to the Allies, who claimed they did not have the resources to bomb the camps, it had the means of at least interrupting the railway traffic. One Polish historian claims that the Poles escalated their attacks so much that by 1943 trains on many lines moved only at certain times under guard or not at all. By 1944, railroad sabotage increased to an average of ten attacks every day. In the first six months of 1944 alone, the Directorate of Diversion was responsible for 179 railroad disruptions, which forced delays on various lines from 2 to 196 hours (ibid., p. 67).

As can be seen from this report, the AK conducted attacks against railroad lines to hamper German traffic, but not specifically to delay transport to the death camps. In order to somehow redeem the Polish resistance, the same historian asserts 'that the AK attacks indirectly and temporarily benefited the Jews by creating logjams in the transportation system. But the Germans were able to restore traffic in a matter of hours or days' (Lukas, 1986, p. 166). Not a single attempt to sabotage railway lines and carriages heading to the extermination camps packed with Jewish men, women and children is mentioned. Since the crematoria were functioning until almost the last days of the war, a delay of a day or two, or even a few hours, could have saved countless Jewish lives.

Sabotaging the railway lines would have had an even greater psychological impact upon Polish society. It would have indicated to the Poles that the underground opposed the extermination of Jews and, theoretically at least, it could have encouraged many more Poles to assist Jews. It can safely be assumed that the absence of such action by the underground was interpreted as acquiescence by the resistance and the government-in-exile in the extermination of Jews.

Furthermore, Warsaw ghetto fighters who escaped into the forests after the collapse of the uprising did not receive any assistance from the Polish underground. After the fighting was over, the Polish underground made only a token effort to rescue the remaining fighters. One group of escapees who managed to gather in the forest near Wyszkow did not enjoy the protection of the Polish underground and many died in 'questionable' circumstances. It has been established that about 70 surviving ghetto fighters managed to reach the forest east of Warsaw. There, many were betrayed – among them Zygmunt Frydrych, who was active during the revolt smuggling arms and men from 'Aryan' Warsaw into the ghetto, was betrayed while leading a group of fighters to a shelter. Others, seeking safety further afield, went towards the forest near Hrubieszów, including the 23-year-old Pesia Furmanowicz. She and her comrades were murdered before they reached their destination (Lubetkin, 1981, p. 300).

> A group of Jewish combatants broke through to a tunnel and reached Otwock railway line. They settled in an abandoned villa in the woods between Michalin and Jozefow. Two days later, on 22 April [1943] the villa was surrounded by German and Polish police, the way having been pointed out by a local Polish police official. Back on Muranowska street, a third combat group of seven members had found a hiding place and remained there from Tuesday till the following day. A son of a Polish watchman, a member of the Miecz i Pług resistance organisation, Andrej Michno, summoned the Gestapo and the Polish police who surrounded the building and killed all the Jewish fighters.
>
> (Ber, 1975, p. 33)

From the middle of 1941 till the end of 1942, when masses of Polish Jewry were being exterminated, the leadership of the Polish underground acting under the orders of the Polish government-in-exile, assumed an official position of inaction regarding the Jews, while a significant section of the Polish underground took part in operations aimed against the Jews.

At this stage, when some Jews took up arms in the forests against the Germans, the Poles could no longer accuse the Jews of cowardice. They found another reason for their anti-Jewish attitudes. Most revealing in this respect is the vocabulary found in the Polish underground press, which was published directly either by the Office or by the Chief Command of the Home Army. Jewish partisan detachments are referred to as 'gangs' – a term routinely applied by the Nazis – or simply bandits.

One underground publication comments on Jewish partisans: 'nearly all the Jews of the Lublin district have been murdered. But a few are hiding in the woods and organising themselves to make holdups.' Another publication is more explicit: 'the gangs which are exclusively Jewish are notable for their atrocities' (Gutman and Krakowski, 1986, p. 122).

A decisively negative turn in the attitude of the Home Army towards Jews came in the summer of 1943 with the appointment of Tadeusz Bor-Komorowski to the post of Chief Commander of the Home Army, and with the admission of the fanatically anti-Semitic National Armed Forces (NSZ) into the Home Army ranks. General Bor-Komorowski, who was to lead the Polish Warsaw rebellion in August 1944, in a message to Polish headquarters in London on 31 August 1943 reported that he had issued an order that the leaders of these [Jewish] gangs be eliminated. The assault of the Home Army against the Jewish partisans had the official sanction in General Bor-Komorowski's further order no. 116 of 15 September 1943, explicitly commanding the liquidation of Jewish partisan groups fighting in the forests (Krakowski, 1977, p. 29).

The murder of Jewish partisans by the units of the Home Army are documented by numerous accounts of former Jewish partisans, as well as by many Polish sources. On 9 February 1943, in the region of Ostrowiec Świętokrzyski, 15 Jews were murdered by a unit of Związek Odwetu, an organisation which acted under Home Army orders. The group had succeeded in escaping from the Ostrowiec labour camp and intended to turn to the Home Army for help. One of the better-known cases is that of the Częstochowa ZOB unit. Jews fled from Częstochowa into the forest in the Koniecpole region with the intention of forming a partisan unit. On 10 September 1943 the unit was surrounded and attacked by an AK detachment under the command of Leon Szymbierski. Most of the Jews were murdered (Prekerowa, 1992, p. 183).

In the vicinity of a village called Majdan Tyszowski, Tomaszow Lubelski county, a Jewish partisan unit commanded by a Jew from Lublin named Cadok established contact with the local unit of the Home Army. After a successful joint operation, the Home Army unit invited the Jewish combatants for a feast. The Jews were first served poisoned vodka, and then fired upon. No one survived. In the Cracow district, a Jewish partisan unit commanded by Szymon Draenger (a Zionist) was attacked by local units of the Home Army under the command of Mikulski. In the autumn of 1943 detachments of the Home Army murdered a number of survivors of the Sobibor uprising. Two such survivors, Yitzkhak Lichtman and Yehezkel Menche, witnessed the murders (Gutman and Krakowski, 1986, p. 128).

The attacks of the Home Army units upon Jews intensified in early 1944. Often the members of local Home Army units provided the Germans with leads to forest bunkers occupied by Jewish partisans. On 5 May 1944 there appeared in Giebutlow, Miechow county, a Home Army detachment of about 50 men. They dragged out Jews who were hiding in an underground bunker on the farm, escorted them to a nearby forest and shot them there (ibid., p. 239). This from an account by two survivors – Mordechai Herszkowicz and Aharon Mutuszynski – (see *Sefer Izkor Miechow*).

The NSZ

The second most important resistance group was the NSZ (National Armed Forces), with the Rampart Group (Grupa Szańca) and the Union of Salamander (Związek Jaszczurczy) forming its core. Their main publication – *Szaniec* (The Rampart) – was imbued with an intensely nationalistic and anti-Semitic spirit.

On 7 March 1944 an agreement was signed subordinating the NSZ to and merging them with the AK. General Bor-Komarowski welcomed the soldiers of the NSZ into the ranks of the AK. But a new split developed in the leadership of the NSZ. Some supported the agreement, while others refused to obey its terms. As a result, some 10,000 to 15,000 soldiers of the NSZ joined the ranks of the AK, while many more remained in the NSZ. This is a clear indication that the NSZ formed a significant part of the Polish resistance movement and was not, as Polish historians claim, a small splinter group.

The remainder of the NSZ concentrated in the Kielce district and, following a reorganisation, was renamed the Swiętokrzyska (Holy Cross) Brigade. During the closing days of the war, on 13 January 1945, the 850-strong Brigade began, with German approval and under German protection, the trek westward through Silesia to Czechoslovakia. On 6 May 1945, the Holy Cross Brigade made its way to the American-occupied zone of Germany.

The NSZ did not accept Jews into its ranks, and units of the NSZ were constantly on the lookout for Jews hiding in the forests. The NSZ was also responsible for the killing in Warsaw of two officers of the High Command of the AK – Jerzy Makowiecki and Professor Ludwik Widerszal – both of Jewish origin (Korbonski, 1978, p. 137). On 14 July 1944, two other members of the Bureau of Information and Propaganda of the High Command of the Home Army – Professor Marceli Handelsman and a well-known writer, Halina Krahelska – were abducted from their offices by the NSZ and delivered to the Germans (ibid., p. 105).

The operations of the NSZ had the tacit approval of the German military authorities and in many cases their full cooperation. There was in fact a silent understanding that as long as the NSZ did not engage in any acts of sabotage against the Germans, it would be allowed to operate against Jewish partisans. The area of operation of the NSZ was the district of Radom controlled by the Holy Cross Brigade. The operations by the NSZ were to be conducted under the old slogan of Judaeo-communism, which meant that every Jewish partisan was a communist and should be liquidated. It was in fact part of a war against the Jews who escaped death by the Germans. The collaboration of the NSZ with the Germans is confirmed by documents kept in German archives.

The originals of the documents are located in the Federal Archives in Koblenz (Bundesarchiv Koblenz – BAK) in a file designated as R 70 Polen/194, which contains correspondence, service notices, etc. of the office of security police and security services for the Radom district of the General Government (Der Kommandeur der Sicherheitspolizei und des SD fur den Distrikt Radom), and its branches (Aussendienststelle) in Tomaszow Mazowiecki, which today are part of the Piotrkow, Radom and Skierniewice regions of Poland.

These documents reveal the mode of operation of the Nazi secret police whose main objective was the suppression in Poland of any resistance against German occupation. Since the German objective of liquidating the Polish left-wing resistance movement coincided with the objective of the Polish nationalist resistance movement to fight the Jews as communists, it led to close mutual cooperation.

As Polish nationalists we are eager to cooperate with the Germans ... We wanted to have in Poland a national government free of Jews. Had we had such a government immediately after the end of the September [1939] campaign, cooperation with the Germans would have possibly been good for us. Now, however, for us nationalists, it is very difficult to propagate such cooperation because today there is almost no Polish family in which one or more of its members was not imprisoned or executed by the Germans.

Therefore, we must conduct our cooperation with the Germans in a most careful manner so as not to provide our adversaries ... with the opportunity to exploit against us this [cooperation] in their propaganda.

(*Polityka*, 14 Nov. 1992)

The above segment of a testimony by Wiktor Marczynski, a member of the NSZ in Tomaszow Mazowiecki, faithfully reflects the perception of many of the soldiers of this underground formation. The following statement by Marczynski appears to have been given as part of the mutual agreement between the NSZ and the German authorities.

Piotrkow [Trybunalski] 1 February 1944. Statement by Marczynski Wiktor Stanislaw [alias Piotr Piotrkowski] born in Tomaszow Mazowiecki 17/10/1918, Pole, Catholic, member of NSZ since April 1942, detained by the gendarmerie in Sulejow on 31/1/1943 about 23.00 as a suspected member of a gang.

' ... in the Przysuchy and Drzewicy region we killed a number of Jews who belonged to the communist gang "Lew" – later called "Lewek" ... Our unit stumbled upon the "Lew" gang in August or September in the woods near Przysuchy or Brudziewic. Out of 20–30 men, we shot 19 Jews including the commander of the "Lew" gang ...

... As I said before ... we did not attack the German police or their offices, neither did we perform any act of sabotage ...'

The above statement carries the signatures of Wiktor Marczynski and of SS-Hauptsturmfuhrer Altman. The final report dated 15 February 1944 confirms that Marczynski's deposition was found correct.

Especially active in effecting the policy of cooperation with the NSZ were SS-Hauptsturmfuhrer Alfred Spielker in Warsaw and Paul Fuchs in Radom. Both received special authorisation from Himler and from the Central Security Office of the Reich (RSHA) to pursue their contacts with the Polish resistance. Their efforts led to establishing secret contacts with the head of the Department II of the NSZ General Command Wiktor Gostomski and his deputy Otmar Wawrzkowicz, as well as with some regional commanders, especially in the Radom district.

According to Zbigniew Siemaszko, tactical understandings between the various units of the NSZ and the German police or military authorities began in the second half of 1943 (Siemaszko, 1982, p. 108). The headquarters of Sipo and SD in Radom noted as early as May 1943 attempts by the Polish nationalist organisations to establish contacts with (German) security police (*Dzieje Najnowsze*, 1985, No.1, p. 230).

Particular initiative in this respect was demonstrated by Hubert Jura (code-named by the Germans 'Georg'), the Chief of Special Action of the Radom district – and from mid-1943 the head of NSZ Special Action in the area. Under his direction, the 'Sosna' unit (later 'Las') of the NSZ fulfilled the objectives of 'Special Action no. 1'. The objective of this action was, among others, 'the cleaning of the territory of subversive and criminal gangs, and of hostile minority [meaning Jewish] formations' (*Archiwum Akt Nowych*, VI, vol. 207/4–31).

A letter from Hubert Jura to the German military authorities characterises the activities of the NSZ:

> Polish (Dywersyjny) Department 'Sosna' 3.9.1943. Gendarmerie post in Nowe Miasto ... In one particular instance I was very close to liquidating a Jewish gang, which caused trouble in the proximity of Sady-Bizuchowa, but I was prevented by the gendarmes and soldiers of the Luftwaffe who arrested a priest (completely innocent) and a peasant who wanted to help us in our task.
>
> At the moment I lost track of the gang, but I found already another one.
>
> Regardless of the above, if the German authorities are not against my activities, I very politely ask to free two innocent men arrested in Sad ...
>
> At the same time, I once more assure you of the sincerity of my intentions and ask that, for obvious reasons, the content of my letter remain an official secret. I hope that the gendarmerie and other German authorities will not cause any difficulties for me, but on the contrary, will render assistance in the attainment of our common objective.
>
> (BAK, R 70 Polen/194, k. 3,3a)

Later, the German authorities concluded the following agreement with Jura ('Georg'). It was signed by the SS-Hauptsturmfuhrer Altman:

As long as his unit operates within the Piotrkow area, he will remain in contact with me and will notify the precise location of his unit so as to avoid incidents. At the same time he will inform me of his activities in the Piotrkow powiat and will hand over the more important individuals – alive if possible – into the hands of the Sicherheitspolizei.

(BAK, R 70 Polen/194, k. 61–9)

'Georg' faithfully adhered to the agreement, and according to the SS-Sturmscharfuhrer, Wiese, informed the Germans about the activities of the NSZ unit as well as of its precise location. On 22 February, Wiese reported a statement by 'Georg':

My unit will remain until the end of the week 26–27 February in Ruda-Papiernia. From here it will proceed to the area of Bialaczow, temporarily to Opoczno and then to action in Kozienice ... 'Georg' drives a green Mercedes car OST 1376. Signed – Wiese, SS-Sturmscharfuhrer.

(BAK, R 70, Polen/194, k.46)

And on 14 March 1944, 'Georg' reported the following:

In the Pietrykow area were executed on 9 March 1944: Majer Rabinowicz, a Jew from Opoczno who lived with Jan Julkowski. Rabinowicz, born on 28.6.1920, son of Lejb and Szangla, and Szlama Lewkowicz [a Jew] from Opoczno also lived with Julkowski. Lewkowicz was born 3.9.1924, son of Izaak ... (Branch office [ekspozytura] in Tomaszow. IV A-2/44 gRs)

In some cases, the NSZ directly intervened with the German police when a member of the NSZ was arrested, as can be seen from the following letter date 17 December 1943.

To the Chief of Sicherheitspolizei and SD in Tomaszow
On 14 of this month were arrested in the gmina Stuzno the following persons: Mieczyslaw Gil, Jan Pluta and Raczynski. I wish to inform you that Pluta and Raczynski directly participated in the elimination of two Jews in Adamowo and two Jews in Krzyżówka near Gielniow. All three always helped us in uncovering Jews and communists ... [if] you approve the action of eliminating Jewish-communist gangs you will allow the above mentioned three men

to continue this activity in freedom.

(BAK, R 70 Polen, k.2)

By the end of 1943 and beginning of 1944, the cooperation between the NSZ units and the German police in the Radom district acquired a permanent character (original letters can be found in BAK, R 70 Polen/194). The anti-Jewish activities of the NSZ and partly of the AK, are also documented in many testimonies of Jewish partisans and generally of Jews hiding in the forests.

The war of the NSZ against Jews was waged on all fronts, including a war in print conducted by all NSZ publications; from the occasional and minor papers to the major one under the direct control of the NSZ, *Szaniec*. An excerpt from *Szaniec* quoted by the Polish historian, Piotr Lipinski (*Gazeta Wyborcza*, 24–5 Sept. 1993), says: 'The solution of the Jewish question is almost as important for the future of our nation as the regaining of independence. The loss of independence and the continuation of Jewish presence in Poland are both an equal danger of slow death for the Poles.'

Szaniec was not a marginal paper, but a theoretical and ideological organ of the leadership of the NSZ. Another NSZ publication which expressed similar views was *Praca i Walka*. The latter was a central youth section of *Szaniec* and was listed in the top 65 largest and most important papers published under the occupation, according to Tadeusz Wyrwa – an associate of the French Centre National de la Recherche Scientifique, and the author of a major work entitled *Polski ruch oporu i polityka europejska*.

An excerpt from *Praca i Walka* quoted in a letter to the Polish President dated 27 March 1944 said: 'The accursed Jewish devil has left so much poison in the blood of the civilised world, has caused so much evil and misfortune, that the time has finally come to mete out the much deserved punishment, which will prevent the Jews once and for all from engaging in a destructive conspiracy.' It should be noted this was written at a time when 'the accursed Jewish devil' had already been mostly annihilated; when there only remained a handful of Jews who escaped death. It was against those few survivors that the call for 'deserved punishment' was directed. That call led to the further murders of many surviving Jews.

Such murders, however, have not been recorded. Here and there one can find fragments of personal memoirs which reveal this part of the activities of the NSZ. Wacław Zagorski, an AK officer, for example, in his book of war memoirs entitled *Wolność w niewola*, published in 1971, describes his encounter with an NSZ unit led by a lieutenant code-named 'Grot'. One of the soldiers of this unit admitted to Zagorski that his commander executed unarmed Jews captured in the woods in front of the unit.

The main source of information about the activities of the NSZ are witnesses who saw what was happening within the Polish underground. The most authoritative source in this respect is the testimony of Stefan Korbonski, the last Delegate of the government-in-exile. He stated: 'it would be very difficult to present a list with dates and names of Jews murdered by the NSZ. This does not prove that such murders were not committed. I know of these shameful acts of the NSZ from the underground reports. Besides, the NSZ did not keep it secret. Some of its members have actually boasted about it' (*Zeszyty Historyczne* nr. 34, 1975). Korboński repeated the accusations in a book entitled *Jews and Poland in World War II*, published in 1989.

The subject of the NSZ surfaced on the pages of the Polish press in November 1992; and after the publication of an open letter from the Australian Jewry to the Polish President in *Gazeta wyborcza* in March 1993, there was some discussion on that subject on the pages of *Gazeta wyborcza* and sporadically in one other journal – *Rzeczpospolita*.

The Warsaw uprising of 1944

The outbreak of the Polish uprising in Warsaw in 1944 was met enthusiastically by Jewish survivors hidden on the Aryan side, and many came out of hiding to join the Polish fighters. On 3 August 1944, the former commander of the Jewish Warsaw uprising, Cukierman, issued an appeal in which he called the surviving fighters of the Warsaw ghetto uprising to join the ranks of the Polish fighters. 'Through the struggle to victory for a free, independent, strong and just Poland!', was one more declaration by the Jews of solidarity and common aspirations in fighting the enemy.

However, despite the eagerness to participate in the uprising, many survivors faced open resistance and even violence from the Poles. Many met with difficulties in joining the Polish fighters because of the reign of prejudice against the Jews within the AK. It is for this reason that during the Polish Warsaw uprising, most of the Jews who joined the Polish units concealed their Jewish identity. We learn of the manifestations of this anti-Semitism through the testimonies of Jews and Poles alike.

Mieczysław Fuks, who participated in the revolt, describes the reaction of the Polish population to Jews who ventured out from their hiding places at the outbreak of the revolt: 'The population pointed their fingers at them. They did not sympathise with them at all ... They were amazed that they had managed to stay alive but mocked them nevertheless ... Because of the population's negative attitude to the Jews, many Jews lost their lives' (Krakowski, 1977, p. 282; YVA, file 0–16/450).

Irena Palenkier, who participated in the Polish revolt, testified to similar phenomena: 'despite the fact that the Zoliborz quarter was in the hands of the rebels and not under German rule, here too the Jews had to be certain that they would not be discovered because the reaction of the Polish population could have been tragic for the hiding Jews' (ibid., p. 283; YVA, file 0–3/2518).

Margolis-Edelman, the wife of one of the leaders of the Warsaw ghetto revolt, reports:

A group of Jews, who participated in the Warsaw insurrection, remained in the Zoliborz quarter after the departure of its inhabitants ... At the time of the Warsaw insurrection, when they thought that it was safe to come out of hiding into the temporarily liberated part of Warsaw, they have formed an armed unit in Zoliborz and took position on the Mostowa street ... [but] in some units of the AK insurgents, anti-Semitism was prevalent and to reveal one's Jewish identity was very dangerous. Marek Edelman, a survivor and former commander of the Ghetto uprising after the death of Anielewicz, tried it and was severely beaten up in the Old City. Julek attempted to do the same and nearly paid with his life.
(Margolis-Edelman, 1997, p. 173)

Tzadok Zvi Florman, who commanded a company in the uprising passing as a Pole under the name of Tadeusz Kaniowski, told the story of Ya'akov Puterrmilch, Baruch Spiegel, and the engineer Bronislaw Topaz – three fighters from the Jewish Fighting Organisation (ZOB) who came out of hiding and approached the command of the AK to be attached to a combat unit. According to Florman, the soldiers in his company opposed the acceptance of the Jews. Two soldiers turned to Florman and said: 'Lieutenant, why do we need Jews? We will take them to a dark corner and beat them on the back with an iron pole.' In this case, the three ZOB fighters were accepted and were saved from death only by the stand of Florman, whose soldiers did not know that he himself was a Jew (Krakowski, (1977) p. 285; YVA, file 0–3/2993).

Some Polish sources see the situation of the Jews during the uprising in quite a different way: 'In the suburbs of Warsaw under the control of the Polish fighters, Jews could finally emerge from their hiding places after years of vegetation and fear for their lives. They could finally feel free and fight against the murderers of their brothers ...' (Arczynski and Balcerak, 1983, p. 188). As with other similar statements, no evidence or witness accounts are available in support of the assessments.

Cases of a positive attitude on the part of the Poles were rather rare. In his memoirs Haim Goldstein describes a case that occurred during the construction of a barricade on Mostowa Street by a group of prisoners who had just been liberated from the prison on Gęsia Street. They were still wearing the typical dress of German concentration camp inmates. Suddenly screams were heard: 'Death to the Jews!' After the screams there were shots. Two Jews were killed. There were shouts: 'We do not need Jews. Shoot every one!' However, several Poles intervened and by a miracle managed to save the other prisoners (Goldstein, 1962, p. 118).

Wladka Miedzyrzecka describes a murder which was carried out on the fifth day of the revolt in the railroad worker's house on the corner of Żelazna and Chmielna streets, where several Jews tried to find shelter from shelling by the German artillery. Three of them had a Jewish appearance and were arrested by an AK patrol. They were told that in liberated Poland there was no place for Jews. Yehoshua Salomon was killed, the other two managed to escape, although one of them, Lutek Friedman, was wounded (quoted in Krakowski, 1977, p. 286).

Waclaw Zagorski describes the murder of 7 Jewish women on the initiative of Captain Stryjkowski ('Hal'), the commander of the 1st Battalion of the Chrobry II group (Zagorski, 1957, pp. 287–9). This was not the only instance of the killing of Jews by Captain Stryjkowski's soldiers. With the permission and under the direct command of Lieutenant Okrzeja, on 10 September 1944 a group of 8 soldiers from the 1st Battalion killed 14 Jews who were in a house on Prosta Street (Ber, 1954). The killing at the hands of the NSZ of approximately 30 Jews at 25 Dluga Street and a murder in the military hospital at 22 Zlota Street by the AK military police are also recorded.

After two months of fighting, on 1 October 1944, the commander of the uprising, Bor-Komorowski, told London: 'Warsaw no longer has any chance of defence. I have decided to enter into negotiations for surrender with full combatant rights, which the Germans fully recognise.' According to the terms of surrender, the AK soldiers were treated as prisoners of war in accordance with the rights of the Geneva Convention. Civilians were not to be persecuted, and their evacuation from Warsaw, demanded by the Germans, was to be conducted in such a way as to minimise suffering. The Germans took Bor-Komorowski and his staff to Ozarow, where they boarded a train to their internment at Gasenstein.

The fate of the Jews was quite different. Those who were recognised as Jews or denounced by other Poles were shot immediately. The Jews, whether they were fighters or unarmed civilians, sought various escape routes. Most of them left Warsaw and tried either to mingle with Polish civilian population or to reach prisoner-of-war camps, as long as they could conceal their Jewish identity.

One Polish source contradicts the above assessment: 'During the uprising, liberated Jews shared a common fate with the Poles. The situation of the Jews was similar to that of the evacuated Polish population sent to the temporary camp in Pruszkow and then for compulsory work in Germany' (Arczynski and Balcerak, 1983, p. 191).

APPENDIX: Jews in the Polish Army

At the time of the German invasion of the USSR in June 1941, the Polish government-in-exile was headed by general Sikorski. Previously, due to the Katyn affair, the USSR cut its diplomatic relations with Poland, but Sikorski, although not favourably disposed towards the Soviet Union, nevertheless consented to renew relations. On 14 August 1941 a Polish–Soviet military agreement was signed.

An important point of the military agreement was the formation of a Polish army on the territory of the Soviet Union. The Polish general Anders was appointed as the commander of the Polish forces and his headquarters were established at Buzuluk on the Samara river east of Kuybyshev.

The terms of the agreement also included an amnesty for all former Polish citizens kept in labour camps in different parts of Russia. Some of the inmates of these camps were soldiers and officers of the Polish army caught by the Russians during their march into Poland in 1939, but the great majority were people arrested on the occupied territories and deported during the months of June and July of 1940. Among them were many Jewish refugees from Nazi-occupied Poland who refused to accept Soviet citizenship.

Following the agreement, tens of thousands of former Polish citizens were released from the camps, and all military internees were sent to Buzuluk to be incorporated into the Polish army. As soon as the news spread about the formation of a Polish army in Buzuluk, scores of Polish citizens began to flock to this town in order to join the armed forces. Polish Jews were no exception. As in the past, they attempted to express their solidarity with the Polish nation and to share the objective of fighting a common enemy.

This met with resentment from the Poles who were liberated from the Soviet labour camps after the Polish–Soviet accord. According to Polish historians, Polish soldiers and officers 'who remembered the behaviour of the Jewish population in Eastern Poland in 1939–1940, were inclined to retaliate by vilifying Jewish soldiers.' (Prekerowa, 1992, p. 194).

The number of Jews willing to join the Polish army was quite significant and there was apprehension among the Polish general staff that a large percentage of Jews might join, thereby making the army less Polish and depriving it of its Polish character. General Anders made strenuous efforts at keeping the number of Jews enlisted in the army to a minimum.

We stood in a queue in front of the recruiting office waiting our turn. My new friend was the first to enter the office to be interviewed. He came out after about twenty minutes. Before I had a chance to make a move towards the door, he pulled me away to prevent me from entering the office.

'What happened?', I asked, 'were you rejected?'

'It is not as simple as I thought', he said, 'you see, the first question they ask you is about your religion. When I told them that I was Jewish, I could see that I was in trouble. They began to speak amongst themselves in a low voice and I guessed that I would be rejected. Of course, they didn't tell me straight out the reason, but a few minutes later after I was examined by a doctor, I was told that I am unfit for military service. But I have an idea how to get over the problem. Just wait for me here I will be back soon.'

He returned a short while later armed with tips as to how to beat the apparent anti-Jewish rules in the newly formed Polish army.

'It's very simple', he said, 'to be accepted, all we have to do is to declare that we are Catholic. We don't have to prove it because no one has any documents anyway. I just spoke to another Jew who did just that. After having been rejected in the morning he appeared again before the commission and was accepted. Since I am not going to convert, I have a clear conscience.'

I said to him, 'you may do what you like, but I am not going to pretend that I am Catholic. If they don't want me as a Jew, I am not going to impose my presence upon them. I am not following you.'

At this we parted company.

(Author's recollections)

Polish historians place the blame for this state of affairs on Soviet authorities who are supposed to have tried to prevent contacts between the Polish representatives and the Jews.

To avoid unfavourable publicity and an adverse reaction of world public opinion, the Polish army command allowed a token number of Jews to enlist, and a few hundred Jews managed to join at Buzuluk and Totsk – another centre of recruitment. However, after a few weeks many had been forced to leave or simply to desert because of the harsh treatment to which they were subjected by the Polish officers and soldiers.

There was an incident in the town of Kiermin, where a number of Jewish army volunteers were beaten up by Poles as revenge for the Soviet occupation of Poland. The officers who witnessed the beating stood nearby laughing. (Sprawozdanie z Działalnosci Reprezentacji Żydów Polskich z lat 1939–1945). The secret order issued by general Anders in this matter reveals the real situation. The document was dated 30 November 1941 and signed by the general.

Headquarters of the Polish Armed Forces in the USSR.
Confidential.
Buzuluk, 30 November 1941.
In connection with order No. 1730 of 14 November 1941, regarding Jewish participation in the Polish Armed Forces, I wish to clarify the matter as follows: ... I can well understand the reasons for the anti-Semitic incidents within the ranks of army personnel – they are a reaction to the disloyal, often hostile, behaviour of Polish Jews, especially in the period of 1939–1940. I am not surprised that our patriotic soldiers react so sharply ...

However, our present policy ... must appear to contain positive features regarding Jews on account of their significant and important influence in the Anglo-Saxon world. All our soldiers must understand that state interests require not to antagonise the Jews, because anti-Semitism at the present time can bring the Polish cause incalculable harm. Therefore, I am recommending to explain to the troops our position in a discreet and proper manner and to warn the hot-headed that, at present, all manifestations of animosity against the Jews are categorically forbidden and will be severely punished as harmful to our cause. The day when we are our own masters, after our victory, we shall settle the Jewish question in a way that will be compatible with our sovereignty and the greatness of our fatherland as well as simple human justice.

Signed:
Gen. W. Anders.
Confirmed as correct: Bielecki (captain)

(Ros, p. 31)

The testimony of a Jewish soldier in Anders' army clearly depicts the attitude of the Polish soldiers and officers toward their Jewish comrades.

> Our situation as Jews was terrible. We were subject to constant attacks and beatings by the Poles. A few of our Jewish fellow soldiers were even murdered. I was once beaten up by a group of Poles in the camp. The officers were aware of what was going on by did nothing to put an end to this odious practice.
>
> There were a few Jews who managed to conceal their Jewish identity. I remember a certain Karolicki whom the Poles suspected was Jewish. One evening, he was surrounded in the dormitory by a group of Poles who forced him to lower his pants. He got a terrible beating. There were also a few Jewish converts but their lot was no better. They were the subject of constant ridicule from the Poles who did not believe in their sincerity.
>
> The Poles claimed that everything that happened to Poland was the fault of the Jews. Another reason for attacking the Jews, one that came from a Polish priest, was that the Jews had killed Jesus. When I told them that they were praying to a Jew – one who died as a Jew – they became very upset and angry. They were ready to give me a trashing. I said to them: 'let us ask the priest, he will tell you', but the priest was reluctant to confirm the truth of my statement.

(Testimony of L. R., interviewed by the author)

The situation of Jews who joined units of the Polish army and found themselves in England was not any better. According to one Jewish historian, 'there was a general reluctance among Polish Jews to serve under the Polish flag; the cause was not lack of patriotism, but a widespread belief that there existed among Polish soldiers and officers a certain sympathy with the anti-Jewish aims of the Nazis.' The behaviour of the Polish troops often confirmed these suspicions (Wasserstein, 1979, p. 125).

The Board of Deputies of British Jews published a memorandum in which it was alleged that at a meeting of Polish officers, the Polish Deputy Commander-in-Chief had announced that Jews who remained in Poland after the war should be killed. A Polish army chaplain was said to have declared that a total British victory in the war might not be desirable because it would leave power in the hands of the Jews (ibid., pp. 125–6; Board of Deputies memorandum sent to Dr I. Schwartzbart, Sept. 1943, BD C 11/7/1/6).

The situation of Jewish soldiers in the Polish army worsened to such an extent, that in 1944 a number of Jews deserted from the troops stationed in Britain. They declared the reason for desertion to be the anti-Semitic excesses of Polish soldiers, and wanted to join the British army instead.

In January 1944 a group of 68 Jewish soldiers in the Polish army deserted, complaining of anti-Semitism among Polish troops. Particularly offensive was the anti-Semitic behaviour of Polish soldiers who, while fighting for the Germans in Tunisia, were caught by allied troops and subsequently permitted to join the Polish army in Britain. The Jewish deserters claimed they had been told by Poles that all the Jews left in Poland at the end of the war would be massacred. The Jews threatened a hunger strike and suicide unless they were transferred to the British army. In February a second group, numbering 134 men, deserted and made similar complaints and demands (*Jewish Chronicle*, 14, 28 April and 5, 12, 19 and 26 May 1944)

A Polish commission of inquiry confirmed that soldiers were responsible for such behaviour. 'Specifically, Polish soldiers who served in Russia and those who had been forced to serve in the German army were the sources of most of the anti-Semitic behaviour' (Lukas, 1986, p. 137).

The desertions have obscured the fact that in many Polish army units Jewish soldiers considered themselves Polish citizens. They fought in all Polish units in the East and the West, and participated in all battles. In many Polish military cemeteries (including Monte Casino) one finds Jewish names.

8
Saviours – Righteous among the Nations

He who saves one life is as if he had preserved the entire world.

(Sanhedrin 37)

The preceding two chapters depicted the situation of the Jewish population in occupied Poland. It described the conditions of a population surrounded by the might of the German army and separated from the rest of Polish society not only by a brick wall, but by a wall of indifference and in many cases pure hatred. To remain within the ghetto enclaves meant certain death while the routes of escape were largely closed. For those who left the ghetto before it was too late and for those who managed to cross onto the 'Aryan' side, life in hiding demanded tremendous courage and ability to change one's conduct in public places. It meant facing the danger of being denounced by the 'szmalcowniks' and blackmailers. Under such circumstances, for many Jews survival was only possible when help was offered by a Pole. The provision of safe houses and 'Aryan' documents was the only way of evading the fate of most Jews. The fact that some Jews survived the war in hiding is one of the tangible proofs that some help was forthcoming.

While there is much evidence to show that the prevailing general attitude of the Poles had contributed to the death of many Jews, it is also an indisputable fact that there were a number of Poles who for various reasons undertook the dangerous task of saving Jews. It is perhaps the most controversial aspect of the history of the Holocaust in Poland because of contrasting claims made by Polish apologists and by those who argue that the extent of help rendered by Poles was insignificant and in most cases motivated by other than humane considerations.

If the question of saving Jews is confined to a comparison of

163

the number of cases of humane behaviour and those involving denouncements, blackmail, murder or robbery, than the balance would certainly tend to lean to the negative side. The question needs to be investigated on its own, and a rational judgment made as to whether such help represented the general attitudes of the Polish society.

Another aspect of the problem is the motivation of those who helped save Jews. It has been established that individual Poles acted for various reasons. Some were motivated by a sense of humanity, solidarity with the persecuted, or a perception of a common bond. Many acted as personal friends. Sometimes it was a combination of several motives (Arczynski and Balcerak, 1983, p. 69). There were also those who received financial rewards for helping Jews to escape from the ghetto, for hiding them or for providing food. This category of saviours might raise reservations as to the moral value of their acts, but one must not forget the reality of the general poverty of the population. Many Poles who wished to offer help to Jews could simply not afford it. There is one undeniable fact: regardless of motive, Poles endangered their lives and the lives of their families and close friends. 'The price of life is generally incommensurable' (ibid., p. 70).

A historian searching for the motivation of saviours encounters the dilemma of deciding whether the action of saving a Jew was motivated by a sense of humanity or whether there were personal reasons involved. Although in ethical terms being rewarded for a humane act diminishes the value of such deeds, it is nevertheless true to say, according to the ghetto historian Emmanuel Ringelblum, 'that no amount of money could recompense the sacrifice of the helpers'.

The debate about the nature and the extent of help rendered by Poles is still going on. The point of departure in this debate is the fact that of all European countries under German occupation, Poland is known to have the smallest percentage of survivors. (See Table 8.1.)

Poland ranks second after Holland in the number of individuals awarded by the Israeli government the title 'Righteous among the Nations of the World' for saving Jews. Whether by the design of the planners or by coincidence, the first thing that attracts the attention of a visitor to Yad Vashem in Jerusalem is the entrance to the Avenue of the Righteous among the Nations. In the area of the history of the Holocaust where it is difficult to pinpoint anything positive, this is living proof that there are exceptions to this rule. In that avenue one immediately notices trees with plaques bearing the names of those who during the war rendered help to Jews. A large number of these plaques carry names of Poles, including members of the Polish

Table 8.1

	Jewish population		
	Before 1939	Alive after 1945	Percentage of survivors
Poland	3,500,000	60–80,000	1.7–2.3
Romania	850,000	300,000	35.3
Hungary	400,000	200,000	50.0
Czechoslovakia	360,000	50,000	13.9
France	300,000	180,000	60.0
Holland	150,000	30,000	20.0
Belgium	100,000	30,000	30.0
Italy	50,000	20,000	40.0
Greece	75,000	10 000	13.3

Source: Grayzel, 1968, p. 674.

organisation Żegota that was active in saving Jews during the war. Many of them were awarded medals.

The exceptionally harsh nature of the German occupation combined with the prevalent anti-Semitism among the broad masses made it much more dangerous for Polish rescuers to reach out to Jews in distress in Poland. The amount of courage, determination and above all compassion demanded of a saviour in Poland was much greater than in any other German-occupied country in Europe. Consequently, the stories of saving Jews emanating from Poland are the most glorious in the history of the Holocaust and deserve special appreciation (Meyer, 1987).

This was recognised by the Israeli government in the Martyrs' and Heroes' Remembrance (Yad Vashem) Law passed by the Knesset in 1953, eight years after the end of the Holocaust. However, it was not until 1962, after the Eichmann trial that the provisions of the law began to be implemented. A committee created for the purpose of awarding medals and planting trees in honour of saviours established criteria for bestowing the award. There were two conditions. One was that a beneficiary of the rescue action must present his or her testimony in person or in writing. The second was that the rescuer must have acted without financial benefit.

The last clause was very often difficult to apply. In Poland, which has accounted for about a quarter of all Righteous honoured, many saviours during the war barely managed to feed themselves and their families. Accepting money for supplying food to a Jew in hiding was, therefore, fully justified. There were, however, cases when this was not so clear-cut and a significant amount of money was paid in advance. The Committee had the unenviable task of deciding whether such a payment constituted a financial inducement, or was simply intended to cover the cost of feeding a few hidden Jews for several months. Mordechai Paldiel, a former head of the department for Righteous Gentiles at Yad Vashem, spoke of numerous cases where the truth of what happened at the time was closely linked to the real motivation of a saviour. In some cases it was established that a Pole saved a Jew and later was involved in killing Jews. In another case, a Pole killed Jews, but with the inevitability of German defeat, actually helped to save them. The head of the Haifa committee, Alexander Bronowski, a survivor of the Warsaw ghetto, told about the help he received from a member of the dreaded Polish Blue Police (Meyer, 1987).

Table 8.2 shows the breakdown by country of cases and individuals investigated by the committee from 1962 until December 1986. Poland clearly is among the countries with the greatest number of individuals and cases. Polish historians emphasise the fact that among the 4,000 individuals who received the distinction, over 1,000 are Poles.

Table 8.2

Country	Cases	Individuals involved in all cases
Holland	1,579	2,972
Poland	1,202	2,074
France	303	429
Belgium	247	415
Germany/Austria	214	290
Russia/Ukraine	55	79
Italy	89	136
Lithuania	88	144
Hungary	80	110
Czechoslovakia	46	95
Greece	39	60
Yugoslavia	32	57
Romania	20	29
Bulgaria	10	10
Latvia/Estonia	9	13
Other countries	29	35
TOTAL	4,042	6,948

Source: Meyer, 1987

Another aspect of the debate is the number of Polish Jews who survived the Holocaust. Based on the incomplete registration effected in 1945 by the Central Committee of Polish Jews, historians offer various assessments ranging from 40,000 to 80,000. Subsequent assessments put the number of survivors at between 80,000 and 120,000, and in addition 350,000 survived by fleeing to the Soviet Union and other neutral countries. According to this calculation, approximately 87 per cent of Polish Jews perished. However, if survivors outside of Poland are removed from this estimate, than the number of survivors constitute only 2.3–3.4 per cent of the pre-war Jewish population. In other words, about 97 per cent of the Jewish population in Poland were exterminated – the largest proportion of any occupied European country.

Faithful to the principle of defending the honour of the nation, Polish intellectuals are asserting that the small number of Jewish survivors in Poland is not due to any anti-Semitic attitudes but to the German terror which punished with death those who helped to save Jews. During the period between 13 August 1942 and 25 may 1944 (almost two years) the Germans executed about 200 Poles for hiding Jews (Berenstein and Rutkowski, 1963, p. 48). Another Polish source claims that 'Available documentation allows us to establish a list of about 900 names of Poles who were executed by the Germans for sheltering Jews' (Prekerowa, 1992, p. 160).

According to views expressed by Polish apologists, one gets the impression that 'rendering assistance to Jews had been quite prevalent, within the possibilities under the terror of occupation'. They also claim that were it not for assistance by Poles, not one Jew would have survived. Polish historians interpret the relatively large number of Jews who perished by claiming that the percentage of survivors depended on the total number of Jews in a particular country – the larger the number, the greater the number of victims. For example, they say that in Belgium, where half of the Jewish population survived, it was due to the fact that 36,000 Jews lived among a population of 8 million. According to this reasoning, it was impossible to save half of the Jewish population in Poland (Prekerowa, 1982, p. 324). However, Polish historians fail to consider how many Jews could have been saved if the general attitude of the Poles had been different.

A further difficulty in estimating the number of survivors is the fact that many Jews continued to conceal their Jewish identity after the end of the war. They still lived in fear for their lives due to a hostile environment which did not offer complete safety for Jewish survivors in Poland. Their number cannot even be estimated.

An attempt to determine the extent of help given by Poles has been made by the well-known writer, Teresa Prekerowa, in an article published in a leading Polish newspaper (Prekerowa, 1987). She estimated the number of Jews hidden under false identity at between 80,000 and 120,000, of which only half managed to survive. She also made the assertion that to save one Jew it was necessary to obtain the cooperation of two to three Poles. In this way the total number of all Poles who may have taken part in the saving of Jews may constitute 1–2.5 per cent of the Polish population.

According to Prekerowa, not every Jew who searched for help among the Poles managed to survive – only less than half remained alive. This raises another question: why did half of those who were hidden on 'Aryan' papers perish? There is no answer to this question from Polish sources. Jewish historians claim that they perished because they were denounced. The denunciation usually occurred when a Jew was known to be Jewish to those who betrayed him, or did not have the required looks and proficiency in the Polish language.

This is usually used as an argument to show how difficult it was to save a Jew. Many Jews either did not speak Polish, or spoke it badly. Only 10 per cent of the Jewish population was assimilated while another 10 per cent integrated to some degree (Tomaszewski and Werbowski, 1994, p. 29). It was easier for Poles to save a Jew who could pass for an Aryan, who blended in with their environment. Appearance was an important factor, but fluency in Polish, familiarity with customs, as well as general mannerism and style, often played an even greater part. This could also provide a partial answer to the question of how many Jews could have been saved had they not been betrayed by Poles.

The pre-war Jewish leader, Zerubavel, was one of the first to visit Poland after the end of hostilities in December 1945. He reported in much detail what he saw and heard from Jewish survivors. He specifically noted the humane behaviour of a number of Poles who risked their lives to save Jews. However, his final conclusion was that:

> They were a few drops in the ocean of Polish anti-Semitism. When one speaks to Jews from various circles, one can hear a statement without any reservation that the death of 50, or perhaps 75 per cent, of Jewish victims can be ascribed to the Poles. It was not that they served the Germans. They did what they did for personal motives, and due to the perception that whatever happens Poland will be rid of the Jews.

> (Zerubavel, 1948, p. 131)

Admittedly, the percentages mentioned in Zerubavel's account are probably vastly exaggerated, and in any case impossible to quantify, but it indicates the general impressions of survivors. For a researcher into this question the most difficult task is to assess the number of Poles who offered assistance. A Jew in hiding rarely spent the entire period of German occupation in one house or apartment; due to various circumstances he was forced to change his place of abode several times and other Poles may have been involved in helping him. House searches and the fear of being denounced necessitated the frequent transfer of hidden Jews from one hiding place to another. Furthermore, some Poles have sometimes rendered assistance to several escapees from the ghetto. Many Jews hiding on 'Aryan' papers survived exclusively thanks to their own endeavours in obtaining false papers, to having 'good looks', and to the possibility of earning a living; they did not have recourse to Polish helpers.

Prekerowa's estimate of the need of an average of 2–3 persons to help one Jew was probably close to the truth. Generally a Jew was hidden by one couple, and sometimes another member of the family was involved. To solicit the help of a larger number of people presented an increased danger of being denounced. The general atmosphere reigning within the Polish population was one of hostility toward Jews, and a Pole would be most reluctant to admit to anyone that he was hiding a Jew. Estimates – admittedly very approximate – allow us to put the number of Polish helpers at about 160,000–360,000.

Most Jews were hidden among the urban population where they could melt into a large number of Poles. It was here that the help was most needed. Often it was necessary to change the place of hiding of Jews. It was also necessary to provide them not only with food, lodging, or with appropriate documents confirming their 'Aryan' origin, but also to assure protection from blackmailers and collaborators.

The rural population was helpful to Jews on a much smaller scale. Hiding Jews in the villages was very complicated. Polish sources ascribe the difficulties in hiding Jews in the villages to frequent German raids rather than the animosity of the inhabitants. They admit nevertheless that it was relatively easier for a Jew who had pre-war connections in the village and personally knew some of the villagers. They quote examples of villages in which the inhabitants were hiding Jews (Berenstein and Rutkowski, 1963, p. 46).

The question remains whether the estimated number of Poles who tried to save Jews justifies the claim that 'not much more could have been done'. Polish literature on that subject generally presents those Poles who demanded money for the help they provided as simple criminals motivated by greed and a feeling that they were beyond the law and would not be punished. Some Polish sources admit that it was a lack of interest in the fate of Jews that made crimes against Jews easier to commit.

Between the two extreme groups of those who helped Jews and blackmailers was the overwhelming majority of the Polish population, who did not take any part in 'Jewish affairs'. Their attitude toward Jews was uneven. Part of this segment of the Polish population may have been favourably disposed toward Jews, although for various reasons they were not actively helpful; they did not consider themselves morally justified to risk the lives of their close relatives, and not everyone was able to overcome the fear of the consequences of rendering assistance to Jews. Next to those who were favourably inclined were also Poles who, although they sympathised with Jews, isolated themselves from the problem by saying 'it is not our concern'. Furthermore, not every Pole came face to face with the problem of helping Jews or found himself in a situation in which active participation was required.

In their defence, Polish analysts point to the death sentences and executions of blackmailers by members of the Polish underground. The reality, according to the reports of the Polish underground, is that such sentences were carried out as late as the end of 1943. During 1943–4, a handful of blackmailers were executed.

Most accusations against Poles who betrayed Jews to the Germans, may be found in Jewish memorial books consecrated to the memory of Jewish communities in Polish towns and villages. Such books are published by the dispersed Jewish communities and contain testimonies of survivors. They quite often mention the names of Polish peasants, shopkeepers or policemen who took money from Jewish escapees and then threw them out to a certain death – sometimes handing them over to gendarmes. In many cases they murdered the Jews they robbed.

Many Polish historians claim that one should be cautious of accepting testimony at face value. Most testimony was presented many years after the war, reconstructing events of which the witnesses heard while in hiding. Most survivors were children at the time. Many were influenced by the views and suggestions of 'foreign and anti-Polish' elements. However, even when one concedes that such memories are partly exaggerated and inaccurate, they cannot be rejected. Their number is too great and they could not all have been invented. 'History is built up out of individual testimonies. The historian's skill is to fit them together, like pieces of a jigsaw puzzle, so as ultimately to offer a whole picture' (Goldbloom in a Foreword to Tomaszewski and Werbowski, 1994, p. 3).

Such are the arguments of well-intentioned Polish intellectuals. However, it remains a fact that the enlightened majority of the Polish population (according to such intellectuals) did allow the anti-Semites, who 'more often than not originated from the most primitive strata of Polish society', to publicly state their opinion and to demand (successfully) that everyone else follow their example.

According to one Polish commentator: 'Good intentions not trans-lated into action are nothing to be proud of, but to express anti-Semitic views while the Jewish people are being exterminated, deserves unequivocal condemnation. Defending oneself against some-times far reaching accusations, one must not loose sight of the fact that ... our history of German occupation contains, together with some marvellous pages, also many dark ones' (Prekerowa, 1987).

Jewish children on the Aryan side

A special chapter of the Jewish saga during the German occupation of Poland is the fate of Jewish children whom some parents tried to save by sending them to the Aryan side to be sheltered in a Polish family – often against a monetary reward. The cost of hiding a Jewish child in the summer of 1942, when there was a massive attempt to send chil-dren out of the ghetto, amounted to 100 zlotys per day. Usually, a Pole willing to hide a Jewish child would demand six-months' payment in advance, because he feared that in the meantime the parents might be deported and he would not be paid. Some demanded a one-year advance payment. Understandably, only the very rich could afford it. There were cases when the Polish hosts, after having received a signif-icant amount of money, evicted the child into the street. In some extreme cases, the Polish hosts handed over the child to the Polish Police or to the Germans, who would send him or her back to the ghetto.

Emmanuel Ringelblum reports:

I know an eight-year-old boy who is hiding in a Polish family – friends of his parents. The child lives in constant fear of being discovered by neighbours or visitors. Very often he listens to anti-

Semitic remarks by young Poles who come to visit the daughters of the host. He once heard one of the visitors boasting that Hitler had taught the Poles how to handle Jews and that they would liquidate any Jew who survived the war. The child had to run to the kitchen in order to conceal his feelings. At present the boy is hidden in a small bunker, but is happy to be together with his parents.

Hiding children in Polish families sometimes had sad consequences after the war. In most cases, when the parents of a child perished, it was converted to Christianity, but even when a child was claimed by a surviving relative, the influence of Christian upbringing could still be detected.

I could see that all her attempts to show motherly love to the child remained without any visible response. The behaviour of the little girl seemed at times quite hostile. The full tragedy revealed itself a few moments later when the young mother tried to introduce her daughter to those sitting around the table.

'My darling,' she said to her, 'come here, meet my good friends'. The reaction of the little girl filled me with horror.

'You are not my mother,' the girl shouted in reply, 'you are a filthy Jewess. You are all filthy Jews!'

'They are not filthy Jews,' she said, 'they are my good friends. Say hello to them.'

It was to no avail. The girl turned away from us.

'Filthy Jews! Filthy Jews!', she repeated twice as if to make her point stronger.

(Author's recollections)

It was one of the many cases of survivors who in desperation, in order to save a child, left it in the care of a Polish family and who later had to endure the results of their influence upon the child.

A number of Jewish children were placed in Polish orphanages. However, according to Ringelblum, in other places, particularly in convents, the acceptance of only the very young – up to 6 years old – would indicate an intention to 'save souls' rather than to save the children. Such was the case in the Częstochowa convent (Ringelblum, 1985, p. 355).

Some members of the Catholic clergy organised shelter for Jewish children in Catholic institutions, but the results were rather poor. There were attempts to hide them in Polish homes for children, but they were abandoned for fear of denunciation by the personnel of these institutions. According to Ringelblum, the fear of Polish anti-Semites was greater than the fear of Germans. Ringelblum displayed his rather considerate attitude toward the Poles when he said: 'We put the blame for the death of innocent human beings who could have been saved, on the conscience of the Polish anti-Semites.'

In contrast to the above, according to Maria Kann, who was active in saving Jewish children, 'the help for Jewish children met with a favourable reaction and understanding by Polish society. Some churches issued birth certificates of prematurely dead children to Jewish children, which was far better than false documents. Children that could not be accommodated in private homes had been placed in orphanages and convents.' One of the most devoted to the task of saving Jewish children was Jadwiga Strzalecka (code-named 'Niunia'), who was the director of the orphanage in Sadyba near Warsaw. One-third of all children in the orphanage were of Jewish descent.

The Polish clergy

A more positive attitude of the Polish clergy toward Jews would have certainly saved many lives. There is evidence of humane behaviour of some members from the clergy. One example is the Catholic clergy in the Vilno region, where some priests offered shelter to Jewish fugitives of the Ponar massacre. A number of members of the Zionist movement Hashomer Hatzair found refuge in a nunnery in Vilna thanks to the intervention of Polish Catholic scouts. Ringelblum considers it a rare example of a Polish organisation helping a Jewish organisation (Gutman, 1994, p. 107).

There are other testimonies of noble action by Catholic priests in the region of Pieklo-Compinos, where the local priest tried to save Jewish camp inmates. The priest held several sermons in which he called the faithful to render assistance to the Jews. As a result of his appeals, there were many cases of local peasants helping the Jews. They threw bread over the fences. There were some priests who came to the rescue of Jews at the risk of their lives, especially at a later stage of the extermination. Some of them were known for their pre-war anti-Semitic views. Father Marceli Godlewski, for example, a former anti-Semite, was very active in saving Jews (*Materiały i studia*, 1973, p. 110).

Humane behaviour by Polish anti-Semites in saving Jews is not uncommon. The motivation for such benevolent acts is sometimes difficult to determine, but in most cases it was due to personal connections rather than for purely idealistic reasons.

A letter from Warsaw announced the visit of pani Maria O., the saviour of my cousins. She arrived a few days later. We sat down in the lounge to reminisce on those terrible times when my cousins were hiding on the false papers she had provided for them. After a while, the topic of the conversation began to revolve around Catholicism, which my cousins had to pretend to exercise while in hiding. When the conversation touched upon one particular incident in Radom during the Christian Easter, pani Maria expressed her belief that Jews were using Christian blood to bake the unleavened bread for Passover.

I could not believe my ears. How could an intelligent lady, educated in France, hold such outdated beliefs? And if she believed it, why did she save my cousins?

'Pani Maria,' I said, 'tell me, do you really believe that my cousins or myself, would do these things?'

'Oh no,' she answered without the slightest hesitation, 'I am not saying that every Jew would use Christian blood, but it has been proven that some do. If I knew that Pola or Leon did that, I would not have saved them.'

(Author's recollection)

Generally it can be said that saving Jews was a result of individual acts, rather than a collective effort. In many cases it was motivated by material interest and required a substantial amount of money. An illustration of the tragedy of some Jewish intellectuals, who could have been saved but for the lack of funds, is the fate of the well-known Jewish historian and former member of the Polish parliament, Dr Itzhak Schiper. He could not raise enough money to pay for a hiding place on the Aryan side and was deported.

Those who worked to save Jews did so without support from other Poles; indeed, they were forced to keep their activities secret from neighbours, friends and relatives. As the Germans could not distinguish between Jews and Poles in Poland, the fear experienced by Jews in hiding on the 'Aryan' side was a fear of Poles.

Żegota

Polish sources usually, and with good reason, emphasise with pride the activities of the so called 'Żegota' – an organisation established for the purpose of saving Jews. They stress the fact that Poland was the only country where such an organisation came into being and functioned until the last days of German occupation. (An organisation similar to Żegota aims was established in Belgium. It was named the Committee for the Defence of Jews.) They often emphasise the indifference of the world in the face of the extermination of Jews in Poland and contrast it with attempts by Żegota to save Jewish lives.' [The saviours] knew, as did the condemned Jews, that the world was indifferent.' As one of the co-founders of Żegota wrote: 'Anyone who remains silent is an accomplice; he who does not condemn, condones' (Tomaszewski and Werbowski, 1994, p. 13).

Initially, the organisation began its activities in Warsaw in August 1942 as a Provisional Committee named after Konrad Żegota. A possible catalyst to the formation of Żegota was the publication of a leaflet entitled *Protest* written in the same month by the well-known Polish writer Kossak-Szczucka. Its aim was to awaken the conscience of Poles to the fate of Jews, but its content was ambivalent to say the least. In fact Kossak-Szczucka has been known for her negative attitude toward Jews and this was clearly expressed in the article. It presented Jews in a stereotyped and negative way as unfriendly 'strangers', but at the same time called for Polish solidarity and 'love for thy neighbour'.

> We, Catholic Poles, are raising our voices. Our feelings toward the Jews have not changed. We do not cease to consider them as political, economic and ideological enemies of Poland. Even more, we realise that they hate us more than they hate the Germans, that they hold us responsible for their misfortune ... Such feelings do not absolve us from our duty to condemn crime. We do not want to be Pilates, but we have no possibility to actively counteract the German crimes. We protest from the depth of our hearts ... Who does not support our protest is not a Catholic.
>
> (Prekerowa 1992, p. 162)

In a similar vein, Kossak-Szczucka later expressed her position in an underground publication: 'it is not possible to like the Jews, it is possible to wish that they emigrate from Poland after the war, but as long as they are persecuted, they must be helped even at the risk of ones own life' (ibid., p. 163).

During a meeting of the delegates of various political groups, including the Catholic group FOP, and the Jewish National Committee in December 1942, the official establishment of the Rada Pomocy Żydom (RPZ – Council of Help for Jews), which acquired the code-name 'Żegota', took place. The act of establishment of Żegota, 'being an expression of the mood and attitude of Polish society toward the fate of the Jewish population', had been approved by the Delegatura and subsequently by the government in London. The Council consisted of representatives of a number of Polish organisations as well as two representives of the Jewish community. It is clear that the leadership of the Council consisted mostly of left-wing activists (PPR-WRN, Stronnictwo Ludowe) as well as a Dr Leon Fainer (Bund) and Dr Adolf Berman. Only one member of the AK, Henryk Wolinski, is mentioned.

Cooperation between the Delegatura and Żegota was effected by Witold Bienkowski and his deputy Władysław Bartoszewski, both of the FOP (Front Odrodzenia Polski – a Catholic organisation). According to Polish sources, the government-in-exile in London allocated a modest amount of money for the organisation (between 50,000 and 400,000 zlotys per month). More significant contributions came from Jewish organisations abroad. One Polish source asserts that 'it was much easier for American Jews to send money to western Europe ... a Committee for the Defence of Jews in Belgium could simply draw funds from Belgian banks' (Tomaszewski and Werbowski, 1994, p. 79).

During its early operations from the end of August until December 1942, the Committee took care of 180 persons of which about 70 per cent were children. It would be difficult to quantify the help Żegota provided for Jewish children. Some estimates put the number of Jewish children in the care of Żegota at about 2,500 (Arczynski and Balcerak, 1983, p. 119). After the collapse of the Warsaw ghetto uprising and until the Polish Warsaw uprising in 1944, RPZ rendered assistance in Warsaw alone to about 4,000 persons (Berenstein and Rutkowski, 1963, p. 71). Other activities of Żegota from the end of 1942 until the outbreak of the Polish Warsaw uprising in August 1944, include the supply of 50,000 false documents, of which 80 per cent were obtained by Jews.

According to Polish sources, it was to a great extent thanks to Żegota and its members, who provided help to the Jewish population, that many Jews survived the war on Polish territory. 'Under the conditions prevailing in Poland it was a lot; Żegota could rightly claim of having fulfilled its humane and patriotic obligation of saving ... Jews and providing assistance to its co-citizens.'

Beside material assistance, Żegota was also active in the propaganda field. The propaganda was mainly aimed at attracting the attention of the Polish population to the activities of the so-called 'szmalcowniks'. Polish historians claim that blackmail was a rare occurrence 'within the general atmosphere of patriotism and sacrifice. The practice of blackmail and extortion cannot be qualified as the expression of the attitude and views of the Polish society' (Arczynski and Balcerak, 1983, p. 96). However, Polish historians admit that even if blackmail was applied by relatively small number of individuals, it had tragic consequences. One individual could blackmail many Jews and Poles. By his action he also created the impression that there were many of them, thereby putting the burden of responsibility upon a much wider circle of Polish society. To counteract the activities of the blackmailers, Żegota claims to have published a number leaflets and posters in which it condemned such crimes and called for the stigmatisation of such individuals. Between December 1942 and October 1943, it published 3 leaflets of 25,000 copies each and distributed them among the Polish population. However, moral condemnation of blackmailers alone did not have the desired results – blackmail continued to ravage the Jews – and other measures became necessary. In view of the imperative to apply other means of combating this scourge, Żegota approached the Delegatura with a request to punish those engaged in blackmail and denunciation in order to reduce the constantly widening circle of such activities. It suggested capital punishment of such criminals. The Delegatura, while not opposing this suggestion, did not, however, display an eagerness to circumvent a lengthy judicial procedure before a sentence would be pronounced. It also refused to publish any death sentence already pronounced, which would have scared the blackmailers. It took the underground until 1943 to announce the death sentence specifically for crimes against Jews. Twelve Poles are said to have been executed soon after this proclamation, their names publicly announced.

One Polish historian admits that the leadership of Żegota considered the attitude of Polish society and the degree of its willingness to engage in saving Jews as the decisive factor. Attempts at helping Jews were hampered by an indigenous anti-Semitism fostered by the Germans.

> it must be remembered that some circles of Polish society entered the period of the war with a luggage of prejudices and anti-Semitic senti-ments ... In order to be able to render assistance to the Jews, ... it was indispensable not only to refute German propaganda, but also to effect a reduction in animosity and prejudices against the Jews ...
> (Arczynski and Balcerak, 1983, p. 197)

According to one Polish historian, the general animosity and preju-dice toward Jews sharply declined during the war. The Jews as the first object of persecution and extermination became partners in the adversity of co-citizens killed by a common enemy. 'The help rendered by Żegota ... he claims, contributed to the reinforcement of links between the Jews and the Polish society. It must be remembered that Żegota had in its ranks representatives of Jewish underground organisations, which was proof of the cooperation between the Polish and the Jewish underground' (ibid., p.198).

The theme of Polish solidarity with Jews in defence of Polish honour is prevalent in Polish society. Most Polish publications about the Holocaust, and particularly during the communist period, emphasise that:

> All democratic parties and political groups not only clearly isolated themselves from the anti-Jewish policy of the German authorities, but openly manifested their condemnation and called on Polish society to show solidarity with the persecuted and to help them ... Thanks to the help of the democratic resistance forces, and individual help of a segment of the Polish society, a large number of Jews were hiding on the 'Aryan' side.
>
> (Berenstein and Rutkowski, 1963, p. 56)

In support the above statement, one Polish source quotes a report by the Jewish organisation Bund sent to London in May 1942. The assertion about the attitude of the Polish left is probably correct, but in reality the 'democratic' forces were very weak and had practically no influence on Polish public opinion. The vast majority of Poles wholeheartedly supported German anti-Jewish policy as well as the position adopted by the Polish underground leadership.

The existence of Żegota is beyond doubt, but there are no independent sources which indicate the extent of the activities of Żegota and especially its achievements. We must therefore rely on the testimonies of its founders and some of its members. From the information at hand, it would appear that the results of the activities of Żegota were rather modest, but regardless of what it achieved, it was a most extraordinary attempt at helping Jews given the general anti-Jewish atmosphere.

According to one Polish source, the activities of Żegota enjoyed the support of a wide socio-political cross-section of Polish society, and were carried out in cooperation with the Jewish underground. 'It contributed to a large degree to saving the Jews by obstructing the German plan of the total extermination of Polish Jews.' Żegota, established and operating in the most difficult period of Nazi occupation, apart from rendering direct assistance to the Jews, also mobilised underground organisations, the underground authorities and all of Polish society by 'invoking the historical traditions of patriotism and humanism of our nation.' Żegota also tried unsuccessfully, according to the same source, to appeal to the conscience of the world. It was this apparent indifference that is used by Polish intellectuals as an argument in defence of Poland.

> Those who admonish the Poles and constantly accuse them of anti-Semitism, were not inclined to act, although their life was not at stake. They kept silent, but raised their voice after the war. Distorting facts, they began to accuse the Polish nation of anti-Semitism – a nation which with its two-thousand-year-old history, proved that anti-Semitism was never able to influence its feelings and deeds.
>
> (Arczynski and Balcerak, 1983, pp. 5–6)

Consequently, it is claimed, the help rendered to persecuted Jews was not an extraordinary event. 'During those terrible and critical moments of mortal danger, Jews saw the helping hands of Poles, while many other nations remained indifferent. In no other occupied European country had the Nazi terror been applied against those who tried to save Jews as in Poland. The Dutch, the Danes or the French could publicly demonstrate against the anti-Jewish repression without much risk.'

Żegota also claimed to be instrumental in raising the alarm in the western world through the intermediary of the Polish government in London. It sent many reports about the situation of the Jewish population in Poland. One of the emissaries, whose services were exploited by Żegota when it was established, was Jan Kozielewski, code-named Karski. In November 1942 he went to England as a courier with information about the situation in Poland. Before going to England, Karski visited the Warsaw ghetto and discussed the situation with leaders of the Jewish underground.

In their description of the activities of Żegota, Polish historians quite often make assertions that are clearly meant to embellish the noble actions of this organisation and at the same time widen its humane spirit to Poland as a whole.

> The material assistance provided by Żegota was an important factor of psychological support not only for those in hiding but also for those who provided them with a place to hide. They felt the backing of the nation ... The fact that on the day when the Polish Warsaw uprising erupted there were about 50,000 Jews in hiding, can be attributed to a great extent to the activities of Żegota.
>
> (ibid., p. 95)

There are only a few testimonies by survivors confirming the activities of Żegota; to most Żegota was unknown. It still is widely unknown today, despite several books written in Poland on the subject of Polish–Jewish relations during the war. Which is not really surprising given the conspiratorial nature of its activities. Its operations could only have been known to those whom Żegota actually helped. To spread the knowledge of its existence was tantamount to it being liquidated.

The testimonies of those who survived are the main sources of information on which we can base our assessment of the extent of activities of Żegota, but as one probes deeper into this subject, one realises the conditions under which this organisation functioned. It had to face not only the German terror, but to an even greater extent the constant menace of being uncovered and denounced by indigenous Poles. To assess the merits of the operation of Żegota based on numbers alone would not do justice to its achievements. The idea of forming such an organisation and the intentions behind it fully justify its recognition as 'Righteous among the Nations'.

What is also significant, is the attitude of Poles toward those who actually saved Jews during the war. There was a clear reluctance by the few courageous Poles to admit their good deeds for fear of being admonished by their friends or neighbours. In some cases Poles who saved Jews did not know at the time that they were hiding Jews, and expressed their feelings after the war when they found out the truth. Margolis-Edelman reports such a reaction:

> The Biglards ... We went to see them as soon as the war was finished. We had difficulties in finding their address. They lived on the fourth floor of a dilapidated building in Praga ... Mother wanted to thank them – it was after all thanks to them that I was alive. We rang the bell. It was Biglard who opened the door. He looked at me, he looked at mother – and he slammed the door.
>
> (Margolis-Edelman, 1997, p. 85)

Maria Hochberg-Marianska, in her book *Children Accuse*, writes: 'I wonder whether outside Poland it is possible to understand the fact that having saved an innocent child from the clutches of a murderer may be a cause of deep embarrassment, even infamy' (Smolar, 1987, p. 47).

There were instances when Poles who hid Jewish children were ostracised by other Poles for doing so. There was the case of a nun who was refused absolution by the priest after confessing that she hid Jewish children (Wilk, 1995, p. 21). Another case is that of Irena Sendler, a

Polish woman, who was a director of the Children's Department of Żegota. She is said to have participated in hiding about 2,500 Jewish children for which she was awarded in 1983 with the medal of the Righteous among the Nations of the World. In 1967 and 1969 she experienced discrimination when her two children could not pursue their music studies because of her involvement in Żegota. 'Mother, what have you done that we have to suffer for it?' they asked (ibid.).

The existence and activities of Żegota as well as the many cases of saving Jews, are very often used by Polish commentators as evidence of the ungratefulness of Jews. Criticism of Polish behaviour is considered as evidence of inherent anti-Polish sentiments among Jews.

However, the number of Jews denounced to the Germans due to personal interest or pure hatred, was so high that it erased in the minds of the survivors the sacrifices of all those Polish Christians who had the courage to act against the general current. It is indisputable that every Jew saved represents the participation of many honest individuals who risked their lives in a humanitarian act. 'Their memory [that of the righteous Poles] should be cherished for they were not only exposed to extreme danger from the Germans, but even more to the risk of being denounced by some from among their own people' (Cooper, 1987).

Part IV
Beyond the Great Catastrophe

9

The Last Blood Libel in Poland – Kielce 1946

> therefore I have said to the people of Israel, You
> shall not eat the blood of any creature, for the life of
> every creature is its blood; whoever eats it shall be
> cut off ... (Leviticus 16:14)

> So Jesus said to them, 'Truly, truly I say to you, unless you
> eat the flesh of the Son of man and drink his blood, you
> have no life in you; he who eats my flesh and drinks my
> blood has eternal life, and I will raise him up at the last
> day ... ' (John 6:54)

With the approaching end of the war and the liberation of territories bordering the USSR, the political future of neighbouring countries became an important issue for the Soviet Union. At the end of 1943 Stalin still claimed to support the principle of granting 'to the liberated peoples of Europe, full rights of freedom to decide for themselves the question of the system of their governments' (Stalin, 1967, p. 125). He insisted, however, that the security of the Soviet Union required that it be surrounded by regimes that are not hostile to it. Regarding Poland, he demanded 'a government which will pursue a friendly policy toward the Soviet Union and not one of a "cordon sanitaire" against the USSR' (ibid., p. 201).

The American position was to preserve the United States' economic interests in Eastern Europe. Although they did accept Soviet special interests in border areas, they perceived the understanding reached in Yalta regarding the organisation of eastern Europe, as leading to western-type democracies, and demanded the inclusion of representatives of democratic elements and the holding of free elections (Alperowitz, 1966, p. 148).

While the political future of Poland was being debated among the allies, the Polish underground in Poland resorted to many acts of hostility toward the advancing Red Army aimed at preventing the installation of a communist-dominated government. The underground also fiercely objected to the formation of the so-called People's Democratic Government and to the first official document, the *Manifesto of the Polish Committee of National Liberation* published on 20 July 1944 in Lublin. The document stated, among other principles, 'that the Jews who were murdered by the occupant in a barbaric way, will have the restoration of their existence and their legal and real emancipation guaranteed by law' (Rudavski, 1986).

This was considered by the Polish population at large as evidence that Jews were communists. Reacting to the Manifesto, the Polish underground and particularly the priests began to warn the Polish population of the Jewish and communist menace threatening the nation.

The resistance against the new regime consisted mainly of the remnants of the National Armed Forces (NSZ), former members of the Home Army (AK) and various nationalist elements directed by the politicians in exile in London. With the imminent collapse of Nazi Germany, the Polish underground consolidated all its efforts against the communists and the Jews. In December 1944, as the Red army advanced on all fronts and was about to enter the town of Pabianice, the local priest addressed the congregation:

> My dear brothers! It is my duty, especially today, to warn you of the imminent disaster that we all face. I have been informed by the Germans that a great Russian offensive is imminent. If this were true, we can expect very soon to be under the rule of the Jewish communists who were always the enemies of the Church. As our dear cardinal said at the time, Jewish influence is immoral ... This is why, my dear Polish brothers, if you should meet a Jew, take revenge as long as there is time. Tomorrow might be too late. The Jews and the Russians are coming!'
>
> (Marc, 1985, p. 17)

In addition to the fear of the communists, the bulk of the Polish population, particularly in the villages and small towns, feared the return of the Jewish owners of houses or apartments. Numerous testimonies of survivors who attempted to reclaim their possessions confirm the hostility of the Poles towards the survivors.

After the liberation of Auschwitz, I began the search for my family. I went to Jędrzejow, a small town near Kielce, where I was born and raised, to see whether I could recover some of my parent's and grandparent's properties. As I entered the house that belonged to my grandfather, I immediately noticed the familiar furniture, the table and the chair on which grandfather used to sit; every inanimate object was in its proper place except for the living who were no longer there.

As soon as I identified myself, I noticed that they adopted a hostile attitude. While I spoke to them they alerted their neighbours, who soon surrounded the house. 'Kill the Jew!', I could hear them shouting. I managed to escape by jumping into the backyard through the window. They gave chase but could not catch up with me … Many like me, who returned to their towns and villages, were not as lucky as I was; they finished up as dead bodies in the cemetery.

(Marc, 1985, p. 91)

Elinor Brecher, who interviewed inmates of Schindler's camp (known from the film *Schindler's List*), quotes testimonies of survivors who attempted to return to their towns.

Henry Slamowicz: 'I came to the place where I had lived, the hello was: "are you still alive? what are you doing here?" They didn't even tell me, "come on, have a glass of water." Even the people who knew us! I was there maybe ten days, then one night, they surrounded the house with a gun [and] they start[ed] killing us' (Brecher, 1994, p. 352).

Sam and Edith Wertheim report: 'I said I would not stay in Poland one more day. Hate was not even the word I had for them. My mother and brother were shot because of one Pole who pointed out where they were hiding, in Skala, in a stable and covered with hay … There were some very few Poles who saved Jews, but most were very anti-Semitic and were happy what happened to us' (ibid., p. 388).

Henry Wiener and Abush Reich decided to go to Cracow: 'There I found out nobody from my family was alive, but they told me Sally was alive! … Henry went to find Sally, and Abush went to a farmer who'd kept some of his family's belongings. The farmer, says Henry Wiener, hacked Abush Reich to death with an axe. Reich was twenty-three years old. I felt horrible. After all that we suffered together. This was our first encounter in Poland'. (ibid., p. 401)

There were very few exceptions. After the liberation Maurice Markheim went straight to Cracow: 'I went to our house. The housekeeper was still there. She couldn't believe it. She almost fainted. She said, "You're my son! You're not going nowhere. You're gonna live with me. I'll give you everything" ... Her name was Jednejowa Bartyzel' (ibid., p. 321).

The murder of six million Jews by the Nazis in Poland with the active assistance of their Polish collaborators, did not signify an end to the persecution of the few surviving Jews in Poland after the end of the war. Murder was perpetrated on survivors who returned from the death camps, from the forests, from Russia, as well as on Jewish soldiers returning from the fronts. Jews were killed individually as well as in groups when taken off buses and trains, and inside their apartments. During the years immediately following the end of the war, Jews could not show themselves in many places at the risk of their lives (Rudavski, 1986).

Early in 1946, convoys of Jews repatriated from the Soviet Union began to arrive. One convoy was attacked after passing the Soviet–Polish border and seven Jews were killed including a 4-year-old girl. In most cases there was cooperation between the attackers and the train conductor, who slowed down at a predetermined spot (Tenenbaum, 1948).

The murder of individual Jews who returned to their places of birth continued through the rest of 1945 and well into 1946. Between February and September 1945, 85 Jews were murdered in the district of Kielce, 75 in the district of Warsaw, 165 in the area of Lublin, 41 in Białystok, 37 in Rzeszow, 29 in Lodz and 14 in Cracow. It was estimated at the time that from the liberation of Poland until May 1946 more than 1,000 Jews were assassinated (Marc, 1985, p. 135).

Nowy Targ, a small town not far from Cracow where 40 Jews found a place to live after the war, became the scene of mass murder of survivors. The first to be murdered in April 1946 was a certain David Grassgrun. Found on his desk was a message scribbled on a piece of paper: 'David Grassgrun and other Jews, your country is Palestine. Leave while you still have time. We are ready to kill you all.' Of the 40 Jews living at the time in Nowy Targ, 21 left town during the night leaving all their belongings behind. For five young men it was too late. Their bodies were found on the road leading to Nowy Targ. They all shot at close range and two showed signs of being tortured. Every Jew with the exception of a certain Ludwig Herz left Nowy Targ. 'I will not be leaving as long as there is one single Jew to defend himself', he

said. He never did. He was murdered a few weeks later.
In Sosnowice, Silesia, a Jewish doctor was shot dead in his surgery.
The murderer had called and asked to see the doctor. When he was
admitted he fired at him and escaped. He left a paper saying that the
'death sentence' had been carried out by order of the Nationalists.
Some Jews made an attempt to escape from Poland, sometimes with
disastrous results. On 14 April 1946, 18 young men took a bus that
would take them closer to the border with Czechoslovakia. On the
road between Krościenko and Nowy Sącz the bus was stopped by men
in Polish uniforms. They gave an order for the Jews to leave the bus and
the execution began. The attack resulted in 11 dead and 7 wounded.
A train between Nowy Sącz and Cracow was stopped by men in
uniforms on 12 June 1946. After checking the identities of the passengers they shot 5 Jews. The train continued to the station of Zaretta where
the 5 bodies were unloaded onto the platform.
Isaac Sternberg was lucky to be alive after an attack on a bus in
which he was travelling.

I went to Piaski by bus. We were about thirty passengers. A few kilometres past Lublin, the bus was stopped by a gang of men the
commander of whom wore a uniform of the Polish army. Two Jews
were forced off the bus and shot on the spot in full view of the
passengers. I did not look Jewish and that saved me.

(Marc, 1985, p. 247)

Incidents such as these, and murders on a scale not seen since the
Nazis were defeated, were occurring in Poland with increasing
frequency. As a result, every Jew felt threatened by the activities of the
former Polish resistance. The constant danger of being attacked forced
most survivors to retain Polish identities acquired in hiding during the
war. Even those who returned from the Soviet Union forged their
identity documents to change to a Polish-sounding name.

When I showed my repatriation documents to my cousin who
survived on Aryan papers, he was horrified. 'With such a name you
are a dead man if you are caught on a train by the underground!'
He immediately managed to erase my name and to change it to
Leon Miedzinski the son of Kazimierz and Jadwiga.
   A few weeks later, while travelling by train to Warsaw, I and two
other young men were arrested by the Polish military police and
taken to the local army headquarters. It appeared that being of

military-service age, we were supposed to register with the appropriate authorities. In the course of a personal search, my identity document showing a Jewish name was found. This in itself did not present any particular problem – I together with my two Polish companions were released after an intensive interrogation – but the fact that my Jewish identity became known to them, placed me in an awkward position.

Although they turned out to be very friendly and did not make any reference to my Jewish identity, my thoughts were busy with the question whether I could trust my companions who knew that I was Jewish. What would happen if the train was ambushed by the soldiers of the underground? How could I be certain that they would not denounce me? I was now searching for a way of getting rid of them.

When we boarded the train I took the seat closest to the door. A loud whistle and the sound of closing doors announced the departure of the train. At this moment I took a decision. I stood up pretending to look out, but as soon as train started to move, I quickly opened the door, grabbed my suitcase and jumped off the moving train. A few minutes later I was again sitting on the platform and waiting for the next train to arrive. I was relieved.

(Author's recollections)

Jewish men and women were not the only target of Polish anti-Semitism. Equally tragic was the plight of Jewish children who survived the Holocaust hidden among Polish families. Although in the vast majority of cases it was done against monetary reward, there were nevertheless some Christians who for purely humanitarian motives saved a number of children. It was the task of the Jewish Committee, immediately after the war, to find as many children as possible in order to reunite them with the surviving members of their families or with relatives abroad.

Prior to their departure from Poland the children were kept in camps organised and supported by the Jewish Committee. One such camp was located in Rabka, a small town south of Cracow. It was transformed into a sanatorium for the rehabilitation of sick children. In early September 1945 it was attacked in the middle of the night. Several grenades were thrown at the building. The Rabka camp was evacuated soon after.

A few weeks later it was the turn of the Jewish orphanage in Zakopane in the Polish Tatra mountains. Letters began arriving almost daily calling for the orphanage to be removed. 'Jews! you poison the atmosphere of Zakopane! Leave as soon as you can otherwise we will burn you down!' It became clear to the management of the orphanage that the lives of the children was in danger. A decision was taken to transfer all the children across the border into Czechoslovakia, but not before another attack on the orphanage took place. During one dark night, all the children and their supervisors crossed the border.

There was little official information about the true state of affairs in Poland, and the extent of involvement in these activities by the Polish resistance and the population at large was unknown. The Polish government press did not report any particular incidents in which Jewish lives were lost; they were classified as acts of fascist opposition. It was the pogrom in the town of Kielce with all its cruelty that revealed the tragic situation of the remnants of the Holocaust in Poland.

The Blood Libel

During the closing days of the war, another factor in the anti-Jewish campaign – one reminiscent of the history of the Middle Ages – appeared in Poland. Jews, in addition to being branded traitors, communists and being accused of other crimes, had now become perpetrators of ritual murder.

The history of the 'ritual murder' slur is as ancient as the history of the Jews. The first mention of it can be found in the writings of the historian Josephus Flavius (first century AD), who attributed to Apion the charge that Jews sacrifice a Greek every year to symbolise the Temple service. It was many centuries later, however, that the blood libel began to be used to stir up the masses against the Jews. In the Christian world, the original charge was that at Easter the Jews martyred a young boy in mockery of the Passion of Jesus. An elaboration was later added that the blood was used in the preparation of the unleavened bread or in the Passover night rites.

Because Poland was relatively late in adopting Christianity, the occurrence of blood libels came also much later than in western Europe. The first recorded case goes back to 1399 in the town of Posen and in Cracow in 1407. The Polish king, Stephen Batory (1576–86) sharply attacked blood-libel accusations, and his successor Sigismund III protected Jews from Church – especially Jesuit – persecution. Ritual-murder charges recurred in the seventeenth century and were particularly prevalent under the Saxon kings (1697–1763), when a series of trials took place. After Poland regained her independence in

1918, ritual-murder accusations occurred from time to time. They were raised in 1926 in Dobrzyn after a dead child was found in the Jewish cemetery. Subsequently it was established that the child was beaten to death by his father. As a result of the accusation, Jewish shops were looted (*The Jewish Chronicle*, 18 Nov. 1927).

In 1928, the disappearance of a Christian Pole who was employed by a Jew at Pluk near the town of Siedlce, led to a blood-libel outcry in the village. The local priest and teachers convened a meeting in the course of which eye witnesses testified that the missing man had been sold by his employer, Dvosh, for 20 zlotys in order to extract blood for Passover. Needless to say the missing Pole was found alive and well (*The Jewish Chronicle*, 12 April 1928).

At Nowowileika a woman servant disappeared. A Polish mob attacked the house of a man named Grinberg when a few witnesses stated that they saw Grinberg killing the servant. In the midst of the attack she appeareds safe and well (*The Jewish Chronicle*, 11 April 1928).

Ritual-murder accusations were especially prevalent prior to or during Jewish Passover.

> If some Jews forget that Passover is approaching, they are promptly reminded by the Christians who seem always to remember the season for the revival of the ritual libel. A copy of a Catholic journal, *Echo parafialne*, was produced in the Polish parliament by the Jewish member Grunbaum. It published a document dated 1712 describing in detail the preparation for, and the execution of the ritual murder with an illustration of how captured Christian boys get fattened during a period of forty days preceding Passover. The journal also reported that in Lithuania alone thirty jars of Christian blood were used each Passover.
>
> (*The Jewish Chronicle*, 1 March 1929)

Trzeciak, a well-known Catholic priest, said during a public speech that 'in Ostrołęka [a small town in Poland] there lies the dead body of a Christian child murdered by the Jews for ritual purposes'. The speech was widely reported in the Polish press in November 1936.

Ritual-murder charges resurfaced in Poland after the end of the war. As early as 1945, the ritual-murder slander had been spreading among the Poles like wildfire, and was giving rise to grave fears among the Jewish population in many towns. Generally, the Church declined to denounce the baseless charges against Jews. An exception was Bishop Kubiny of Czestochowa, who was prevailed upon to issue an appeal in which he denounced the ritual murder charges as untrue.

In August 1945, leaflets began to appear on the streets of Cracow near the Jewish synagogue: 'The Jews are our eternal enemies. They kill our children in their synagogue.' Acting on such rumours, thousands of Christian Poles launched an organised attack against Jews. A mob attacked the synagogue on Miodowa street during the Sabbath service. Liba Zindel, who returned to Cracow from a Nazi camp, described the attack on the synagogue on that Sabbath in August 1945:

> They were shouting that we had committed ritual murders. They began firing at us and beating us up. My husband was sitting beside me. He fell down, his face full of bullets. The synagogue was set on fire and the Holy scrolls desecrated in front of the synagogue in a fashion reminiscent of Nazi practices.
>
> (*Polska zbrojna*, 12 Aug. 1945)

The crowd also broke into several apartments and attacked the occupants. In the process, a Jewish woman was killed, as was an unidentified man who was found with his head smashed in. The number of victims is not known for it was never officially reported. During the first seven months after the end of the war there were 350 anti-Semitic murders on Poland. The British ambassador in Warsaw reported that anyone in Poland with a Jewish appearance was in danger (Johnson, 1988, p. 513).

The Kielce pogrom

If there is a black day in Polish history it would be 4 July 1946. For on this day, long after the Nazi crematoria had ceased to smoke, the Polish nation expressed its determination to continue the Nazi task of exterminating the Jewish people. It was the culmination of vicious anti-Jewish acts of violence perpetrated by many Poles against the remnants of the Jewish community in Poland.

Before the war Kielce had a Jewish population of 27,000. Only 200 had returned to the city after the war. Some came back from the Soviet Union; a few were survivors of Auschwitz. The majority lived in a two-storey building at no. 7 Planty Street – allocated by the Polish authorities to those who were unable to recover their former apartments from the Poles. In the same building were located the offices of the Jewish Committee, of the Jewish religious congregation, a communal kitchen and a kibbutz of some 35 young Jews who were preparing themselves to go to Palestine. On the day of the pogrom there were about 200 men, women and children within the building. As early as April 1946 it was felt that something was brewing. It was common knowledge that pogroms had taken place in some of the surrounding towns and that a number of Jews had been murdered. The chairman of the Jewish Committee, doctor Severyn Kahane, himself a survivor and a former fighter in a partisan unit operating in the Kielce region during the war, intervened on several occasions with the Polish security forces regarding the menacing situation in Kielce.

There were good reasons to be apprehensive. In December 1945, a grenade attack on the building resulted in three people being slightly injured and some property damage. It created an atmosphere of fear which prompted a member of the Committee, Yechiel Halpert, to ask the police for protection. An officer at the police station said he could not help, but suggested they approach the priest of the diocese, Monsignori Kaczmarek, who had great influence over the Christian population. After some difficulties, Halpert, accompanied by his friend Eisenberg, were received by Kaczmarek, who did not show any willingness to intervene with his flock, but instead continued his long diatribe against the Jews.

About six weeks before the Kielce pogrom, a Jewish delegation headed by Rabbi David Kahane and Professor Michael Ringelblum, went to see Cardinal Hlond in order to make him aware of the dangerous situation of Jews in Poland. A memorandum handed over to the Cardinal warned the head of the Polish Church about the consequences of the Church's silence in this matter. Cardinal Hlond returned the memorandum through his secretary and refused to see the delegates.

The celebration of the 170th anniversary of the Declaration of American Independence in Warsaw on 4 July 1946 was in full swing. Diplomats, journalists and politicians of many western and east-European countries were assembled at the reception given by the American ambassador in Hotel Polonia – the only one remaining intact in Warsaw after the war. It was during the reception that news of a massacre of Jews in Kielce began to circulate amongst the invited guests. Questioned by some journalists, the Polish authorities attempted to minimise the extent of the tragedy, while the evening newspapers did not mention it at all. Slowly the truth started to filter through from eyewitness accounts and from some foreign journalists who managed to get into Kielce during the following few days. A correspondent of the London *Jewish Chronicle* who went to Kielce to investigate reported:

I am writing in Kielce. Today the city is quiet, and were it not for the armed guards at every corner you would not think that anything was amiss in this town of 50,000 inhabitants. People going about their daily business seem to be completely unaware that barely 300 yards from this hotel lie the bodies of 36 Jews and Jewesses murdered yesterday in the biggest and most savage pogrom that has taken place in liberated Poland.

... In the mortuary I saw today 36 terribly mutilated bodies, with battered faces, crushed bones, broken legs, and limbs almost torn off. It is hard to believe that such injuries could have been caused except by a shell or a bomb. But they were human hands – if indeed, one could call them such – that perpetrated these horrors, hands of Poles who but a short while ago were themselves the victims of German brutality. Today, they carry on the work of their former enemy.

On top of the pile of twisted misshapen bodies lay that of a tiny baby, born dead after its mother, whom I saw lying in the hospital, had been kicked in the abdomen and wounded in the head and face. The dead were being laid out in rows and identification tabs put on them.

(*The Jewish Chronicle*, 12 July 1946)

Subsequent reports from the police and eyewitnesses allow one to reconstruct the train of events leading to and during the pogrom. The pogrom began at about 9 a.m. on Thursday, 4 July. The previous Monday, a 9-year-old Christian boy named Henryk Blaszczyk, the son of a local labourer, disappeared from home. The boy came back on Wednesday night. Asked where he had been, he said that he 'had been kidnapped by Jews, kept in a cellar where he saw about 15 other Christian children already murdered'.

According to the police, the father and son went to the police station, where the boy repeated his story. When asked to tell where he had been held he said that it was the house of the Jewish Committee at no. 7 Planty Street. The police, acting on the boy's accusations, took him to the office of the Jewish Committee located in that building and asked him to point out 'which Jew' had detained him. The boy pointed to a well-known Jew who happened to be in the office with many others. The police at once took him to the police station. In the meantime, crowds began to gather around the Jewish Communal building. The arrest convinced the people outside that the Jews had done something wrong and served further to incense the crowd, which seemed to grow by the minute. The building was also surrounded by members of the local police, but it was obvious that the police instead of calming the mob, incited them to violence.

Doctor Severyn Kahane, the head of the Jewish community, sensing a blood-libel incident and the danger that this posed to the occupants of the building, tried to contact the bishop. He only got through to his secretary. Kahane then tried to get Security. They told him that the security forces were exhausted by a night operation against the 'guys in the forest' (a popular name for the Polish resistance to the Soviets). Doctor Kahane then telephoned the Vice-Governor (the Governor was ill) for protection. The Vice-Governor got in touch with the militia and a force of several hundred was sent to the scene. In the meantime, a few policemen followed by some civilians from the crowd burst into the building searching for the basement where, according to the boy's account, he had been kept. The house had no basement. After checking the premises the policemen left. By this time a hail of stones and rocks hit the windows shattering the glass. The front door was pushed open by the pressure of the crowd and the mob invaded the building. They dragged out a number of people and killed them. Some of the victims were thrown out of the windows on the heads of the crowd and were killed on the square.

A unit of the internal security forces, sent to the scene of the pogrom, did not change the situation. Told earlier that Jews were killing Christian children, they soon became part of the mob. Soldiers armed with automatic weapons ran up the stairs and began breaking down doors and shooting at the people inside. The first to be shot at point blank was doctor Kahane. Meanwhile agitators appeared on the scene, and told the crowd that the Jews had 'killed 15 Christian children' and that it was high time 'to finish off' all the Jews.

The carnage was only stopped at five in the afternoon when a large army unit arrived from Warsaw. But even later, while the wounded were taken to hospital, the open wagons in which they were transported became the target for stone throwers. Some estimates put the number of Poles who participated in the pogrom at 25,000 out of the town's 50,000 inhabitants – about half of the population. The pogrom resulted in 42 deaths and over 80 injured.

The wounded, some of whom died later, were taken to the local hospital. Many had face and head wounds. Their account of the pogrom was at times even more terrifying than what was reported in the press. One of the girls, Neta Fishel, bearing the concentration camp number 53625 on her arm, said that she was more terrified during the pogrom than she ever was in the camp, and she had spent three years in Auschwitz.

> I was in Auschwitz and witnessed the extermination of thousands of Jews in the gas chambers, but the cruelty of the Polish mob killing Jews, defies any description. The victims were beaten with spades and iron bars, cut with knives and left to die a slow and painful death.

A British correspondent who visited the scene of the pogrom described what he saw:

> Today, there were still signs of the pools of the victims' blood on the square ... I also saw some of the bloodstained bricks with which the Jews were battered to death by the mob, and a radiator pipe thickly covered with blood which had obviously been used as a weapon in the pogrom. A few pieces of torn clothing, smeared with blood, some letters and papers belonging to the victims, some pictures, all bloodstained, provided for the gruesome evidence of the butchery that had taken place.
>
> (*The Jewish Chronicle*, 12 July 1946)

Not all the Jews in the building were killed. The soldiers did eventually manage to reach the building and save 35, who were taken to the police station for protective custody.

While the carnage was taking place on Planty Street, other parts of the town and its area were the scene of more murders. Two uniformed policemen, Mazur and Nowakowski, dragged Regina Fish and her three-weeks-old baby out of her house on 15 Leonard street, then took them to a nearby forest and shot them.

Jews were hunted down from trains arriving at Kielce and executed. At the station of Piekuszow, 7 Jews were murdered, including a 70-year-old woman who had just returned from Russia. She was dragged from the train and stoned to death. Rumours flew from station to station, with the result that Jews were set upon wherever they were found. The railway guards, it was alleged, frequently took part in the pogroms. The real number of victims of the Kielce pogrom and in the surrounding district was never made public.

The victims were buried with military honours on 8 July at a public funeral which was attended by several thousand Poles. Representatives of the government, the Central Jewish Committee and foreign press were present. At the funeral, doctor Berman tried to express his feelings when he said: 'we are not accusing the whole Polish nation for this horrible crime'. The army Rabbi Colonel Kahane was more outspoken: 'It is the duty of the Polish clergy to put an end to the anti-Semitic agitation in this country.' While the caskets with the bodies of the victims were lowered into the ground, a Polish professor, Gorecki, an elderly, grey-haired man, expressed his sorrow and regret about what took place in liberated Poland. He cried out: 'Polish Christians, our hands are stained with the blood of innocent Jews. We are all responsible for this crime. Never, never must we forget. The burden of this crime will weigh forever on our conscience' (Marc, 1985, p. 302).

In the aftermath of the pogrom the world press reported on these events. The *New York Times* commented: 'anyone who visited the town of Kielce after the pogrom will search in vain for an expression of regret or shame on the faces of the population. With the exception of official posters, there was not a person who expressed any regret about the massacre.'

The trial

The trial opened on 11 July before the Supreme Military Tribunal, which was especially sent from Warsaw. 12 Poles, among them one woman, were charged with the murder of Jews during the pogrom. In addition to the 12 facing trial, 120 officers had been arrested, including a number of agitators who spread the ritual-murder rumours.

The speed with which the government proceeded with the trial was, to a certain degree, motivated by the fear of western reaction. The image of Poles as a martyr nation took a severe knock.

On the table in the courtroom were displayed evidence of the massacre: blood-stained axes, stones, iron bars as well as the blood-soaked clothes of the victims, but the full horror of the event came into the open during the questioning of the accused. Antonina Biskupska, a young woman of 26 and mother of a 4-year-old child, admitted having marched in front of the crowd and shouted 'death to the Jews'. She also admitted inciting the crowd to kill Jews and throwing stones into the building. In a trembling voice she confirmed the facts as disclosed in the indictment. When she heard that Jews were killing Christian children she could not retain her emotions and joined the mob.

Edward Jurkowski, 40 years old, a cultured man, a member of the Kielce symphony orchestra, admitted to conducting the mob as if it were an orchestra. 'Let us go and kill the murderers of our children!' he shouted at the time. He claimed that he was drunk.

Julian Pokrzywinski looked at a blood-stained shirt and told the court how he had stamped on the belly of a woman thrown out of the window while she was lying in a pool of blood. He added a few more details: 'I must have been seized by an attack of madness. Actually, I don't hate the Jews. But I thought that they were no longer in Poland, that the Germans had finished them off once and for all. Then I saw them all coming back, I don't know where from. This is why I and other Poles became terribly angry.'

Stefan Mazur, a policeman, who thought he was accomplishing his patriotic duty by killing a few Jews, was more contemptuous than the other accused. He acted as if he were facing a simulated trial that would end soon. Perhaps he had hoped that the 'guys from the resistance' would come to his rescue. The judge questioned him on the murder of Mrs Fish and her three-week-old child: 'And the child? Why did you kill the child?'

'I killed the mother. I could not have left the child by itself.'

Nowakowski and Śliwa, the other accused in the murder of Mrs Fish, were as defiant in their attitudes: 'Yes, we do recognise the facts. But after all, she was only Jewish.'

Then came the turn for the defence to present its case. Chmielewski, the attorney for the defence, argued that 'the accused went to Planty Street to see if Polish children were kept there and whether a murder had been committed. The people who went to Planty Street had acted out of their paternal instinct to protect their children. This reaction of self-defence must be taken into consideration by the tribunal.'

While waiting for the verdict, a crowd of Poles began to form in front of the court-house. There was an atmosphere of tension in town. A leaflet began to circulate promising the death of 100 Jews for each Pole condemned to die. 'The Polish nation will never accept the death of Polish patriots because of Jews.'

In his closing speech, the prosecutor said that there were still people in Poland with Nazi ideas. The Kielce criminals had committed a worse crime than the Nazis. A handful of Jews who had escaped from the German hell had returned to their native town. Among them were officers and men of the Polish Army who had fought bravely against the Germans. This argument found little sympathy among the Poles. The problem here was that Poles as a nation did not consider the Polish Army in the USSR as fighting the Germans but assisting the Soviets in conquering Poland.

The tribunal, after a short session, rejected most of the arguments presented by the defence. Nine of the 12 Poles, including one woman, were sentenced to death. An appeal for clemency was rejected by President Bierut, and the 9 condemned men were executed by firing squad.

A sequel to this terrible pogrom was the arrest, on the orders of the Minister of Public Security, of the Commandant of the Security Police, Sobczynski, and the Military Commander, Lieutenant-Colonel Kuzminski, for 'failing to act energetically in subduing the riots'. They, together with 40 others, were tried for neglect of duty, and also alleged to have been involved in the pogrom (*The Jewish Chronicle*, 19 July 1946).

The Church

The only authority that refrained from commenting on this terrible event was the Catholic Church. A letter read in Churches after the pogrom failed to condemn the violence; it expressed its position in such terms as to obscure the real issue, which was Polish anti-Semitism. The Archbishop of Kielce, Karczmarek, who refused to do anything that could have prevented the pogrom, and refused to answer the calls for help by doctor Kahane when the mob surrounded the house where the pogrom took place, also refused to condemn it when it was over.

The American ambassador, shocked by the events, asked the Cardinal to issue a statement to the press. To no avail. The church remained silent all over Poland. Finally, on Sunday 7 July a letter was read in the church in Kielce:

> On 4 July our town became the theatre of a terrible tragedy due to a coincidence of various events. Given the fact that the immediate causes of this sad event are not known it must be deplored that it took place in the presence of children. The diocese asks the Catholic population to preserve the peace.

The swiftness with which the Polish authorities brought the accused to trial and the execution of the sentences set the Catholic Church a severe test. As a 'state within a state' it had to take a position from a Christian point of view, but at the same time was reluctant to express herself in a way that went against the sentiments of the majority of the Polish nation. It adopted complete silence. *Tygodnik powszechny*, the organ of Cardinal Sapieha of Cracow, and other Polish Catholic papers, refrained from even mentioning the pogrom.

Great disappointment was felt by the Jews when the Pastoral Letter sent by Polish Bishops to be read in all churches failed to condemn the murder of Jews in Poland. The letter was issued after a meeting of Poland's two cardinals and some 30 archbishops and bishops in Częstochowa. It spoke of 'violence and crime' and appeals for their cessation, but omitted any reference to Jews being murdered by Poles.

The Catholic Church was approached several times by Jewish leaders, who appealed to them to add their voices to the condemnation of anti-Jewish crimes. It was felt that had the Church taken a stand against the terrorists, the government's task would have been much easier. The silence of the Church was actually interpreted by the terrorists as, if not exactly support, at least tolerance of their action. In fact, the nationalists were considered by the Church and the wider public to be heroes fighting the Jews and the 'godless' communists. Killing Jews was not a crime but an act of Polish resistance.

As to the question of the blood hysteria that led to the pogrom, the Archbishop of Lublin, Wyszynski, who became Cardinal after Hlond's death, had this to say: 'During the trial of Beiliss [in tsarist Russia] many Jewish Scriptures were submitted to deny the practice of using Christian blood for ritual purposes, but there was no proof that it wasn't practiced.'

Numerous appeals to Catholic authorities by the leaders of the Jewish community in Poland remained without response, with the sole exception of Kubina, the Archbishop of Częstochowa, who had the courage to condemn not only the violence but the accusations of ritual murder.

There were attempts in the United States to obtain a statement in this matter from the Pope. The American Jewish Committee sent a letter to President Truman urging him to ask his representative at the Vatican, Myron Taylor, to appeal to the Pope to issue a statement to Polish Catholics condemning anti-Semitism. The Pope expressed his position in an article published in *Ari,* the official organ of the Vatican: 'The anti-Jewish incidents in Poland were a result of political passions provoked by the measures adopted by the "Jewish authorities". The attacks against the Jews cannot be seen from the point of view of racism, as the Polish government tries to imply' (*The Jewish Chronicle*, 19 July 1946).

The great exodus

In the final analysis, what the Germans did not achieve, making the city of Kielce *Judenrein* – (free of Jews) the Polish population succeeded in doing within a few days. Those who survived the assault on the building at Planty Street no longer trusted government protection and began secretly to leave town. Trucks provided by the government for the evacuation of Jews from Kielce to more secure locations in Warsaw and other larger cities left almost empty. Some of the injured were taken by special train to a hospital in the city of Lodz. At the end of July, the Jewish Committee in Kielce was dissolved and its three remaining members, like the crew of a sinking ship, left for Warsaw.

It was the last nail in the coffin, the beginning of the end of Jewish presence in Poland. Those who were still hesitating and postponing the decision to leave Poland, suddenly felt the ground burning under their feet, and even those who lived with the hope of rebuilding a Jewish existence in Poland, were overcome with despair. After the pogrom, most came to the conclusion that Poland had become a country in which there was no future for Jews (Rudavski, 1986).

Faced with increasing evidence of Polish hatred of Jews, the government abandoned its policy of providing protection for the Jewish population. The government came to the conclusion that it could not eradicate the anti-Semitic animosity of the people of Poland, and that protection of the survivors would be politically counter-productive for a regime that wanted to consolidate its power. It chose the easiest way to overcome its dilemma by giving its approval for the mass emigration of the remnants of the Jewish population. It issued directives to the Polish border guards to facilitate the departure of the thousands of Jews who began to flee Poland. But the Poles were not content with the fact that they are getting rid of Jews. Those fleeing Poland were still the subject of attacks and murder.

One particular murder took place on a farm established by the Zionists for young Jews, survivors of the camps, near the town of Zabrze. Young boys and girls were trained in agricultural work in anticipation of departure for Palestine and a kibbutz. The farm was well known in the region for its activities and drew a large crowd of visitors, usually for the Friday evening Sabbath celebration. It was during one of those evenings, while the crowd of members and guests were singing and dancing, that a bullet shot by someone outside the window struck Bluma Wajn, a young girl, the sole survivor of her family. A few minutes later she was dead.

In the aftermath of the Kielce pogrom the exodus of Polish Jews took the form of a mass escape. Thousands of Jews began to move southward towards the border with Czechoslovakia. There was tacit agreement between Jewish organisations and Polish military authorities about the way the exodus would be organised and the procedures to be adopted up to and during the crossing of the borders. Polish border guards were instructed not to put any obstacles in the way of those wanting to leave Poland, while the Czechs had given their consent to let the fugitives enter Czechoslovakia as a transit stage for further travel. No passports or visas were required. The whole operation was to be conducted in close cooperation with Jewish organisations, who undertook to make sure that only Jews were among those leaving Poland. The only control was that the number of persons crossing the border needed to correspond with a list supplied by the Jewish organisation.

The escape usually took place during the late hours under cover of the night, to keep the whole operation secret from the Polish population and to avoid attacks by the Polish underground. Very often the Polish inhabitants of a small town found in the morning to their astonishment and joy that all Jews had left town.

Two crossing-points were established: one at Kudowa on the Polish side, on the road leading to Nachod in Czechoslovakia, and a second one in Friedland, on the road to Braumow. The Kudowa crossing-point was reserved for women, children and elderly people, who were brought up to the border checkpoint in large trucks. After walking a short distance over the no-man's land they were picked up on the Czechoslovakian side by other vehicles to take them further to the nearest railway station. The Friedland crossing was much more difficult, for it entailed a march on foot for a few kilometres and was, therefore, for young people. The surrounding towns of Klodzk, Walbrzych, Swidnice, Rychbach and Bielawa were designated as assembly points for those wishing to cross the border, and were at the same time the local offices of the 'Breikha' (a Hebrew word for 'Escape') – an organisation formed for the purpose of evacuating the Jews from Poland.

The dominant role in organising the exodus of Jews from Poland can be ascribed to Itzhak Zukerman ('Antek'), the hero of the Warsaw ghetto uprising, who also participated in the fighting during the Polish uprising in Warsaw in August 1944. After the end of the war, he became one of the leaders of the Jewish community in Poland and the organiser of the 'Breikha'.

Michael Rudavski, who at the time was a major in the Polish army, reported that in July 1946 he was summoned to the commander of the Polish border military police, the Soviet General Gwidon Tchervinski, who told him that a decision had been taken to organise two secret passages on the Polish–Czech border through which the movement of Polish Jews toward Czechoslovakia would be allowed. The surveillance and responsibility for this operation had been assigned to the Polish Major Chorabik. One of the conditions imposed on the Jewish side was that the entire operation be kept secret from the world press.

The crossings began on 20 July 1946 – some three weeks after the Kielce pogrom. Large groups of Jews appeared at the appointed places and after a brief check were allowed to cross the border. The number of people in a particular group ranged from a few hundred to over a thousand.

The large military truck was packed to capacity; there was standing room only. The convoy consisted of four trucks, their headlights dimmed and painted over as if it were wartime. This was a measure of precaution against being detected by the Polish underground.

The trucks began to move. As we were not allowed to talk, all kinds of thoughts began coming to me. I reflected upon the situation in which I found myself at this very moment and on its significance. A question kept surging in my mind: why do I leave Poland like a thief in the night? If the Poles don't want me why don't they let me go openly?

I looked up and saw above the sky which by then had become slightly lighter, indicating the arrival of dawn. We disembarked and after forming a column of six abreast, started to march. The real significance of what was happening became clear to me as we approached the border. It dawned on me that a chapter of not only my life but of a whole people who had lived in this country for a thousand years was coming to a close. And it also occurred to me that the expulsion from Poland did not come as a result of a royal decree, as was the case in Spain and in other countries from which Jews were expelled. This time it was caused by the concerted action of an entire nation, who had made our existence in this country intolerable. We were being forced to leave not by the will of the rulers but of the people.

We stopped in front of a wooden barrier. A few men in Polish army uniforms stood nearby. We were counted and told to advance. The barrier was raised and I stepped into the no-man's land strip separating Poland from Czechoslovakia. When I was half way through it, I looked behind me. The Polish border barrier was being slowly lowered and when it came to rest on the timber post, it looked to me as if a thick book was being shut, as if the last page of the closing chapter of Polish Jewry was turned over.

(Author's recollections)

The Kielce pogrom has already been described in its gruesome details, but the shocking fact was that it had taken place in broad daylight, and involved ordinary Poles, including almost entire workforce of a local enterprise, and that functionaries of the so-called 'people's militia' who were supposed to protect the Jews had taken part. The question remains: How was it possible, in the middle of the twentieth century, after a bloody war, for thousands of ordinary people to take to the streets and massacre other ordinary people, on the spurious charge that the latter were guilty of ritual murder?

10
Between Tragedy and Infamy – March 1968

The Kielce pogrom was the culmination of the continuous victimisation of Jewish survivors. It succeeded in convincing the majority of Jews that there was no place for them in Poland. After the pogrom the number of Jews in Poland was drastically reduced. A mass exodus took place, and by the spring of 1949 only about 80,000 Jews remained in Poland.

However, even after the flight of the majority of Jews, there was no peace for the remnants of Polish Jewry. An anti-Jewish atmosphere continued to dominate, and consecutive governments began once more to exploit the old-fashioned maxim that Jews were responsible for Poland's ills. The government tried again to redirect the discontent of the masses against the Jews, its proclaimed ultimate objective being to free Poland of Jewish presence (Gutman, 1985, p. 9).

On 1 September 1949, the Ministry of Public Administration announced that Jews who wished to settle in Israel could register for emigration. A deadline of one year was set, later extended to the end of 1950. As a result, nearly 30,000 Jews then left Poland, leaving behind only about 45,000.

The Polish 'Spring' – 1956

The Polish 'Spring' in October of 1956, after the workers' disturbances in the city of Poznan, was a time of consolidation of communist power in the country. Following Stalin's death in 1953 and the secret speech by Khruschev denouncing Stalinist terror, Władyslaw Gomułka, released from prison, was returned to power. The change in the Polish government signified a relaxation of the communist rule, but it did not improve the situation of Jews. Jews were now blamed for

Stalinist 'errors', and in the process of de-Stalinisation thousands of Jews were dismissed from their positions.

At the same time, the new government under Gomułka began appointing to important posts individuals who were not only reactionaries in the communist definition but openly anti-Semitic. Anti-Jewish views were no longer an impediment to reaching a high position in the government. Mieczysław Moczar, who was previously purged for his 'rightist and nationalist deviation', became Deputy Minister of State Security in 1948, and in 1956 Gomułka appointed him Deputy Minister of the Interior in charge of the secret police. Noted for his anti-Semitism, Moczar soon became a powerful factor in Polish politics. His faction, known as 'Partisans', acquired wide appeal among the nationalistic Poles. Moczar was successful in establishing a broad base among the war veterans and soon became the head of their 800,000-member organisation, Związek Bojowników o Wolność i Demokracje – ZBoWiD (Union of Fighters for Freedom and Democracy). Another anti-Semite and activist of the prewar Obóz Narodowo-Radykalny (ONR), Bolesław Piasecki, who was known to have tried to collaborate with the Germans during the war, also obtained an important post in the government.

As in previous periods in the history of the Jews in Poland, the government began to search for a scapegoat in order to divert public attention from its ineffective economic policy. It correctly assumed that by launching an anti-Jewish campaign it would satisfy the concealed wishes of the majority of the Polish nation. The fact that the number of Jews had dwindled in the meantime did not make any difference. Polish anti-Semites saw a Jew in every member of the government and the administration.

It must be emphasised that the anti-Semitic campaign unleashed by Gomułka was not instigated by Moscow, as is claimed by some Polish historians, but was a deliberate exploitation by the government of anti-Jewish sentiments in Polish society, an excuse for the poor economic conditions. In no other east European country under communist rule did such a general anti-Jewish atmosphere prevail. Gomułka's new regime launched a purge of Jews first from the top positions in the party and then from sensitive posts in the government and army (Dawidowicz, 1993, p. 97).

In the summer of 1956, the Polish government in order to demonstrate to the nation its aim of getting rid of Jews, began once more to ease its restrictions on Jewish emigration. Subsequently, seeking to obtain material benefit from Jewish emigration, the government introduced new regulations in 1958 requiring dollar payments from

Jews wishing to leave Poland. This slowed down the exodus of Jews from Poland, but did not stop it.

It seemed at the time that with the exodus of most of the Jews, when the objective of ridding Poland of Jews had been achieved, anti-Semitism would lose its *raison d'être*. Nothing could have been further from reality. The Jewish question, or to be more precise Polish anti-Semitism, had nothing to do with the number of Jews living in Poland. It also had nothing to do with the regime in power. Persecution of Jews in Poland took place under the rule of semi-fascist governments before the Second World War, anti-Semitism was prevalent during the German occupation, and it continued to reign under a communist regime. The official anti-Semitism in Poland found a propitious breeding ground among those who for many years had been obliged to conceal their true feelings and were now eager to give vent to ever-present prejudices. By the early 1960s the endemic Polish anti-Semitism began to surface with increased vigour. The emergence of new and old pre-war anti-Semites is clear evidence that their ideas fell on fertile ground and enabled them, despite their reactionary past, to achieve high positions in Polish government. Anti-Semitism regained its former popularity within Polish society.

A leading role was assumed by the press of Pax, an organisation headed by Bolesław Piasecki. Before the war Piasecki created the Falanga, a Catholic organisation whose members, imitating the Nazi SA Brownshirts, wore green shirts as a kind of uniform. He advocated the expulsion of the Jews as a precondition for a revival of Polish Roman Catholicism. In 1937 he publicly demanded the 'systematic and radical elimination of Jews from Poland'. On 22 June 1971 he was appointed member of the Council of State of the Polish People's Republic – the supreme state authority. An article signed by Piasecki inaugurated the aggressive Jew-baiting campaign. It was directed manly toward Catholic readers, but his call was immediately echoed by all the mass media, including the central and local Party press.

As discontent in Poland assumed alarming proportions, the Party began once more to point a finger at the few remaining Jews. Skilfully exploiting old slogans, the Party set off a witch-hunt. The Jewish question had once more become a universal antidote for Poland's social and economic ills. The image of the old enemy, the perfidious Jew, was revived. In some cases this acquired religious connotations. As one satirical writer said, 'Even people who always denied the existence of Jesus Christ, now became convinced that he was crucified by the Jews' (Ros, p. 7).

The Six-day War

The Israeli victory in the 1967 Six-day War provided the Polish government with a powerful weapon to unleash a new anti-Jewish campaign. It gave Polish anti-Semitism a new twist by disguising it as anti-Zionism. From the point of view of Polish state interests, the conflict between Israel and the Arabs did not directly concern Poland. However, there were many Poles, simple people as well as members of the intelligentsia, who received the news of the Israeli victory with enthusiasm. Their joy had not been caused by a sudden burst of love for the Jews, but by the setback suffered by the communist enemy. They saw the defeat as proof of the inferiority of the Soviet armaments supplied to the Arabs, and the failure of Soviet military and political strategy. Some Poles were happy that 'our Jews' – that is Jews who used to live in Poland – had taught the Soviet rulers a lesson.

Gomułka, on the other hand, saw in that rejoicing a clear sign of revolt. In June 1967 during a conference of professionals, he criticised the Jews for rejoicing after the Israeli victory and branded them as a 'fifth column'. The accusation of treachery had been deleted from the official text remitted for publication, but those at the head of the anti-Semitic campaign among the 'partisans', as well as the Catholic organisation Pax under the leadership of the pre-war anti-Semite Piasecki, saw in the words of Gomułka encouragement for waging an anti-Jewish crusade.

When Gomułka presented Polish Jews as a potentially treacherous 'fifth column', as people having 'two fatherlands' and a 'double allegiance' who therefore could not be trusted, he used it as a rationale for purging Poland of Jews. It was an official, public statement of collective responsibility – all Jews were guilty. This served as a pretext to remove from the party and from administrative posts a group of Polish citizens defined as being of 'Jewish origin'. The government launched a widespread propaganda campaign through the mass media accompanied by an economic terror, the aim of which was to facilitate citizens of 'Jewish origins' to take the only desirable decision – to emigrate. Anti-Semitism in the form of anti-Zionism was to become a new faith for those who had never seen a Jew. The marriage of Polish nationalism with the Polish road to socialism has given birth to a new monster: anti-Semitism without Jews.

The previously sporadic campaign had by June 1967 become well organised and systematic. The Party ordered a general reissue of membership cards accompanied by verification of the entire membership. A malicious smear campaign was directed against anyone with a Zionist-Jewish connection. A similar campaign was going on in the mass media.

The then Minister of National Defence, Marshal Spychalski, although not Jewish, fell victim of the campaign. Spychalski's dark hair and appearance offered an excuse to label him a Semite; to be Jewish was by then again considered a crime in itself. In Spychalski's case the rumour was not restricted to the allegation that he was Jewish, he was at the same time accused of maintaining secret contact with Israel, as well as selling state secrets. Some army officers publicly demanded the dismissal of 'the Jew' from the supreme military command, and that the ministry and the armed forces be purged of 'alien' elements. Subsequently, Spychalski lost his post.

A mass purge began wherever there was a Jewish presence. Workers' meetings were conducted according to guidelines sent to all Party organisations ordering them to purge themselves, as well as factories, of Zionists. The better-known victims of such purges were listed on the front page of the Party central newspaper. In the course of a few months several thousands were dismissed because of their Jewish origin.

From the available documents it is clear that the Ministry for Internal Affairs had beforehand prepared lists of people of Jewish descent, although the lists included details not of only Jews, but of people who for a long time had ceased to be Jewish and only according to Nazi racist principles could have been considered so (Skarbek, 1969, p. 31). Long before the 1967 anti-Semitic campaign, the Ministry of Internal Affairs had begun to compile files on Poland's Jewish citizens. In the ministry, headed by General Mieczysław Moczar, the Department of Nationalities was responsible for this operation. From 1966 onwards the Ministry of Internal Affairs had a 'Jewish section' headed by Colonel Tadeusz Walichnowski, the author of writings of an anti-Jewish character, who was known as the Polish Eichmann. His staff of over 200 was kept busy compiling 'genealogical charts' of the Jewish population. The chart listed – as far as possible – parents, grandparents and sometimes even great-grandparents.

It must be noted that according to the then Polish law, identity documents did not contain a mention of religion. Unlike the situation in Poland between the two World Wars, it was not compulsory to declare one's religion or to define one's nationality. There was now no possibility of officially ascertaining the Jewish or non-Jewish origin of a citizen. The list of citizens of 'Jewish origin' was therefore established according to confidential information supplied by Poles who knew that a person was Jewish. Walichnowski's officials screened all the archives at their disposal with scientific precision (Banas, 1979, p. 90). Virtually all public institutions were supplied with lists of names of Jews in their employ. Such lists were based on a card index compiled previously by a section of the Nationalities Department in the Ministry of Internal Affairs, headed by Walichnowski. In many cases people heard for the first time that they were of Jewish extraction when they found their names on such a list. Some on the list were Jewish orphans who survived the Holocaust thanks to Polish families who had subsequently adopted them, or those who were hidden in Roman Catholic convents and brought up as Christians. Children who were ignorant of their origin, were suddenly informed of their true identity.

There were cases of people being discriminated against by Polish authorities because they had 'Jewish looks' or a Jewish sounding name. Some of them had to prove their 'pure' Polish origins by showing family graves in Catholic cemeteries. A document proving that their fathers served during the war under the Nazi occupation in the so-called Blue Police, in which there were no Jews, was sufficient evidence of their non-Jewish origin.

The campaign resulted in a new wave of Jews leaving Poland. In order to prevent a prospective migrant from ever returning to Poland, he was handed a form which contained a statement that the applicant wished to renounce his Polish citizenship. At the final stage of this operation, in June–July 1968, the Polish authorities, realising that such an application had all the hallmarks of coercion, specified that all emigrants must lodge the application in their own handwriting. They were also asked to declare that they felt more affinity with the state of Israel than with Poland. In this way, even those Jews who were never Zionists and had never intended to emigrate to Israel, had to sign the application in order to obtain travel documents. All this served to confirm the Party's thesis that Jews have double loyalty and are therefore enemies of Poland.

At that time, the Jewish community in communist Poland numbered about 30,000 in a population of 32 million. The great majority were assimilated, spoke perfect Polish and had close ties with Polish culture. They constituted 0.1 per cent of the population and could hardly be defined as a national minority. This, however, did not protect them from the hate campaign organised by the government, which had all the features of racist persecution. Anti-Semitism became a matter of faith for Party activists and a programme for administrative action. Even the reduction of the number of Jews living in Poland had not closed this chapter in Polish history. The anti-Semitic campaign in Poland entered into a new phase – it changed its form but not its content.

The campaign and the words of encouragement from Gomułka provoked reaction within the party itself. Edward Ochab, the President of Poland and the person who made the return of Gomułka to power possible, resigned from his post in March 1968. 'As a Pole and a Communist,' he said, 'I deplore with all my heart the anti-Semitic campaign in Poland organised by the dark forces of the ONR and their contemporary followers' (*Polityka*, vol. 28, 11 July 1981).

A joke was circulating at that time in Poland: 'What is the difference between past anti-Semitism and today's anti-Semitism? The answer: in the past, anti-Semitism was not compulsory.' Another joke spoke of Jews who were hidden by Poles during the war, asking them if they could once more use their hiding places in case of need (Gutman, 1985, p. 120).

Jews were again defined as enemies and as people whom one could not trust, except those whom Gomułka singled out as genuine Polish patriots. However, Poles of the Moczar kind did not attempt to segregate the Jews according to Gomułka's classification. Moczar claimed that only he would determine who was a bad and who a good Jew.

A number of 'experts' such as Kąkol, Szydor, Ruszyński, Walichnowski and others, began to spread their findings about Jewish crimes against Poland. The radio and television dedicated special programmes to the subject. They also spread incredible news on the model of Nazi propaganda: 'Moshe Dayan is not Israeli, but a Nazi war criminal.'

Another subject that kept creeping up without respite was that Jews were ungrateful. All Jews who survived the war were saved by Poles and now they were denigrating the country and the Polish nation.

Linked to the anti-Semitic campaign, was the appearance on the book market of novels about crime and morals in which Jews were the villains. The weekly *Walka młodych* printed excerpts of the well-known anti-Jewish book *Prawdziwe oblicze syjonismu* (The Real Image of Zionism). In Gdansk, a booklet circulated as the text of a 'Lecture for the Association of Atheists and Freethinkers' entitled *Zionism, its Ideological Sources and its Influence on Polish Medicine*, presented some grotesque ideas:

> The ideological sources of Zionism are derived from the monstrous double ethics of the Talmud, which divided humanity into 'the chosen people' and the so-called goyim (gentiles), beasts with

human faces who should be totally subordinated to the interests of the 'Supermen' – the Jews ... For thousands of years the double ethics of the Talmud have given the Zionists superior strength over the nations of the goyim because they have kept the Talmud secret. Insidiously they won control over big capital all over the world ... The Zionists also invented and spread the absurd notion of anti-Semitism. In fact, anti-Semitism is a fiction ... Even the Nazi extermination of Jews could not be considered anti-Semitism.

(Banas, 1979, p. 151)

The anti-Jewish campaign was waged on the pages of *Żołnierz Wolności*, a publication of the political department of the army. The journal was notorious for printing anti-Zionist cartoons depicting characters with Semitic features similar to those found in Nazi publications. On 22 July 1968, on the occasion of Poland's independence day, the annual prize for best cartoonist was awarded to Zbigniew Damski, the author of anti-Semitic cartoons.

Particularly aggressive was the organ of the Association of Polish Lawyers – *Prawo i Życie* – edited by Kazimierz Kąkol, a close confidant of general Moczar. Equally vicious was the weekly of the Union of Socialist Youth, *Walka młodych*, and some Party periodicals, especially in large cities such as Lodz, in which there still existed a small Jewish community.

Andrzej Werblan, head of the Department of Education and Science in the Central Committee of the Party, subsequently promoted to Deputy Chairman of the Sejm, in an essay published in the popular journal *Miesięcznik Literacki*, argued for the necessity of purification of the party and administration of Jews: 'no society would tolerate the participation of a national minority in the state elite, especially in the organs of national defence, security, propaganda and foreign representation' (Werblan, 1969). 'Based on historical experience,' he asserted 'it was necessary to get rid of Jewish influence in the Party and in government ... The Jews who had once been reluctant to defend Poland's independence with all their strength were now just as reluctant to do their best for Poland's advancement'. Gomułka supported the author by saying his essay provided a good basis for discussion. The Party ideologist, Kliszko, did not contradict him; and *Trybuna ludu*, the organ of the Party, printed excerpts of his essay.

State propaganda also put forward the idea that Jews were responsible for Poland's loss of territory in the aftermath of the Second World War. It argued, not unlike Hitler who blamed the Jews for the 'stab in the back', that Jews were responsible for Poland's loss of the towns of

Vilno and Lvov, and that were it not for the Jews, Poland could have obtained better borders (Ross, pp. 9–10).

The notorious *Protocols of the Elders of Zion* were published at least twice with no publisher mentioned. But the layout, paper and print all pointed to the printing presses of the publishing house of the Ministry of National Defence. Thus the Polish population was constantly fed texts and pictures in mass circulation. Old-time anti-Semites – people who had been forced to conceal their true feelings for twenty years or more – could now at last openly display their accumulated hatred.

Simultaneously with the anti-Jewish campaign, there was also a campaign whose objective was to revise the history of the Jewish community in Poland and its role in Polish history. New light was thrown on the history of the Second World War, on the German occupation, on the armed struggle and the resistance movement, and on the assistance to the Jewish population. The revision consisted mainly in a complete denial or lessening of Jewish participation in events, and in placing on Jews responsibility for all the mistakes committed by the regime.

March 1968

The catalyst to a new wave of anti-Semitism, which caused the final exodus of Jews from Poland, came from an unexpected source – the staging in Warsaw in early 1968 of a classic drama by the greatest Polish poet Adam Mickiewicz, entitled *Dziady*. It is a play about tsarist oppression and contains a reference to 'the rascals sent to Poland from Moscow'.

The first performance brought thunderous applause from the audience. Trying to counteract the clearly anti-Russian attitude of the Poles, the Polish authorities banned all further performances. This led to violent protests by university students, writers and intellectuals. A demonstration organised by Warsaw students protesting 'against censorship, arbitrary arrests, and suppression of freedom' took place on 8 March. The demonstration was attacked by armed police and Party militia. During the university upheavals, hundreds of students were arrested, but only students with Jewish-sounding names were brought before the courts.

On 9 March 1968 students of the Warsaw Polytechnic in turn called for a protest rally. Outside the University campus, police started to beat up passers-by. On that day, dubbed in Poland 'the longest day of the month', the streets of Warsaw presented a picture resembling that of the SS raids during the Nazi occupation. During the next few days the press, radio and television reported that the 'riots' had been instigated by Zionists and nationally alien elements. *Słowo Powszechne*, the daily newspaper of Bolesław Piasecki and his Pax movement, set the tone by appealing to the patriotic sentiments of Polish youth and inciting them against the 'Zionists'.

In Warsaw and in other cities, including Lodz, a leaflet was distributed in which it was said:

> Whom are you supporting? Look at them closely, remember them, compare what you read here with their behaviour.
>
> Adam Michnik, son of Ozjasz Szechter . . . Alexander Smolar, son of Grzegorz, the editor of *Folks-sztyme*, the newspaper of the Social and Cultural Association of Jews in Poland . . . Henryk Szlajfer, son of Ignacy . . . Jozef Dajczgewand, son of Fajga and Szlomo . . . Krystyna Winawer . . . Alina Godfarb . . . [all Jewish sounding names] . . . Read this and pass it on.
>
> (Banas, 1979, pp. 117–18)

Student protests spread to the Jagiellonian University in Cracow, where students adopted a resolution demanding adherence to the constitution, in particular to article 71, paragraph 1, which guaranteed freedom of speech. On 13 March 1968, a mass rally of students from all Cracow institutions of higher education was held with the participation of the Rector of the Jagiellonian University. On 15 March a state of emergency was proclaimed in Lodz which remained in force for two months.

During interrogations of those arrested in the course of the disturbances, the police attempted to influence Polish students against fraternisation with Jews. Some clubs such as the Bobal Club, one of many clubs for intellectual youth in Warsaw which some Jews used to patronise, was described as a nest of enemies of the state. Simultaneously with the arrests, the names of those arrested were publicised in the press, radio and at public meetings of workers. Most of them were Jewish-sounding. The campaign by the government was aimed at an alleged Zionist conspiracy which 'strives to harm the cause of socialism in Poland'. In most universities where student protests took place, there were no Jewish students at all, and among the listed protesters were individuals who lived abroad at the time. Many Poles were completely ignorant of what Zionism was, and many who were born during the war or after, had never met a Jew.

It was obvious that the lists of the arrested had been falsified. The student community had for so long been infiltrated by spies and police informers that the security organs knew the *curriculum vitae* of virtually all students considered to be Jewish. The government through its secret service apparatus kept a watchful eye on Polish society, and more often than not kept particular individuals under constant surveillance. The then chief of the Ministry of Internal Affairs, Mieczysław Moczar, who during the first post-war years had been the head of security in Lodz, knew who was Jewish, which made the racial purge much easier (*Wprost*, 8 March 1998, p. 27).

A letter by a certain Beata Dąbrowska addressed to the First Secretary of the CC of the KZPR, Władyslaw Gomułka, on 23 February 1968, prior to the March events, clearly indicates the extent of spying and pressure applied on private citizens in order to incite them against the Jews:

> I am a third-year student of the philosophy faculty. On 16 February at about 8.00 p.m. I was detained by members of the Security Service of the Ministry of Interior Affairs and brought to the Mostowskich Palace. I was shocked by what I heard and I would like to report to you, and quote accurately some of it. This is what I was asked and heard:
>
> Why do you work among Jews?
>
> How many Jews have signed a paper in connection with the performance of *Dziady*?
>
> You are so intelligent and you did not notice the inundation of your faculty by the Jews?
>
> You do understand that we Poles must finally have our say, because as long as the Jews occupy all the positions, Poles cannot achieve anything, and for you, for example, there won't be enough positions for lecturing.
>
> All through the interrogation, the interrogator used the word 'Żyd' [Jew] as an insult ...
>
> (Soltysiak and Stepien, 1998, pp. 362–3)

It is not known whether Gomułka replied to this letter; but another document speaks of a further interrogation, as a result of which Beata Dabrowska wrote another letter to Gomułka.

> On 4 May I, together with Andrzej Duracz, was arrested ... During the second interrogation I heard: 'how much did the Jews pay you

for defending them?' It was asserted that I am a tool in the hands of my colleague-Jews.

In the course of the last interrogation the situation of the Jews in Poland was described as follows: 'Jews have brought about the economic difficulties because they are interested in their own pockets. This is a race which is able in any situation, and in any country to find a favourable place for itself. Why do you defend these 'Deutchgewands and Schleifers' [Jewish names]?

(Ibid., pp. 360–1)

The following reports, marked 'secret', indicate the extent of Polish secret police surveillance. The report mentions several individuals and their movements, travels, meetings with other people, etc. The emphasis is on people of Jewish descent.

Ministerstwo Spraw Wewnętrznych, Gabinet Ministra. Załącznik do Biuletynu Wewnętrznego nr 62/68 [Warsaw, 5 April 1968]
SECRET
In the circle of Warsaw lawyers of Jewish descent, there are noticeable negative remarks about the Polish nation and government authorities. The lawyer Wurcel, for example, is spreading the view that events at the universities were provoked by the government in order to instigate anti-Semitic sentiments in Poland. A similar attitude is adopted by the lawyer H. Zajączowski. He asserts that the 'role of the Poles during the occupation has been disgraceful. There were a number of cases of denunciation of Jews to the Germans.'

(Ibid., p. 260)

While the government devoted its attention to student protests, Party organisations in Lodz factories, offices and institutions held extra-judicial show trials at which Jewish employees were expelled from the party and dismissed from their jobs. One report notes that workers at the 'Tewa' semi-conductor factory were incensed by the fact that the director of the experimental section of the factory, Artur Nowak, stated in his *curriculum vitae* that he was a member of a Zionist organisation before the war. The workers reproached Nowak for favouring persons of Jewish nationality by placing them in managerial positions. He was dismissed.

Among those ousted from their positions were the Deputy Rector and a number of scientific workers of the School of Medicine. The Internal Diseases Clinic at the School of Military Medicine lost its chief physician, Professor Himmel, while at the Ophthalmological Clinic all physicians had to produce their certificate of baptism. The well-known film director Aleksander Ford, the manager of a film studio, R. Brudzynski, and the manager of the *Ruch* newspaper and book distributor lost their jobs. An educational film-producing company dismissed its editor-in-chief as well as two film directors, Etler and Kokesz. Etler was dismissed because his films – one of them, *The Remu Graveyard*, had won an international award – dealt exclusively with Jewish subjects. A. Postolow, director of the publishing house Wydawnictwo Łódzkie, was forced to leave because his firm was blamed for dealing with 'Jewish subjects and the martyrology of the Jews', and neglecting 'peasant strikes in pre-war Poland'. The journalists' club in Lodz banned Jewish newsmen from its premises. The events of that time closely resembled the climate in Germany immediately after Hitler's seizure of power.

A local newspaper published an article which mentioned 'old Jewish religious customs' and 'unverified stories about the use of Christian children's blood for matzos', and the official Party daily printed an open letter to Golda Meir in which its author, P. Goszczyński, claimed that Dayan was in fact Otto Skorzeny, while she herself was hiding Martin Borman.

On 19 March 1968, Gomułka spoke at the Congress Hall of the Warsaw Palace of Culture. Not only did he repeat the most absurd propaganda lies, but in addition embellished them with many details, most of them concocted. He asserted that among the instigators students of Jewish origin had played a major role. Referring to the student demands raised during the meeting in the University, he said: 'The resolution was read out by Irena Lasota-Hirszowicz, of Jewish extraction, and by two ... well, of ours, Poles.' By saying this, Gomułka publicly differentiated between Jewish Poles and 'our' Poles. Throughout the speech Gomułka never missed an opportunity to add the description 'of Jewish extraction' whenever he mentioned a Jew by name.

In his speech, Gomułka divided the remaining Jewry in Poland into three groups. In the first group he included Jews who had close connections with and were favourably disposed toward the state of Israel. This kind of nationalistic Jew, Gomułka said, would sooner or later leave Poland. According to this hypothesis, they had divided loyalties and were hostile to Poland.

The second group consisted of Jews who, despite being converted to Catholicism, held universal-humanistic views – that is, they were 'cosmopolitan'. This type of cosmopolitanism was a feature of most

Jews in Poland, and deprived them of the ability to call themselves Polish patriots.

The third group included Jews who saw in Poland their only motherland and who contributed to the building of a new Poland (Blit, 1969, pp. 30–2).

The last classification was clearly intended to defend Poland from accusations of anti-Semitism. However, when one takes into account the fact that there were only about 30,000 Jews left in Poland at the time – hardly a number capable of 'setting Poles against their patriotic responsibility' – then the only explanation is that anti-Semitism had been exploited for political purposes; and this can only have been possible because it met with the general approval of the Polish population (Dawidowicz, 1993, p. 110).

Gomułka, nevertheless, made one concession by opening the doors to emigration. Letting the Jews leave the country they had lived in for over a thousand years earned him abroad the reputation of a 'moderate'.

Recently published secret documents prove that the anti-Semitic campaign of March 1968 was the build-up to a previously prepared and planned attack on the Jewish population. The government had simply been waiting for an opportunity to begin the campaign. In March 1968, the government seized the opportunity to blame Jews for the disturbances by unleashing an anti-Semitic barrage which charged that the 'Zionists in Poland intend to set intellectuals and youth against . . . the patriotic responsibility for People's Poland'. This period is known in Poland as the 'March Events'. It should be noted that the events began with an expression of Polish patriotism and resistance against a foreign power. It had nothing to do with the Jewish question, but Gomułka attempted to explain to party activists the reason why 'the slogan of struggle against Zionism' emerged.

Many Polish commentators on the March 1968 events assert that the renewal of persecutions of Jews in Poland had been ordered by Moscow. If this were true, then the same process should have taken place in other 'fraternal parties'. They did not. Jews were not blamed for the Stalinist aberration in Hungary in 1956, despite the fact that many communist leaders were Jews.

Nationalism and anti-Semitism became useful once more. Nationalism requires the existence of an enemy of the nation; anti-Semitism served the purpose. The government correctly assumed in 1968 that the Polish people were spontaneously and generally anti-Semitic, and that anti-Jewish slogans would secure popular sympathy for the government. This might well explain why, even after the first great purge, the anti-Semitic campaign still continued. The purges and the ensuing loss of livelihood endured by thousands of Jewish families brought about an increase in the number of applications for exit permits, particularly since Gomułka in his 19 March speech had expressly offered emigration as a solution.

The only thing not applied to Jews was physical force. The psychological terror, the anti-Semitic propaganda campaign and administrative pressure resulted in the emigration of entire families, including the 'Aryan' spouses of the exiled, while their children were disgraced. Usually, the general atmosphere was a sufficient reason for leaving Poland, but an additional factor was the loss of a job and of earnings. A number of Jews who either did not lose their employment or decided to stick it out, managed to remain in Poland.

The emigration of the Jews as a result of pressure and terror included full, half, one-quarter or one-eighth Jews registered in the card index compiled by Walichnowski's department in the Ministry of Internal Affairs.

Jews were encouraged to emigrate by anonymous letters, phone calls and threats, sometimes by display in their neighbourhood of small posters on walls and trees, with announcements running more or less along these lines: 'Adam Weinberg, son of Isaac, because of his imminent departure for Israel, will sell his furniture and other household articles', followed by his address and phone number. In this way many Jews discovered for the first time that they intended to emigrate. As a result, a new trade emerged by leaps and bounds: buyers of Jewish property could purchase household goods at ridiculous prices, as the sellers were pressed for time. Organised gangs of such buyers showed themselves eager to exploit the plight of others.

Many Jews assumed an attitude of resigned indifference towards all material possessions. The great sale began. Jews disposed of their property at ludicrous prices, well aware that they had been left with no choice. Not only private purchasers but even state-owned, especially antique, shops were eager to avail themselves of this unique opportunity. As during the German occupation, several thousand Poles obtained better-paid jobs, and several thousand people occupied flats abandoned by Jews.

The Poles had a great deal of experience in this respect. They still remembered the 'good old days' under the German occupation, when Jewish assets could be had at bargain prices from the starving Jews in the ghetto. The Polish authorities did not interfere in this trade because it made them popular.

Rumours that one day it might be too late drove many undecided people to apply for an exit permit. Such rumours were presumably circulated deliberately in order to accelerate the exodus. It was not the work of individual officials alone. On 11 June 1969 all Polish newspapers published the following short communiqué issued by the official Polish Press Agency, PAP:

> In order to facilitate the departure of people who consider themselves attached to Israel rather than Poland, a special simplified procedure has been introduced. The Polish Press Agency has been advised that the temporary procedure for issuing documents to people wishing to settle in Israel permanently will remain in force till December of this year.
>
> (Banas, 1979, pp. 172–3)

A detailed questionnaire which a prospective emigrant had to fill in contained a question about nationality. Someone who tried to enter the word 'Polish' was told that Poles were not supposed to emigrate to Israel. This was just another example of duplicity; Polish officials in the passport department were well aware that most applicants had not the slightest intention of settling in Israel.

Each prospective emigrant was handed a form with a printed request to the Council of State, asking for release from Polish citizenship. Such a declaration deprived an emigrant of the possibility of ever returning to Poland and of his entitlement to old-age pension. Before leaving Poland, an emigrant received a document which stated: 'The holder of this certificate is not a Polish national'. Only after having signed this document, which was supposed to provide evidence of lack of affinity with the Polish nation, could he get his exit permit. Subsequently, the rule was changed, and a prospective emigrant was instructed to submit a handwritten application. He was warned in advance that the only reason for leaving the country was a declaration stating that the applicant considered himself attached to the state of Israel rather than Poland.

Among the exiles were men and women who contributed to Poland's culture, art, literature and science. The well-known actress Ida Kaminska, who received in 1967 an Oscar for her role in the film *Shop on the Main Street*, was forced to leave together with almost the entire ensemble of the Yiddish theatre.

The racial purges affected cultural institutions, publishing houses, the press and radio: 800 persons employed in the media were checked as to their racial 'purity'. The best-known television presenter, Jan Serafimowicz, managed to tell the viewers that he was going to Israel before a member of security cut him off. Forty employees of the State Scientific Publishing House and its director Adam Bromberg were dismissed.

Even ordinary people in small towns were exiled. In Mragow (population 1,000), Wera Lechtman, the only paediatrician in town, lost her job. In the port city of Szczecin, a nurse and a gardener were dismissed because they could not prove their 'Aryan' origins. An employee of a supermarket in the town of Bytom, Władysław Pasternak, died of a heart attack when he was informed that 'as from tomorrow' he could no longer work because he was a Jew. Before he died he managed to ask his wife, Stefania, to leave Poland in order to save herself and the children. Adam Koński, the son of one of the few Jews who survived the Kielce pogrom and decided to stay in Poland, was forced to emigrate.

Especially dramatic were the March events in Lodz. The local Committee of the PZPR, headed by Józef Spychalski, adopted a resolution to make Lodz *Judenrein* and worked out a plan to achieve this objective within two months. Among those dismissed were directors of large enterprises, Przemysława Granas, Mieczysław Srebrnik, Stanisław Nowicki, Israel Rabinowicz, Bronisław Rakowski, Jan Sokal, and Henryk Łokieć. The rector of Lodz University, Professor Stanisław Piatowski, Professor Jerzy Szapiro and Leon Lichsztajn of the Academy of Medicine, were dismissed. The March purge affected even Jewish children, who were thrown out of kindergartens.

The anti-Semitic campaign caused countless personal tragedies reminiscent of the Nazi campaign of the thirties. Some Jews committed suicide, couples became separated, and there was a case, or perhaps cases, where a woman claimed that her Jewish husband was not the biological father of her son.

The damage caused to Poland's image abroad by the anti-Semitic persecution induced the Polish authorities to initiate a counter-propaganda drive abroad. On 12 April 1968, Jan Druto, Polish ambassador in Paris, claimed that nobody was persecuted in Poland for racist reasons; 'the majority of the tiny Jewish community was deeply attached to their country'.

Government emissaries were sent on propaganda tours to Great Britain, the Netherlands and Austria; they held press conferences bitterly complaining against the 'fabrications' of western and Israeli press. Among the emissaries were some people who distinguished themselves in word and deed as champions of anti-Semitism:

Zbigniew Soluba, Władysław Machejek, Wilhelm Szewczyk, Czesław Plichowski and others, some of whom were active in the pre-war anti-Semitic movements in Poland.

During the 1970s still more Jews emigrated, leaving only a few old men behind together with a number of totally assimilated young men and women. Today Poland is virtually free of Jews, though by no means free of anti-Semitism. The handful of Jews still living in Poland will soon die out. The problem has been solved, the ancient history of the Jews in Poland has drawn to its end. Ironically, many Poles today are eager to go to Israel to work because they can earn more than they would in Poland. In fact there are many more Poles in Israel today than Jews in Poland.

Conclusion

The last wave of the exodus of Jews from Poland came after the infamous March 1968 vigorous anti-Jewish policy adopted by the Polish government. Since then the number of Jews in Poland has dwindled to only a handful – perhaps a few thousand. The final disappearance of the Jewish community in Poland in the years 1944–68 is one of the most tragic chapters of European Jewry after the end of the Second World War (Gutman, 1985, p. 10).

The March events in Poland can only be explained in the context of Polish endemic anti-Semitism. The Polish communist rulers understood that only by unleashing an anti-Jewish campaign could they achieve two major objectives: to divert the attention of the population from economic failure, and to gain popular support for the Party. They turned to a national heritage – anti-Semitism (Smolar, 1987, p. 62).

The Polish March 1968 was an extraordinary event in post-war Europe. A civilised country in the centre of Europe applied repression against its citizens based on racial criteria. Over 20,000 persons – remnants of the survivors of the Holocaust in Poland – were expelled. Those who were forced to emigrate were deprived of Polish citizenship, were not allowed to take with them their assets, and were even forbidden to return to Poland.

The post-March repression lasted twenty years, years of blatant violation of human rights and international conventions (*Wprost*, 8 March 1998, p. 28). Most of those forced to emigrate found refuge in Denmark which took 3,500 persons; Sweden took in 2,500, Israel 4,000 and the USA and Canada about 10,000. A small number settled in France, Germany and Australia.

11
Anti-Semitism without Jews

Today in Poland, after the expulsion of the remnants of a once vibrant community, one is faced with a phenomenon of anti-Semitism without Jews. It is a sad reflection of Polish society that in Poland, where three and a half million Jews lived before the war and where only five or ten thousand remain today, anti-Semitism still exists.

According to some very rough estimates, the number of 'minimally affiliated' Jews might reach as many as 10,000, but despite their small number, searching for Jews in Poland seems to be a national sport. Many Poles believe that there are many more hidden Jews. In the Polish city of Szczecin, author Zdzisław Zalewski has produced a book claiming that the Jewish population of Poland numbers 700,000 and that they 'constitute a grave threat to the Polish nation and its true religion – Catholicism' (Davis, 1990).

Anti-Semitism in contemporary Poland manifests itself in different forms, the most widespread of which is the assertion that Jews rule Poland and are responsible for everything that happened to Poland. Some Poles seem to think that a real Pole must be anti-Semitic; a Pole who is against anti-Semitism reveals his Jewishness. As a result of this perception, a Polish Jew or a Pole of Jewish origin feels threatened (Chrostowski, 1991, p. 11). 'Anti-Semitism or more precisely anti-Jewishness, lies slumbering in the thoughts, attitudes and behaviour of the so-called man in the street. What we are witnessing today is not only anti-Semitism but general tolerance of its symptoms' (Turowicz, 1995, p. 13).

In Poland the word Jew sounds like an insult – it is a word that exists in isolation from Jews and can even function very well without them. When applied to a non-Jew, it is intended to disqualify and humiliate him, being used as a sinister label. This contrasts with other European countries, where the derogatory meaning of the word Jew is now confined to the dictionary.

Since the last purge of Jews in Poland in 1967–8, anti-Semitic slogans have been appearing in political party programmes, on walls of buildings and subways, in leaflets and brochures given away free or sold, in magazines and in speeches of a more or less public nature. Research by one polling centre indicates that about one-third of all Poles harbour varying degrees of anti-Semitic feeling and belief (Chrostowski, 1991).

In 1974, a book by a Polish historian, Janusz Zarnowski, on Polish society in inter-war Poland, was reviewed in a scholarly monthly, *Przegląd humanistyczny*, by another historian, Jan Borkowski. Most of the review was devoted to the Jewish question and to anti-Semitism. Once more Jews were presented as an 'anti-Polish element' who had not only exploited their fellow countrymen but systematically pushed them out of better-paid jobs. Extracts from the review were published by other papers, indicating a widespread acceptance of the opinion expressed in it.

In June 1976, when workers downed tools to protest against price rises, there were no more Jews to blame, but security officials still beat up strikers to make them confess they had been paid by Jews, presumably from abroad, while the mass media engaged once more in Jew-baiting.

Even after the collapse of communism it did not take long for anti-Semitism to surface once more, but this time in connection with Polish internal politics. It began to be exploited by leaders of political parties, including Lech Wałęsa himself. In 1990 a controversy arose when Lech Wałęsa in an opening speech during a meeting of the Citizens' Committee on 12 June, mentioned that rumours reached him about some new members in the government who were Jewish. He did not comment on these rumours, but when questioned whether he considers the newly established party ROAD as Jewish, he said: why, no, but look who is in that party: Michnik, Turowicz, Geremek ... Why do they conceal their origins? ... ' When asked by a British journalist whether biological extraction is of political importance, Walesa said: 'In a normal democratic country it should not be, but we are only now emerging from communism and we have to be careful' (*Gazeta wyborcza*, 23 Oct. 1990).

Subsequently, during the 1990 presidential election campaign, Wałęsa said again that Poles of Jewish origin should declare themselves. Adam Michnik, a former dissident, who feels entirely Polish and cares little about his Jewish origin, told Wałęsa how much he resented what the latter said. He added: 'It confirms the old belief that true Poles are Catholics and the Jews are alien – not real Poles' (Buruma, 1997, p. 41). In fact, when the subject of Jewishness arose during the election campaign of that year, Wałęsa stated that he was 'a hundred per cent Pole – a Pole from his grandfather and great grandfather' – and that he 'had documents to prove it'.

There is no reason to judge Wałęsa an anti-Semite. It would appear that he simply used anti-Semitic language as a convenient instrument in his battle with political opponents. He thought that this way he could sway an electorate which if not anti-Semitic, at least tolerated anti-Semitism (Warszawski, 1995, p. 11).

Evidence of anti-Semitic sentiments in Poland appeared in September 1990 when the monument erected in Warsaw on the location of the 'Umschlagplatz', from where over 350,000 Jews were deported to the death camps, was defaced by graffiti saying 'a good Jew is a dead Jew'. The Polish minister Alexander Hall expressed his outrage and promised increased protection of Jewish objects, but such protection did not materialise. More graffiti were painted on that monument, as well as on the Warsaw synagogue and on the building housing the Yiddish Theatre. On a visit to Israel, Władysław Bartoszewski, the master of Polish diplomacy, assured Jews that there is no anti-Semitism in Poland, except perhaps in the depths of the provinces. At about the same time in Warsaw, during a demonstration, youths burnt the effigy of Prime Minister Oleksy decorated with a Star of David, shouting that it was necessary to send the Jews to the gas chambers (Cychol, 1995).

In November of that year, a mob attacked the building of the Jewish Historical Institute in Warsaw. Windows were broken and there was an attempt to break the door. The police did not intervene despite the fact that the headquarters of the Warsaw police were located a few hundred metres away. When an attack occurred again a few weeks later the Institute decided to hire a private guard.

It has taken the Polish authorities until the late 1980s to restore the only remaining Nożyk's synagogue in Warsaw. There were a number of attempts to vandalise this house of prayers, the most recent one in February 1997 when it was firebombed. No one was arrested, but representatives of most political parties, except those on the right and the Catholic Church, turned up to protest. Similar acts of anti-Semitism took place in provincial locations but did not even reach the pages of the press. What was more disturbing was the fact that public opinion and state authorities did not react.

Another Polish commentator, Andrzej Osęka (*Gazeta wyborcza*, 10 April 1992), reported that young Poles were distributing in a Warsaw market-place a newspaper called *Myśl Narodowa Polska* – an organ of the Polskie Stronnictwo Narodowe (Polish National Party) – in which a certain Przemysław Dymski in an article entitled 'Judeopolonia jako dramat' (Judaeo-Polonia as a drama) attempted to prove that 'the Jewish struggle to rule over Poland continues in all areas of life and has the attribute of an historical crime ... Jewish doctors and lawyers have worked out a theory and practice of killing Christian children.' Dymski considered the accusation of ritual murder to be proven, and claimed that after 1956 Jews murdered thousands of Polish children. He also quoted the New Testament to prove his point.

Gazeta wyborcza summed up the situation in Poland in the following way: 'To those who continue to assert that only unimportant, isolated groups are spreading anti-Semitism and racial hatred, we say that they are no longer isolated and their opinions are increasingly becoming general opinions. "Clever and good people" with their insanity are amongst us and enjoy a large degree of leniency' (Osęka, 1992, p. 10).

Another newspaper (*The Warsaw Voice*, 16 June 1991), although admitting the existence of anti-Semitism in Poland, regard the frequent accusations as injurious to Polish self-esteem. 'Anti-Semitism is not the only key, and neither can it be the most important one, to the history and current state of Polish–Jewish relations in Poland.' The article points to the fact that even France and Germany are not free of anti-Jewish slogans and excesses.

This latter argument is used in Poland quite frequently, but what the Polish press fail to point out, is that in Germany and France there has been much soul-searching about this matter over the years, and there also was a massive reaction to such excesses, while in Poland, apart from a few individuals, it is not only tolerated but sometimes condoned by government authorities and society.

When, in 1986, Zygmunt Nissenbaum came to visit Kielce in order to place a commemorative plaque at the cemetery for the victims of the pogrom, he was surrounded and later arrested by gun-wielding militiamen. At the police station he was warned not to 'take up the Kielce affair'. It was only after the intervention of higher authorities that he was released (*Gazeta wyborcza*, 5 July 1990).

Although some changes in attitude regarding anti-Semitism have occurred, Jew-hating remains acceptable and undercurrents of anti-Semitism run through political campaigns in Poland. Anti-Semitism has emerged as a potent force in Polish elections, as candidates accuse each other of being Jews. Anti-Semites within the Solidarity group labelled the Polish Prime Minister, Tadeusz Mazowiecki, and labour Minister Jacek Kuron, as Jews. They also pointed out (correctly) that two leading Mazowiecki supporters – Bronisław Geremek and Adam Michnik, editor of the daily *Gazeta wyborcza* – are of Jewish origin. Apparently, being Jewish or of Jewish origin was considered detrimental for holding an important position in Poland. Wałęsa himself acknowledged that he heard 'rumours about waging a war against Jews who allegedly have taken over all key posts in Poland' (*The Jerusalem Post,* international edition, 8 July 1990).

Although Wałęsa denied the allegation of being an anti-Semite, the political struggle at that time led to the proliferation of anti-Semitic publications, including the notorious *Protocols of the Elders of Zion.* These publications were publicly sold at Warsaw University and in a church in Warsaw's central Zagorna Street. The new edition of the *Protocols* contained an introduction in which it was claimed that all of Poland's recent ills had been caused by Jews.

Another anti-Semitic publication is *The Truth About the Carmelite Sisters Convent in Auschwitz,* by Franciszek Wolny, in which he accuses Jews of conducting a hate campaign against the Roman Catholic church in general and the Carmelite Sisters in particular. He condemns the 'ingratitude and arrogance' of Jews and emphasises the gulf between the moral concept of Christianity and Judaism.

The electoral campaign became almost entirely linked to the contest between Wałęsa and Mazowiecki, and it was during election meetings in the presence of Lech Wałęsa that the public began to express its anti-Semitic attitudes. A feature of the exploitation of the Jewish question in the electoral campaign was the rumour that Tadeusz Mazowiecki was Jewish. Wałęsa faced a dilemma when confronting the public. He had to answer questions such as 'when will you throw the Jews out of the government?' As for the shouts of 'Jews to the gas chambers!', he just listened without making any comments (*Gazeta wyborcza,* 23 Oct. 1990).

Nothing could compare to the reaction of the public when during a public meeting the speaker read a question put by someone in the audience: 'When will you, as a president, clean up the government of the Jews who threaten the patrimony of Poland and the Poles? Poland must be ruled by Poles and Poles alone.' It received thunderous applause (*Gazeta wyborcza,* 10–11 Oct. 1990). When anti-Semitic leaflets supporting Walesa's candidature appeared in the Danzig shipyards, Wałęsa's spokesman, Jacek Merkel, said: 'It pains me very much, but this is the price of democracy. What can I do? Call the political police to shut them up?' (*Glos wybrzeya*, 12 Oct. 1990).

Anti-Semitism is still a powerful force among some Catholic clergy in Poland, where individual clergymen, ranging from cardinal to ordinary parish priest, continue to preach the gospel of hate (Dershowitz, 1997, p. 86). 'Anti-Semitism is used not only by secular Poles but also by the clergy ... who used it during the campaign from the pulpits' (*Gazeta wyborcza*, 19–20 Jan. 1991). Gra żyna Kopińska, who collected signatures for the candidature of Mazowiecki in front of a church, reported that many parishioners said they would not vote for a 'Jew', 'Jews', 'Moseks' (*Gazeta wyborcza*, 22 Oct. 1990).

Another witness to the campaign reported: 'I spent two days in front of the St Stanisław Kostki church collecting signatures for Tadeusz Mazowiecki. 'You, you are an Israeli servant! Mazowiecki can rule in a synagogue – but not in Poland! We vote for Wałęsa, he is a real Pole and a Catholic!' Others comments were more benign. For 'him' (the word was accompanied by a gesture indicating a beard) real Poles don't vote. 'The Jews want to rule over Poland! This government is entirely Judaeised!' (*Tygodnik Solidarności*, 16 Nov. 1990).

The church hierarchy remained silent. A Pastoral Letter calling for religious tolerance was to be read in all churches, but the Episcopate Conference in October 1990, which resolved to read the text of the letter in all churches, postponed its reading until January 1991 so as 'not to influence the electoral campaign'.

There were also different voices. Michał Czajkowski, a priest, wrote an article in the popular *Gazeta wyborcza* in which he lamented the manifestations of anti-Semitism in Poland (*Gazeta wyborcza*, 27 Oct. 1990). 'Most disturbing is the more or less concealed xenophobia and anti-Semitism in the programmes of some parties and groups. But most dangerous, however, is what is least visible – the hatred of Jews within a wide circle of society ... I can see prejudice and anti-Jewish propaganda among teachers of Catechism, preachers, theologians and priests.' In Poland, in contrast to west European democracies, anti-Semitism had so far not been delegitimised: 'Here, one can be an anti-Semite and a decent person at the same time' (Warszawski, 1995, p. 13).

It is not surprising that Mazowiecki failed in the first tour of the election. He faced enormous obstacles. He would have had to prove his Polish ancestry, and if he attacked the anti-Semites he would have created more suspicion. The deputy secretary of the Polish Episcopate, Bishop Orszulik, came to his rescue by raising his voice about the alleged Jewishness of Mazowiecki: 'Mazowiecki,' he said, 'has a genealogical tree based on a certificate of baptism going back to the fifteenth century. I have been shown this by the bishop of Plock' (*Tygodnik powszechny*, 4 Nov. 1990).

The anti-Semitic trend in Poland reached its climax when Henryk Jankowski, a priest, held a sermon in the church of St Brigide in Danzig in which he expressed views typical of a Polish anti-Semite. What was significant about his sermon was the fact that among the few hundred people in the church was the President of the Polish Republic, Lech Wałęsa, whom Jankowski addressed directly (Szczypiorski, 1995). 'We can no longer tolerate the fact that we are governed by people who fail to declare whether they come from Moscow or Israel' – a clear hint that there were still too many Jews in the Polish government. He than added: 'The shield of David is intertwined with the swastika in the same way as is the sickle and the hammer.' A few days later he repeated his views in an even sharper manner: 'The Jews, as did other people, have behaved badly in public life, although some behaved correctly ... We can say without any doubt that it was those elements who with their satanical eagerness were responsible for communism and the Second World War.'

Wałęsa did not react to Jankowski's anti-Semitic speech, and when asked said that he did not hear what the priest said. His failure to react created a controversy. It indicated once more that anti-Semitism in Poland is a useful political instrument. Wałęsa came to the conclusion that from the point of view of election strategy, it would be better if he kept silent; that it would be detrimental for him to accuse Jankowski of anti-Semitism. 'Today Jankowski may allow himself to preach hateful ideas in the presence of the head of the Polish state, which makes Poland an exotic place and at the same time a frighteningly wild area of Europe' (ibid.). Aleksander Kwaśniewski, a candidate for president in 1995, was targeted as being Jewish by some newspapers which claimed to have researched his origins. Kwaśniewski, defended himself by saying that his family has had the same name for generations (*The Warsaw Voice*, 9 July 1995). In the minds of many Poles, when someone calls Kwaśniewski a Jew, 'he is calling him a thief or somebody who cannot be trusted', according to Kazimierz Bujak, Professor of Political Sociology at Cracow Jagiellonian University (*Christian Science Monitor*, 13 Nov. 1995, quoted in Dershowitz, 1997, p. 138).

Szczypiorski, a well-known Polish analyst, is one of the few Poles who places the blame for holding such views on the Polish nation rather than on the government in power. 'For an educated Pole, in contrast to a West European analyst, the object of a critical analysis is not the nation but its rulers.' Consequently, the Polish nation is an ideal nation without any faults and anyone who fails to praise it is an enemy of Poland. 'There are many such bastions of fear and ignorance in Poland. The priest Jankowski is not an exception.' Very seldom does anyone dare to say publicly that Polish society is backward, demoralised, uneducated and prone to prejudices. To criticise Poles is very unfashionable. Anyone who dares to raise his voice about civic obligations and independent thought about national problems, is accused of betraying the nation. When Professor Bartoszewski said in Israel that anti-Semitism is a sign of ignorance, there was an outcry in Poland. Someone sued Bartoszewski for insulting the nation and there were cries of 'Bartoszewski to the gas chamber' (ibid.).

Szczypiorski asserts that a large degree of responsibility for the general attitude towards the Jews rests on the shoulders of the Polish intellectual elite. The same elite which has always been in the forefront of a political struggle against the government, is not prepared to wage a war against the ignorance of a significant section of the Polish nation. 'Where educated people remain silent, one can hear the voice of Jankowski and of many other false prophets of the new paganism.'

The Catholic Church in Poland is still not friendly to Jews, despite the attempts by Pope John Paul II – a Pole himself – to mend relations. Old prejudices and intolerance still persist. The simmering animosity of the Church came into the open in 1984 when Carmelite nuns established a convent at Auschwitz. This controversy lasted for a number of years and was finally resolved by moving the convent, but did not entirely disappear.

In 1989 a cross was erected close to Auschwitz as a gesture to Pope John Paul II, who was then visiting Poland. World-wide protests by Jewish organisations led to the closure of the Carmelite monastery on that site in 1993, and in 1998 a number of crosses and one star of David were removed from the area of the gas chambers. This series of events led to a harsh exchange of words between Polish officials and the local Jewish community.

The conflict is focused on opposing views of history. Many Poles feel that the 3 million non-Jews who were murdered during the Nazi occupation, including around 100,000 in Auschwitz, did not receive the honour they deserved, and in fact became invisible because of the magnitude of the Jewish holocaust. Jews, on the other hand, see the presence of the crosses near a camp that stood at the centre of the Nazi extermination apparatus as unacceptable. Jews point out the fact that more than one million of the victims at Auschwitz-Birkenau were Jewish.

The conflict erupted with increased vigour when at the end of 1998 hundreds of crosses were erected outside the site of the Auschwitz extermination camp. The crosses were multiplying outside Auschwitz, many of them only metres from the barbed wire fence still surrounding the site, which for over 50 years has symbolised the Jewish Shoah. Around 240 crosses, some made of wood, others of metal, have been erected by Catholic believers. This was in response to opposition by world Jewry, which arose when the first few crosses were put up. People who have visited the site and climbed the watch-tower describe an 'ocean of crosses' visible from its top (Tal, 1999).

The caretaker of these crosses is Casimir Sviton, formerly member of Solidarity, which helped bring down the communist regime in Poland. Sviton came to the area in June 1998, and since then has lived in a tent. As soon as he arrived, Sviton announced that he had come to the place in order to defend Polish soil from Jewish attempts at domination. He planted the first cross and asked for others to do likewise. Once more Jewish opposition to the erection of crosses stirred up severe anti-Semitic manifestations. 'We don't tell the Jews what to do in their country, and similarly they have no right to tell us what to do in ours', Sviton said: 'I will not leave this place until I receive a signed assurance from the church that these crosses, that honour Polish victims in Auschwitz, will remain forever.'

Over the last few years the camps of Auschwitz-Birkenau have stood at the centre of an international storm of controversy involving conflicting views, Polish and Jewish, concerning all that relates to what occurred in the country during the Second World War. The struggle between the groups has centred on the question, 'who suffered more under the Nazis?' Still, the anti-Jewish rhetoric of Sviton and his colleagues signals a fundamental escalation in the struggle between the two sides, a struggle which, amongst other things, deals with the fear in the Polish community of potential compensation claims by holocaust survivors and their descendants, for property lost during the war. According to many sources in Poland, the claims made by Jewish organisations against Swiss banks, as well as several large German and Austrian companies who used Jewish labour, demonstrate the approaching Jewish threat.

'Sviton represents a marginal element, but perhaps much more widespread than we thought at the beginning', said Polish historian Ladlicki. 'The communists removed crosses from public places, but to remove them today would be the action of a national enemy.' The government finds itself in a precarious situation. The Polish Prime

Minister has promised a number of times to remove the crosses, but despite his promises, and in spite of condemnation by the Council of Polish Churches in August 1998 of the erection of new crosses, no attempt has been made to remove the crosses or to evict Sviton from his tent. The realities of the dispute indicate that any attempt to remove the crosses without legal grounds, will only work in favour of Sviton and his supporters, many of whom are radical elements within the Catholic church itself, and Polish nationalists who have already claimed for many years that the Jews are trying to reconquer the country. Meanwhile, Sviton and his colleagues threatened to continue the fight. 'The Jews want to exploit us, they want to take power in Poland,' claimed Sviton, 'but these Christian symbols prove that we will not submit to their blackmail. We gave up the Carmelite monastery and the Jews are still not satisfied.' Sviton promised that the number of crosses will continue to grow. (At the time of writing, the crosses have been removed by a government decree, but a chapel erected on the site and the Papal cross remain.)

The obsession of present-day Poles with anything that has to do with Jews – especially their pathological fear of Jews and of their alleged attempts at dominating Poland – goes much further than abusing Jews. It attempts to purify Polish culture of any Jewish connection. The latest victim of this trend is the greatest Polish poet, Adam Mickiewicz, because of his alleged Jewish ancestry.

An article by an anonymous writer published in the Polish weekly *Angora* under the column 'Wiadomości kulturalne' (Cultural news) and claiming to represent the views of Polish intellectuals such as Mariusz Chwedczuk, Ewa Likowska, Przemysław Wielgoszcz, Tadeusz Stefański and Jacek Zychowicz, depicts Mickiewicz as a 'womaniser, a filthy, semi-literate adulterer, and above all – a Jew. This is the kind of bard we had and still have' ('Mickiewicz zlustrowany', *Angora*, 21–8 Dec. 1997, p. 3). The article was written in reply to the Polish President, Aleksander Kwaśniewski's, speech on the occasion of the bicentenary of the birth of Mickiewicz, whom the President described as 'the greatest national poet whose creativity had a big influence and was an example of Polish patriotism'. The circulation of the magazine is not known, but the fact that it is reprinted in a number of countries, including Australia, indicates that it enjoys wide readership.

Professor Jadwiga Maurer, interviewed on Polish television in June 1996, clearly indicated the general aversion of the Poles to anything Jewish:

The official study of Mickiewicz does not admit any connection with the Jewish world. But then, all the essential features of the life of Mickiewicz, the birth from a 'foreign mother' ... are linked to the Jewish world. All of them have been simply cut out from the study about Mickiewicz in such a skilful way that there are not even the so-called 'white pages' ... All the 'white pages' have been splashed with patriotic paint.

Paradoxically, the Polish obsession with Jews also contains the phenomenon of interest in Jewish culture. The only operating Jewish theatre in Warsaw is popular with Polish theatre-goers and most actors are Yiddish-speaking Poles. But to see signs of the Jewish past one must travel to Cracow. There, in the old district of the town, one encounters attempts at reviving Jewish life. But these are motivated by commercial considerations rather than genuine interest. In the main square of the former Jewish quarter of Kazimierz are Jewish cafes, bookshops and restaurants, where one can listen to Jewish music. However, music and Jewish dancing are staged for tourists and Poles, with some dancers wearing yarmulkes for greater effect. However, if one takes away the pecuniary interest in the promotion of Jewish culture, one is still left with the attitude of the average Pole toward Jews, which is either hostile or indifferent. An American visitor to Warsaw in 1997 reports:

> This is where I see a bus pull up and disgorge a group of elderly German tourists, who take photographs of freshly painted Hebrew signs and disused synagogues. An old Jewish man with a hat and beard approaches them. The tourists take pictures of him too. One old Jew ... speaks to me in Yiddish. He tells me about his neighbours in Warsaw who turn away when he greets them in the morning. 'every human being is lonely,' he says, 'but we Polish Jews are especially lonely'.
>
> (Buruma, 1997, p. 38)

Such attitude is caused not only by internal politics or the influence of various anti-Semitic groups, but is also the result of a legacy which young Poles have inherited from the older generation who were witnesses to the great tragedy. Most young Poles today have probably never met a Jew, yet the animosity persists.

There was a knock at the door. I opened it and saw one of the cleaning staff, a young Pole I had noticed earlier. He asked me whether he could service the room. I told him in Polish that he should come back later. A few minutes later, when I was leaving, the young man approached me and a conversation ensued. To my question what he was doing in Israel, he replied that he came to work for two years to earn some money. When I asked him whether he liked it in Israel, he said that it is a terrible country and that the people are terrible, he now understands why there is anti-Semitism in this world. He obviously took me for a Christian Pole. Needless to say, I was shocked.

'You mean this is why people don't like Jews?', I said, 'Well, if you really want to know why, you better ask your priest when you go to church' (he told me he attends church every Sunday).

'I know,' he replied, 'because Jews killed Jesus.'

(Tel-Aviv, Nov. 1997; Author's recollections)

It is clear that anti-Semitism in Poland is still widespread. Jan Karski, in an interview on Polish television in June 1996, had this to say on that subject:

On the Polish side, those who defend the good name of Poland feel they have a duty to deny that there is anti-Semitism in Poland. This is absurd; there is anti-Semitism in Poland. But within many Poles anti-Semitism is so deeply ingrained in their mentality that subconsciously they feel innocent of anti-Semitism; they don't understand that the way they think, what they say, the way they reason is anti-Semitic.

Claude Lanzman, the producer of the documentary film *Shoah*, when interviewed in the early 1980s by a correspondent of the *Jerusalem Post*, and asked to comment on the tenacity of anti-Semitism in a Poland where there are almost no Jews left, had this to say:

This is the strength of anti-Semitism; it needs no Jews to exist … One must keep in mind that Poland is a deeply Catholic country. The Poles have absorbed anti-Semitism together with the teachings of the Church. It is the old anti-Semitism of the Church purveying notions like 'the God-killers'. That remains the main reason for the persistence of anti-Semitism there.

As to the question how Poles can live with the memory of their past behaviour, Lanzman said: 'Only by going on hating Jews; otherwise, they would not be able to put up with themselves – with their passivity and complicity with the Nazis, with taking the Jews' belongings … '

Epilogue: Facing the Past

> Whosoever flees from history will be pursued by history.
>
> (Janusz Korczak, November 1939)

> No nation can look to the future without first facing the truth
> about where it has been.
>
> (Ian Macphee, *The Melbourne Weekly*, 22 July 1997)

The history of the Jews in Poland should be an important subject for
Polish historians, and it certainly deserves more space in historical
textbooks than it has at present. Jews have lived in Poland for a
millennium and, as indicated in this study, have always in some way
either actively or indirectly contributed to the development of Poland;
yet one would be hard pressed to find significant work on the history
of Polish Jewry written by a Polish historian. 'It is indeed unfortunate
that there is no one now in Poland who is able to study and revive the
history of Polish Jews – a history that is most important to the Polish
people, for its own sake and because of Jewish participation in or
contribution to Poland's past' (Kieniewicz, 1986, in Abramsky et al., p.
71). Even when Jews are mentioned it is always in a superficial fashion
and more often than not in a negative manner. After the shock of the
Holocaust, there is silence.

> By the time I was growing up, the subject of the Holocaust had
> become surrounded with an aura of taboo ... on the Polish side ...
> the Holocaust had been relegated to the psychic realm of denial
> and numbing. Immediately after the war, both Jews who were
> hidden and those who hid them wanted anonymity. They were
> afraid to reveal their secrets. Whether this was because they feared

other Poles' disapproval or because of some strange sense of shame-
fulness about what had passed is difficult to know.

(Hofman, 1997, pp. 249–50)

If the matter was raised at all, it was only to defend Polish honour
against what was considered unjust accusations of Polish participation
in the murder of Jews during the war. This phenomenon is not really
surprising. A Polish historian who probes into the history of Polish
Jewry, must inevitably come across the sad history of Jewish–Polish
relations. If he is unfavourably disposed toward Jews, he interprets the
history to suit his personal attitude and presents Jews in a poor light.
A Polish historian who wishes to be more objective, cannot present
the historical reality for two reasons. First, for fear of the negative reaction of his colleagues or other members of the Polish intelligentsia,
and secondly, to avoid denigrating so-called 'Polish honour'. He
prefers to remain silent. Some years ago, a work by Jan Jozef Lipski
entitled *Two Fatherlands – Two Patriotisms* provoked a violent response
in Polish circles because it was thought the book stained the Polish
past (Kalicki, 1990).

Polish apologists are constantly devising ways of absolving Poland
of any responsibility, and in the course of such apologies attempt to
deprive the Holocaust of its Jewish character through universalisation.
Divesting the Holocaust of its Jewish content, they hope, will absolve
the Polish conscience, making Poland appear a martyr nation that lost
many citizens, even though the overwhelming majority of those who
perished were Jews. This idea has been taken up with alacrity by the
government of Poland and even more so by the Church. As a result,
almost all evidence of Jewish martyrdom in the extermination camps
has been removed. Visitors to the camps are told about the death of
millions of Poles with only passing mention of Jews.

An acute crisis in Polish–Jewish, and especially Catholic–Jewish relations occurred when the Polish authorities allowed the Catholic
Church to build a monastery on the grounds of the former extermination camp at Auschwitz, while a large cross symbolising Polish
martyrdom was erected. Despite vigorous protests by Jews against the
erection of the cross, the Polish Cardinal Glemp stated that the cross
must remain. It is true that the Vatican, especially the Polish Pope,
after a long delay, came out against the project, and the cross was
moved away from the camp, but judging by the reaction of readers of
the Polish press, this was not welcomed by Poles at large.

The position of the Polish Church until very recently can at best be

238 In the Shadow of the Polish Eagle

defined as ambiguous. It should be noted that more often than not, the Polish Church representatives did not follow the precepts of Rome. The new attitude of the Pope, who began to refer to the Jewish people as the 'older brothers', did not strike a sympathetic chord with a majority of Polish people steeped for generations in quite different beliefs (*Znak*, vol. 2, no. 3, 1983).

There were, however, some exceptions. In April 1983, on the occasion of the fortieth anniversary of the Warsaw Ghetto uprising, Primate Jozef Glemp celebrated for the first time in history a solemn mass for Jews. 'By now, the Jews have ceased to be a political problem. Instead, ... they have become a moral problem for the people of Poland and also for the Polish Church', Glemp said. During the same mass, Father Bronislaw Dembowski affirmed: 'We must admit that the crime of genocide of the Jewish people had its origin in the sin of anti-Semitism' (quoted in Smolar, 1987, p. 68).

The fiftieth anniversary of the Warsaw Ghetto uprising was celebrated by a mass in a number of churches in Poland. In the Church of St Augustine, located in the area of the former Ghetto, the mass was conducted by the Polish Primate Jozef Glemp together with seven bishops. There was a prayer asking 'forgiveness for any hatred in our hearts, for all crimes committed against the Jewish people, for the crime of the Holocaust, for all forms of violence which took place here on the territory of the ghetto ... ' At the same time, however, the Primate also called for more 'objectivity' regarding the Jewish question. 'Just as not every Jew who served in the Soviet Polish army can be considered a communist, so must not the Jews repeat the slogan that a Pole sucks anti-Semitism with his mother's milk' (*Gazeta wyborcza*, 13 April 1993).

There were numerous, albeit feeble, attempts by some Polish public personalities and by members of the Catholic clergy to express regret for past behaviour, but such expressions of national moral responsibility were voiced in rather vague terms. In 1991, in an address to the Israeli parliament, the Polish President, Lech Wałęsa, referred to the Second World War, and declared: 'There were among us those who did evil, those who perpetrated evil. Here in Israel, in the cradle of your culture and renaissance, I ask your forgiveness.' By saying this he went as far as he could in admitting Polish guilt. The reaction in Poland to his statement was in direct contradiction; Wałęsa was sharply criticised for offending his nation.

The Catholic Church, which historically has been responsible for much Polish anti-Semitism, did try to change the attitudes of the

Polish masses toward Jews. A letter of the Polish Episcopate, read in all Polish churches on 20 January 1991, contained expressions of regret 'for all acts of anti-Semitism which have taken place on Polish soil at any time and by anyone'. The letter also begged forgiveness for the Church's position during the Nazi occupation of Poland (*Gazeta wyborcza*, 26 Jan. 1991).

In April 1993, churches all over Poland held special masses to mark the first ever 'Day of Judaism' sponsored by the Roman Catholic Church. The nationwide initiative, designed to bring Jews and Catholic Poles closer together, operated under the slogan taken from a quotation by Pope John Paul II: 'Whoever meets Jesus Christ, meets Judaism.' The Poles were very displeased with this pronouncement. This sounded to many Poles like heresy and a provocation (Szczypiorski, 1998, p. 12).

Facing the past

It is clear that the question of Polish behaviour during the war is still haunting Poland, but it is slow to emerge into the open. It has taken more than thirty years since that period for a Polish intellectual to deal with the problem of the Polish past. An article written in 1985 by Jerzy Turowicz, the editor-in-chief of a prestigious Polish Catholic weekly, used words that had been taboo in Poland since the end of the war. He said:

> Polish Catholics who witnessed the terrible fate of Jews on Polish territory and have seen what anti-Semitism can lead to, are bound to make a thorough examination of conscience as regards the sin of anti-Semitism. I must say clearly, though it hurts me, that in my opinion this examination of our conscience has yet not been thorough enough.
>
> (Turowicz, 1985).

Ten years later, in July 1995, Turowicz was even more outspoken. He tackled head on the question of collective responsibility.

> In the civilised world there is no collective criminal responsibility. An individual is only responsible for what he himself has committed. There is, however, collective moral responsibility – something about which Karl Jaspers in his book *Schuldfrage* spoke. This feeling of guilt should exist and should lead to a situation where anti-

Semitism would not be likely to occur. As we know, it is not only likely but possible.

(Turowicz, 1995)

Another Polish intellectual who also spoke out about the moral responsibility of the Polish nation was Jan Błoński in an article under the heading 'Poor Poles are looking at the Ghetto,' published on the front page of a Cracow weekly in January 1987. The writer, a well-known literary critic, for the first time spoke about the duty of the Poles to 'reflect upon Jewish blood, upon the Genocide for which the Polish nation bears no responsibility, but which took place in Poland and left its mark on the Polish earth ... To honestly face the question of co-responsibility ... ' Błoński concludes: 'we are responsible for our past and we must strive to cleanse it.' In his article, he refers to the poet Czesław Miłosz who in one of his poems calls for the cleansing of the Polish soil, which 'is burdened, bloodied, desecrated ... ' What Miłosz had in mind, according to Błoński, was the genocide, 'which was perpetrated on Polish soil and has stained it for centuries to come. It cannot be erased from the collective memory.' There are voices, especially amongst young Poles, who reject the principle of collective guilt. Błoński was perhaps one of the first to declare that 'we [the Poles] are indirectly responsible for our past. We must carry in us this responsibility, although this is sometimes unpleasant and painful' (Błoński, 1987).

We read or listen to discussions about the Polish–Jewish past, but whenever an event is mentioned that reflects unfavourably upon the Polish nation, we attempt to minimise, to explain or to ignore it ... We are unable to speak about it in a cool fashion because, consciously or unconsciously, we fear accusations directed against us. We fear the question: 'did you help to kill? Or at least did you look calmly at the death of Jews?'

(Ibid.)

A reply to Błoński's attempt at putting the question of Polish–Jewish relations in its proper perspective, was not long in coming. Siła-Nowicki, a well-known Polish lawyer, considered Błoński's article as an approval of the 'rabid anti-Polish propaganda relentlessly waged for decades by the enemies not of the government or the system, but of the Polish nation' (Siła-Nowicki, 1987). In his reply Nowicki exploited the old pre-war anti-Semitic argument that the Jews controlled the Polish economy. 'Who controlled the bulk of wholesale trade and most of the retail trade, most of the capital – the Polish majority or the 10 per cent Jewish minority?'

Referring to the anti-Jewish extremism during the thirties at Polish universities, Nowicki asserted, 'it is a fact that the percentage of Jews at the universities was far greater than their percentage of the total population'. 'My concern,' he said, 'wasn't so much the question of the number of Jews at the universities, as the question of defending the Polish intelligentsia from being overtaken by an alien element' (ibid.).

Regarding the behaviour of the Poles during the war, Nowicki put forward the argument that Jews were passive. It was a view that could be found in many underground publications distributed during the German occupation. He did not provide any new insight into the problem but repeated what the anti-Semitic resistance propagated during the war. The Poles, Nowicki claimed, were much more active than were the Jews. 'For us Poles, it was often amazing to see thousands of Jews led to the railway station by a few guards armed with ordinary rifles. No one tried to escape, although escape did not present much difficulty.' Passivity – searching for salvation in the group and in submission to German orders – was the foremost obstacle to saving Jews. The Germans were fired upon on the streets of Warsaw, but seldom in the ghetto. The Jewish police, especially, were never shot at, although they were 'far more cruel against their own compatriots than were the Polish Blue police'. A rather peculiar statement, coming from a Polish intellectual; strange attempt to equalise the fate of Jews and Poles.

The question of passivity during the deportations appears justified until one looks at the real situation on the ground. An escaping Pole had every chance to disappear in the local crowd or in the nearest village. A Jew could not. Semitic features and insufficient mastery of the Polish language, or even a trace of a Yiddish accent, were tantamount to a death sentence. Jews could not rely on the help of Poles, who in such cases caught the fugitive and handed them over to the Germans – unless they were lucky enough to find a Pole belonging to the 2 per cent who were willing to hide Jews (Prekerowa, 1987).

Another argument runs something like this: the Nazis invaded Poland in 1939, Poland was the first country to offer military resistance to the Nazis, and the only country which never collaborated with them in any way. However, the evidence presented in the present study disproves such assertions. During the war there were many cases of appalling behaviour of Poles toward the Jews. It was not only the szmalcowniks who behaved abominably, but also the average citizen, particularly one who derived material gain.

Hanna Świda-Ziemba has put it more succinctly: 'from the Germans the Jews expected nothing but persecution and terror; in the Poles, however, they wished to see companions and co-citizens united in the face of oppression. They thought that they were on the same side of the barricade as the Poles, and expected from them compassion and solidarity' (Świda-Ziemba, 1998, p. 14).

The few articles that touch upon this sensitive issue, became the subject of attacks against the authors which accused them of denigrating Polish honour and of lacking patriotism. But even this debate was short-lived and, as we have seen, was transformed during an election into a political matter rather than a thorough examination of Polish conscience. Even those Polish intellectuals who have from time to time expressed their opposition to anti-Semitic propaganda in Poland, have shown little desire for an in-depth scrutiny of the question of Polish anti-Semitism.

> Today we live in a free country and are analysing our past. It is perhaps time that we should also honestly reflect on the Jewish problem. Instead we see posters calling for 'Jews to the gas', anti-Semitic references in sermons by the clergy and in private conversation. Parties are appearing with a clearly anti-Semitic character. Finally there is the Auschwitz conflict which shows anti-Jewish overtones. The majority of the clergy, even if it does not express anti-Jewish views, displays reluctance to condemn them. In short, the atmosphere in Poland is as if the Holocaust had never taken place.
>
> (Świda-Ziemba, 1998, p. 15)

There is also a trend in Poland to ignore the role played by anti-Semitism in the behaviour of Poles. Any reference to Polish endemic anti-Semitism is taken as an insult to Polish honour and more often than not, ignored or simply eliminated from the record. Such was the case with the first publication immediately after the end of the war of the unearthed archives of the Jewish historian Emmanuel Ringelblum, when all references to anti-Semitism were removed from the published text.

The blame was placed on the communists who were in power at the time. A similar event took place in the more democratic Poland over fifty years later. *His Holiness*, a best-selling biography of Pope John Paul II, written by Carl Bernstein and Marco Politi, was published in the United

States and in Poland in the Polish language. It was heavily edited by the Polish publishers to remove any references to Polish anti-Semitism. The American publishers, Bantam Doubleday, sued for damages and demanded that more than 14,500 copies be taken off the shelves. 'Clearly, the Polish publishing industry suffers from the same kind of mentality that characterised the communist era,' said Bernstein. 'In this case, rather than being communist censors, there are people who fear some kind of imagined reprobation from the church or Polish readers' (*The Age*, 31 May 1997).

Poles who genuinely believe that it is time to face the past and to examine the question of Polish–Jewish relations are few in number, but recently they have become more outspoken and their voices are being heard much more often.

The Kielce pogrom

The most conspicuous proof of the attempt by Polish historians and commentators to distort facts or to ignore them altogether is the infamous Kielce pogrom, which was deleted from Polish history for many years. The silence was broken only in 1981 – 35 years after the event – by Professor Krystyna Kersten in an article in *Tygodnik Solidarności* in which she commented on the pogrom. Other comments on the pogrom were confined to the question of who was behind it.

A few years later, in 1983, under the sponsorship of the government, a book written by Jozef Orlicki containing an analysis of the 'so-called Kielce pogrom' (Orlicki's definition) and a print run of 50,000 copies appeared in Polish bookshops. In his book, Orlicki puts the blame for the pogrom on the Polish government-in-exile in London. He also implies a Zionist plot: 'we shall wait a long time for a definite answer as to whether the Kielce pogrom was an Anders or Gomułka [Stalinist] provocation – in both cases a Polish provocation – or a Zionist one' (Orlicki, 1983, p. 263). An extensive analysis of the events in Kielce was published in 1990 in *Gazeta wyborcza* – a leading Warsaw daily – under the title *Zabić Żyda* (Kill a Jew) (Kalicki, 1990). After the publication of this article, a number of readers commented on it in letters to the editor. One reader asked the whether the cry 'Zabić Żyda', which the mob shouted during the pogrom, could still become a rallying cry in contemporary Poland. He answered in the affirmative.

Another reader was critical of the newspaper taking up a subject in which few Poles were interested. The letter castigated the paper for attempting 'to denigrate the Polish nation and thereby become a boot-licker of Zionism which tries to dominate the world' (*Gazeta wyborcza*, 4 July 1990).

The latest version of the Kielce Pogrom puts the blame on the communist government of the time. Generally, Polish intellectuals are now flogging the dead horse of communism and putting everything that was done to the Jews in Poland after the war on the shoulders of the communists. What is significant about all the published material in Poland regarding the pogrom, is the diversity of theories on the question of who was behind it. Among the suspects are the communists, the Polish underground, the Polish government-in-exile, the Zionists, and finally the Jews themselves. The former head of the province at the time, Wislicz, when interviewed in 1986 and asked who he thought was responsible for the pogrom, said: 'Today I would like to forget about it, but if you insist on going back forty years ... I consider that the Jews themselves are partly responsible.' Such opinions are not rare even today.

The responsibility for the pogrom is therefore externalised; it is not the Polish population that is considered responsible, but alien forces. So far not one Polish historian has investigated Polish anti-Semitism as a catalyst for the spontaneous eruption of historically rooted religious zeal. Not one commentator has addressed the fact that the 9-year-old boy who catalysed the pogrom already believed that Jews were allegedly killing Christian children and used this as an excuse for his absence.

Today any reference to this tragic event meets with hostility from Poles, who claim that it denigrates Polish honour. On 4 July 1990, the 44th anniversary, a commemorative plaque for the victims of the pogrom was unveiled on the initiative of the President Lech Wałęsa. On the day prior to the unveiling, the tombs of the victims in the Kielce cemetery were desecrated (they were already vandalised in 1960), and during the night the plaque itself was defaced. Since 1990, the anniversary of the Kielce pogrom has received only passing mention in the Polish press.

But despite the passing of time and the attempts at minimising the significance of this tragedy, the spectre of Kielce is likely to haunt Poland for a long time to come.

March 1968

After the events of 1967, when anti-Semitism became identified as anti-Zionism, there was a short respite. Then, suddenly, in 1968, it appeared that Polish anti-Semitism was more and more alive and aggressive. Mieczysław Moczar, who reached a high position in the Polish government and was known for his anti-Semitic views, is said to have initiated a new wave of expulsion of Jews from Poland.

For a number of years it was said that in 1968 it wasn't Poland that expelled the Jews but Moczar and his backers – the Gomułka dictatorship. Today different views are being presented. 'One cannot pretend that the society then had nothing to say; Moczar by himself could not do what he did without the cooperation of a significant segment of Polish society. The year 1968 was a year of shame because only a few defended the honour of the country while many trampled on it' (Szczypiorski, 1998, p. 11). Even people from the AK, who were always fiercely anti-communist, stood behind Moczar – behind 'the dear colleague partisan', as general Radoslaw, one of legendary commanders of the AK and heroes of the Warsaw uprising, wrote about him. March 1968 is proof that even Poles who fought for Poland's independence and were anti-communist fighters, sided with the communist rulers when it came to the Jewish question (ibid., p. 12).

It must also be said that in March 1968 and for some years after March, the clergy did not express a single word of condemnation. The silence of the bishops meant that the Church condoned the anti-Semitic acts of the communist party. Cardinal Wyszynski defended victimised students, but did not condemn the anti-Semites. 'Today from the perspective of the past thirty years and given the changes that have since occurred in the church, the clergy should not have remained silent in 1968, according to Andrzej Szczypiorski, a contemporary Polish intellectual.' In an article published in March 1998, he made a pertinent comment:

> A question that disturbed me for years was why did the Holocaust not become a spiritual shock for the Poles as it was in almost all of Europe and America?

He concludes:

> Jews have the right to make peace with their past, but Christians [Poles] do not have such a right. Jews may allow themselves to forget the Holocaust – Christians [Poles] cannot do that.

References

Abramsky, Ch., Jachimczyk, M. and Polonsky, A. (eds) (1986) *The Jews in Poland* (Oxford: Blackwell).

Alperowitz, G. (1966) *Atomic Diplomacy: Hiroshima and Potsdam* (London: Secker & Warburg).

Arad, Yi., Gutman, Yi. and Margaliot, A. (1987) *Documents on the Holocaust* (Oxford: Pergamon Press).

Arczyński, M. and Balcerak, W. (1983) Kryptonim 'Żegota' Z dziejów pomocy Żydom w Polsce 1919–1945 (Warsaw: Czytelnik).

Arnold, S. and Żychowski, M. (1966) *Zarys Historii Polski* (Warsaw: Polonia).

Auerbach, R. (1952) *Hazahav shel Treblinka* (Jerusalem).

Banas, J. (1979) *The Scapegoats, the Exodus of the Remnants of Polish Jewry* (London: Weidenfeld and Nicolson).

Bartoszewski, W. (1968) *Warsaw Death Ring* (Warsaw: Interpress Publishers).

Bartoszewski, W. (1993) *Los Żydów Warszawy 1939–1943* (Lublin: Towarzystwo Naukowe).

Bauer, Y. (1978) *The Holocaust in Historical Perspective* (Canberra: Australian National University Press).

Bauman, J. (1986) *Winter in the Morning, A Young Girl's Life in the Warsaw Ghetto and Beyond 1939–1945* (New York: The Free Press).

Beauvois, D. (1986) 'Polish–Jewish Relations in the Territories Annexed by the Russian Empire in the First Half of the Nineteenth Century', in Abramsky, Ch., Jachimczyk, M. and Polonsky, A. (eds) *The Jews in Poland* (Oxford: Blackwell).

Benet, S. (1922) 'Der Yidisher ontail in di poilishe oifshtandn', *Australian Jewish News* (22 May).

Ben-Sasson, H. H. (ed.) (1976) *A History of the Jewish People* (Cambridge, Mass.: Harvard University Press).

Ber, M. (1975) *Uprising in the Warsaw Ghetto* (New York: Schoken Books).

Berenstein, T. and Rutkowski, A. (1963) *Pomoc Zydom w Polsce 1939–1945* (Warsaw: Polonia).

Black, E. (1987) 'Lucien Wolf and the Making of Poland: Paris 1919', *Polin*, 2 (Oxford: Blackwell Inc.).

Blit, L. (ed.) (1969) *The Anti-Jewish Campaign in Present-day Poland* (London).

Bloński, J. (1987) 'Biedni Polacy patrząna getto', *Tygodnik powszechny* (11 Jan.).

Bower, T. (1997) *Blood Money – the Swiss, the Nazis and the Looted Billions* (London: Macmillan).

Brecher, E. J. (1994) *Schindler's Legacy* (London: Hodder & Stoughton).

Buruma, I. (1997) 'Poland's New Jewish Question', *New York Times Magazine* (3 Aug.).

Caban, I. and Mańkowski, Z. (1953) *Związek Walki Zbrojnej, Armia Krajowa w okregu lubelskim 1939–1945*, vol. II.

Chrostowski, W. (1991) 'The Jew Within Us', *The Warsaw Voice* (16 June).

Cooper, L. (1987) 'Poland's Guilt', *The Jerusalem Post* (13 April).

Cychol, D. (1995) 'Zabij Żyda', *NIE* (1 June).

Czerniakow, A., (1979) *Prelude to Doom: the Warsaw Diary of Adam Czerniakow*, eds Hilberg, H., Staron, S. and Kermisz, J. (New York: Stein and Day).

Davis, D. (1990) 'Anti-Semitism Fuels Solidarity In-fighting', *The Jerusalem Post*, International edn (8 July).

Dawidowicz, L. (1976) *A Holocaust Reader* (New York: Behrman House, Inc.).

Dawidowicz, L. (1993) *The Holocaust and the Historian* (Cambridge, Mass.: Harvard University Press).

Dershowitz, A. M. (1997) *The Vanishing American Jew* (Boston, New York: Little, Brown and Co.).

Dobroszycki, L. (1973) 'Restoring Jewish Life in Post-War Poland', *Soviet Jewish Affairs*, 3, no. 2.

Dobroszycki, L. and Kirshenblatt-Gimblett, B. (1977) *Images Before My Eyes: a Photographic History of Jewish Life in Poland, 1864–1939* (New York: Schocken Books).

Dubnov, S. (1951) *World History of the Jewish People*, vol. IV (New York: Yiddish Scientific Institute–Yivo).

Engel, D. (1993) *Facing the Holocaust: the Polish Government-in-Exile and the Jews 1943–1945* (Chapel Hill: University of Carolina Press).

Giertych, J. (1938) *O wyjściu z kryzysu* (Warsaw).

Gilbert, M. (1985) *The Holocaust* (New York: Holt, Rinehart and Winston).

Goldstein, Ch. Yi. (1962) *Zibn in a bunker* (Warsaw: Yidish Buch).

Grayzel, S. (1968) *A History of the Jews* (New York: Mentor Books).

Gross, J. T. (1979) *Polish Society Under Occupation: The Generalgouvernement 1939–1945* (Princeton: Princeton University Press).

Gutman, I. (1985) *The Jews in Poland after World War II* (in Hebrew) (Jerusalem: The Zalman Shazar Centre).

Gutman, I. (1993) *Żydzi Warszawscy 1939–1943* (Warsaw: Warsaw University).

Gutman, I. (1994) *Resistance: the Warsaw Ghetto Uprising* (New York: Houghton Mifflin Company).

Gutman, Yi. and Krakowski, S. (1986) *Unequal Victims: Poles and Jews During World War Two* (New York: Holocaust Library).

Gutman, Y., Mendelsohn, E. and Shmeruk, Ch. (eds) (1989) *The Jews of Poland Between Two World Wars* (Hanover, NH: University Press of New England).

Hartglas, A. (1936) 'Walka o równouprawnienie', *Opinja* special issue (1935–6).

Hartman, G. H. (1996) *The Longest Shadow: In the Aftermath of the Holocaust* (Bloomington: Indiana University Press).

Heller, C. (1977) *On the Edge of Destruction: Jews of Poland Between the Two World Wars* (New York: Columbia University Press).

Hertz, A. (1988) *The Jews in Polish Culture* (Evanston, Ill. Northwestern University Press).

Hilberg, R. (1992) *Perpetrators, Victims, Bystanders: The Jewish Catastrophe 1933–1945* (New York: Harper Collins).

Hoffman, E. (1993) *Exit into History* (New York: Viking).

Hoffman, E. (1997) *Shtetl* (New York: Houghton Mifflin Company).

Hundert, G. (1986) 'The Implications of Jewish Economic Activities for Christian–Jewish Relations in the Polish Commonwealth', in Abramsky, Ch., Jachimczyk, M. and Polonsky, A. (eds), *The Jews in Poland* (Oxford: Blackwell).

Iranek-Osmecki, K. (1971) *He Who Saves One Life* (New York: Crown Publishers).

Irving, D. (1967) *Accident: the Death of General Sikorski* (London: William Kimber).

Jasienica, P. (1966) *Polska Piastów* (Warsaw: Państwowy Instytut Wydawniczy).

Jeske-Chojenski, T. (1913) Poznaj Żyda (Warsaw: Drukarnia Spolczna).

Jeske-Chojenski, T. (1919) *Historja Żydow* (Warsaw: Drukarnia Spoleczna).

Johnson, P. (1988) *A History of the Jews* (New York: Harper & Row).

Kalicki, W. (1990) 'Zabić Żyda', *Gazeta Wyborcza* (30 June–1 July).

Kaplan, A. (1966) *Megilat Yesurin* (Tel Aviv).

Karski, J. (1944) *Story of a Secret State* (Boston: Houghton Mifflin Company).

Kermish, J. (ed.) (1986) *To Live with Honor and Die with Honor! Selected Documents from the Warsaw Ghetto Underground Archives 'Oneg Shabbath'* (Jerusalem: Yad Vashem).

Kersten, K. and Szarota, T. (eds) (1968) *Wieś Polska 1939–1948* (Warsaw).

Kieniewicz, S. (1986) 'Polish Society and the Jewish problem in the Nineteenth Century', in Abramsky, Ch., Jachimczyk, M. and Polonsky, A. (eds), *The Jews in Poland* (Oxford: Blackwell).

Kisielewski, T. and Nowak, J. (eds) (1968) *Chleb i krew, moja wieś w czasie okupacji, wspomnienia* (Warsaw: Ludowa Spółdzielnia Wydawnicza).

Klukowski, Z. (1959) *Dziennik z lat okupacji Zamojszczyzny* (Lublin). Translated 1993 as *Diary from the Years of Occupation* (Urbana: University of Illinois Press).

Konic, W. (1938) 'Żydzi a Powstanie Styczniowe', *Ster*, no. 3 (30 Jan.).

Korboński, S. (1954) *W imieniu Rzeczypospolitej* (Paris).

Korboński, S. (1978) *The Polish Underground State: a Guide to the Underground 1939–1945* (New York: Columbia University Press).

Korboński, S. (1989) *Jews and Poland in World War II* (New York: Hippocrene Books).

Korzec, P. (1980) *Juif en Pologne* (Paris: Presses de la Fondation Nationale des Sciences Politiques).

Krakowski, S. (1977) *Halehima Hayehidit Bepolin* (Jerusalem: Yad Vashem).

Landau, L. (1962) *Kronika lat wojny i okupacji* (Warsaw: PWN).

Lewandowski, J. (1987) 'History and Myth: Pinsk, April 1919', *Polin*, 2 (Oxford: Blackwell Inc.).

Lichten, J. (1986) 'Notes on the Assimilation and Acculturation of Jews in Poland 1863–1943', in Abramsky, Ch., Jachimczyk, M. and Polonsky, A. (eds) *The Jews in Poland* (Oxford: Blackwell).

Lipski, J. (1969) *Diplomat in Berlin, 1933–1939* (New York: Columbia University Press). Translation of the 1960 Polish edition.

Lubetkin, Z. (1981) *In the Days of Destruction and Revolt* (Tel-Aviv: Hakibbutz Hameuchad).

Lukas, R. C. (1986) *The Forgotten Holocaust, the Poles Under German Occupation 1939–1944* (Kentucky: University Press of Kentucky Press).

Mac, S. J. (1998) 'Marzec hańby', *Wprost* (8 March).

Madajczyk, Cz. (1970) *Polityka III Rzeszy w okupowanej Polsce; okupacja Polski 1939–1945* (Warsaw: PWN).

Mahler, R. (1942) *Anti-Semitism in Poland: Essays on anti-Semitism* (New

York: Conference on Jewish Relations).

Marc, H. (1985) *Le massacre des survivants en Pologne après l'holocaust – 1945–1947* (Paris: Plon).

Marcus, J. (1983) *Social and Political History of the Jews in Poland, 1919–1939* (New York: Mouton Publishers).

Margolis, M. L. and Marx, A. (1956) *History of the Jewish People* (Philadelphia: Jewish Publication Society of America).

Margolis-Edelman, A. (1997) *Je ne le repeterai pas, je ne veux pas le repeter* (Paris: Editions Autrement).

Mark, B. (1963) *Powstanie w getcie warszawskim* (Warsaw: Biblioteka Narodowa).

Materialy i Dokumenty (1946) *Ruch podziemny w gettach i obozach* (Warsaw: Żydowska Komisja Historyczna).

Meed, V. (1973) *On Both Sides of the Wall* (Tel Aviv: Ghetto Fighter's House Publishers).

Meyer, E. (1987) 'The Making of a Righteous Gentile', *Jerusalem Post*, International edn (22 Jan.).

Mitkiewicz, L. (1972) 'Powstanie warszawskie – z mego notatnika w Waszyngtonie', *Zeszyty Historyczne*, no. 1 (Paris).

Myślek, W. (1966) *Kościół katolicki w Polsce a latach 1918–1939* (Warsaw).

Oberlaender, L. (1935) 'Dziewięć wieków współżycia', *Opinja* (1933–1935).

Oberlaender, L. (1936) '1918–1926–1936 – Refleksje o Antysemitiźmie', *Nasza Opinja*, no. 55 (30 Aug.).

Orlicki, J. (1983) *Szkice z dziejów stosunków polsko-żydowskich 1918–1949* (Szczecin: Krajowa Agencja Wydawnicza).

Osęka, A. (1992) 'Dobre ludzie', *Gazeta wyborcza* (10 April).

Poliakov, L. (1974) *The History of anti-Semitism* (New York: Schocken Books).

Pospieszalski, K. (1958) *Documenta Occupationis*, vol. 6 (Poznań: Instytut Zachodni).

Prekerowa, T. (1982) *Konspiracyjna Rada Pomocy Żydom w Warszawie 1942–1945* (Warsaw: Państwowy Instytut Wydawniczy).

Prekerowa, T. (1987) 'Sprawiedliwi' i 'Bierni', *Tygodnik powszechny* (25 Jan.).

Prekerowa, T. (1992) *Zarys dziejów Żydów w Polsce w latach 1939–1945* (Warsaw: Wydawnictwo Uniwersytetu Warszawskiego).

Ringelblum, E. (1985) *Ksovim fun geto, Writings from the Warsaw Ghetto, volume 1 (1939–1942)* (Tel Aviv: I. L. Peretz).

Ronen, T. (1999) 'The Crosses of Conflict', *Yediot Ahronot* (1 Jan.).

Ros, J., 'Żydzi a walka z okupantem hotlerowskim na ziemiach polskich 1939–1945' (Tel-Aviv: unpublished monograph).

Roth, C. and Wigoder, G. (eds) (1970) *The New Standard Jewish Encyclopaedia* (London: W. H. Allen).

Rudavski, M. (1986) 'Der Blutiker Purim in Przytyk', *The Australian Jewish News* (21 and 27 March, 4 April).

Rudavski, M. (1986) 'Der ershter groiser Yidisher yetziyat Poiln', *The Australian Jewish News* (31 Oct. and 7 Nov.).

Rudavski, M. (1987) 'Der Doikhek in a historishn emes vegn poilishe yidn', *The Australian Jewish News* (12 June).

Rudnicki, Sz. (1987) 'From "Numerus Clausus" to "Numerus Nullus"', *Polin*, 2 (Oxford: Blackwell).

Rymkiewicz, J. M. (1994) *The Final Station: Umschlagplatz* (New York: Farrar, Straus, Giroux).

Schiper, L. (1932) *Żydzi królewstwa w dobie powstania listopadowego* (Warsaw).

Schiper, I. (1935) 'Pierwszy bój Żydów o wolność Warszawy', *Opinja* no. 7 (24 Feb.).

Shirer, W. L. (1960) *The Rise and Fall of the Third Reich* (London: Pan Books).

Siemaszko, Z. S. (1982) *Narodowe Siły Zbrojne* (London).

Sila-Nowicki, W. (1987) 'Janowi Błońskiemu w odpowiedzi', *Tygodnik powszechny* (Feb.).

Skarbek, S. (1969) 'Wyjazd', *Kultura* (Oct.).

Smolar, A. (1987) 'Jews as a Polish Problem', *Daedalus* (Spring).

Sołtysiak, G. and Stepień, J. (eds) (1998) *Marzec 68, między tragędią a podłoscią* (Warsaw: PROFI).

Stalin, J. V. (1967) *Sochinenya* (Stanford: Hoover Institution).

Świda-Ziemba, H. (1998) 'Hańba obojętności', *Gazeta Wyborcza* (17 Aug.).

Sword, K. (1994) *Deportation and Exile: Poles in the Soviet Union, 1939–48* (London: Macmillan).

Szafrański, J. (1960) 'Straty Polski w II wojnie światowej', *Studia i rozprawy*, vol. VIII (March).

Szapiro, P. (ed.) (1992) *Wojna żydowsko-niemiecka, Polska prasa konspiracyjna 1943–1944 o powstaniu w getcie Warszawy* (London: AN EKS).

Szczypiorski, A. (1995) 'Sielska moc ludowej krzepy', *Polityka*, no. 26 (1 July).

Szczypiorski, A. (1998) 'Marzec i Polacy', *Gazeta wyborcza* (28–29 March).

Tal, R. (1999) 'The Crosses of Conflict', *Yediot Ahronot* (1 Jan.).

Tenenbaum, J. (1948) *In Search of a Lost People* (New York: Beechhurst Press).

Terej, J. J. (1971) *Rzeczywistość i polityka* (Warsaw: Książka i wiedza).

Tomaszewski, I. and Werbowski, T. (1994) *Żegota, The Rescue of Jews in Wartime Poland* (Montreal: Price-Patterson Ltd.).

Tomicki, J. (ed.) (1982) *Polska odrodzona 1918–1939* (Warsaw: Wiedza Powszechna).

Turowicz, J. (1985) 'Shoah w polskich oczach', *Tygodnik Powszechny* (10 Nov.).

Turowicz, J. (1995) 'Obojętność nasza powszednia', *Gazeta wyborcza* (1–2 July).

Unity in Dispersion (1998) *A History of the World Jewish Congress* (New York: World Jewish Congress).

Verstandig, M. (1995) *I Rest my Case* (Hawthorn: Saga Press).

Warszawski, D. (1995) 'Gdybym był Żydem, byłbym dumny', *Gazeta wyborcza* (26–27 Aug.).

Wasserstein, B. (1979) *Britain and the Jews of Europe 1939–1945* (Oxford: Clarendon Press).

Werblan, A. (1969) 'Przyczynek do genezy konfliktu', *Miesięcznik Literacki* (June).

Wilk, E. (1995) 'Matka Jolanta od tonących', *Polityka,* no. 39 (30 Sept.).

Wroński, T. (1974) *Kronika okupowanego Krakowa,* (Cracow: Wydawnictwo Literackie).

Zagorski, W. (1957) *Wicher wolności–Dziennik powstańca* (London).

Zerubavel (1948) *Barg khurbn* (Sztutgart: Special issue of 'Najwelt' under EUCOM Civil Division).

Zuckerman, Yi. (1993) *A Surplus of Memory: Chronicle of the Warsaw Ghetto Uprising* (Berkeley and Los Angeles University of California Press).

Zygier, T. and Nadworny, M. (1993) 'Polemika w sprawie NSZ-tu', *Wiadomości Polskie* (26 July)

Index